# EVERYMAN'S LIBRARY

571

## POETRY

Everyman, I will go with thee, and be thy guide,
In thy most need to go by thy side

WILLIAM LANGLAND, the probable author of *Piers Plowman*, lived from c. 1332 to c. 1400.

# WILLIAM LANGLAND

# THE BOOK CONCERNING PIERS THE PLOWMAN

RENDERED INTO
MODERN ENGLISH BY
DONALD AND RACHEL ATTWATER

EDITED BY
RACHEL ATTWATER, M.A.

LONDON   J. M. DENT & SONS LTD
NEW YORK   E. P. DUTTON & CO. INC

# INTRODUCTION

THE POEM.  The work called compendiously *The Book concerning Piers the Plowman* (*Liber de Petro Plowman*) is known in forty-seven manuscripts, in which scholars have agreed to recognize three versions of the text, called respectively the A-text, written soon after 1362; the B-text, written about 1378; and the C-text, written in 1398 or 1399.  Each text contains two distinct parts (though they are not generally distinguished in the manuscripts), namely, The Vision of William concerning Piers the Plowman and the Vision of the same concerning Do-well, Do-better, and Do-best.  The standard editions of these texts are those of Dr W. W. Skeat, published by the Early English Text Society, in four volumes, in 1867–84, and by the Clarendon Press in two volumes, 1886.  The various known manuscripts are written in a mixture of the Midland and Southern dialects of Middle English, somewhat influenced by the Western dialect; but they vary considerably, both in dialect and text.  That on which Professor Skeat based his B-text is MS. Laud Misc. 581 in the Bodleian Library.

THE AUTHOR.  The authorship of this poem has been the subject of a wordy and involved dispute among literary historians and critics.  The traditional view, resting partly on external but mainly on internal evidence, was that the author's christening name was William, for he refers to himself as Will in several passages, and his name is given as William in most of the manuscripts; that his surname was Langland (which is given in two early manuscripts, one of which adds the information that he was son of one Stacy de Rokayle, who held land at Shipton-under-Wychwood); that he was born at Cleobury Mortimer about 1332 (according to a writer one hundred and fifty years later); that he was put to school, probably with the Benedictines at Great Malvern; that he became a clerk in minor orders and wrote *The Book concerning Piers Plowman* (A-text) shortly after he had gone to London, where he later re-wrote and enlarged the poem (B-text); and he lived for many years on Cornhill with his wife Kit and his daughter Kalote (that he married accounts for his not being further ordained); that he earned a precarious and poor living by such clerical means (in both senses) as he might, that he wore the clerical tonsure and dress, and that he was so tall as to be known familiarly as Long Will; that he again revised his poem (C-text), and died we know not when nor where.

With minor variations this account of the writer and the writing of the poem was accepted without question until the beginning of this century, when Professor J. M. Manly produced a theory, supported by textual evidence, that the poem was written not by one but by five persons: not, of course, in concert, but as independent editors and continuers. This provoked a very pretty battle of the kind in which literary historians and textual critics delight. Dr Furnivall and Dr Henry Bradley, with some hesitation, supported the conclusions of Professor Manly; and M. Jusserand led the single-author party, whose case was strengthened by the researches of Professor R. W. Chambers: articles, replies, pamphlets, rejoinders, letters and counter-letters were written and published; Langland was 'on trial for his life,' he was sentenced, hanged, drawn, quartered, and resuscitated— several times over.

But in spite of the difficulties raised by these learned men, it may be said with confidence that the balance of literary, textual, philological, and metrical evidence is still on the side of a single author; and that this author was William Langland has found fresh and valuable support in later investigations of a kind too little used in the solving of literary and historical puzzles, namely, research, inquiry, and observation in the neighbourhood concerned. It appears clear from the work of Mr Allan H. Bright (*New Light on 'Piers Plowman*,' Oxford, 1928) that we may continue to hold undisturbed the traditional account of Long Will, with two important modifications, namely, that he was born not at Cleobury in Cheshire but at Ledbury in Hereford-shire, and that he was the *illegitimate* son of Stacy de Rokayle.

THIS VERSION. Of the prologue and first seven *passus* of the B-text, for the version of which herein I alone am responsible, several translations into modern English have been made. My object in making another was simply and solely to produce a version with the minimum of alteration and verbal substitution of the Middle English text necessary for its understanding by an ordinary reader in the twentieth century. To do this, and at the same time always to retain the original alliterative metre, was impossible; nor did this grieve me overmuch: for Langland himself kept on breaking the metrical rules, either because he was more interested in the sense than the sound, or else because he did not think regularity necessary to make a good poem—he was no 'literary man,' and his academic fame to-day doubtless astonishes him. I paraphrased as little as possible, preferring a few obscurities to excessive messing about with the text. Those who wish for a straightforward version, in prose and with all things made clear, cannot do better than that of Miss Kate Warren (London, 1913); for a metrical version, with the poem sacrificed to the verse, there is that of Professor Skeat (London, 1905): I used both of these for reference purposes, especially Miss Warren's, which is an excellent piece of work.

Without the erudition and monumental labours of Professor Skeat this version would have been impossible, and I have to make acknowledgment to the Delegates of the Oxford University Press for their permission to use his B-text, the minor edition in the Clarendon Press Series, of which the ninth edition was published in 1906. I must also acknowledge my indebtedness for help and information to Mr Allan H. Bright.

THE THEME. Whatever may be the literary, philological, and historical importance of *The Book concerning Piers Plowman*, its interest to the ordinary reader is still the same as it was to its writer, namely, personal. I have said that Langland was not a 'literary man,' least of all in the self-conscious modern sense—perhaps the expression has no other sense: anyway, he was not primarily a man of art but a man of prudence, in fact, a moralist. And his poem is a tract. Therein is its interest to-day as in the fourteenth century; that is why it is republished in cheap editions and read by others beside professors and students. However much human nature may change superficially, men continue to have a bias towards inordinate behaviour in thought, word, and deed, and so long as we have that characteristic, whether the resulting disorder be regarded as 'sinful' or as simply 'anti-social,' so long will moralists, professional or amateur, rise up and endeavour to reduce us to the ways of virtue.

And the miserable sinners, however unwilling we may be to be cured of our distemper, are far from being uninterested in the attempts to do so; some even acquire considerable skill in criticism of the efforts; and this interest in our physicians is not an exhibition of diabolical cynicism. For we know that the moralist is really in the right of it; that the heart of man does tend to be desperately wicked—however you like to account for it; that left to ourselves we shall make a hell of this world and deserve the same in the next; that God is not mocked.

So Langland's poem is read, not indeed deliberately as an ascetical exercise, but because it is a good tract, a bit of moralist's work well done: the poem and the argument are one thing, and that thing gratifies our mind in general and satisfies our conscience in particular.

Those who have never read the book commonly suppose it to be an attack on the iniquities of those in places of power and advantage, especially of spiritual authority: that the author was a morning-star of the Reformation and a forerunner of what is called modern democracy. This is a complete misunderstanding. Langland was a faithful son of the medieval Church, and his politics were anything but 'radical': the State should be governed by a Prince, the personification but not the nominee or the tool of his people, whom he rules with the aid of Conscience and Reason. And his attack on wickedness and abuses was not by way of direct denouncement, of rhetoric (in its improper sense), or a playing on the feelings of a mob; but a logical explanation directed at common sense and right reason. 'This,' he said in effect, 'is how you behave, poor and rich, lowly as well as great. Of course it must follow that the world is in a mess and you are unhappy.' There is none of the demagoguery which flatters our self-esteem and tickles our lust for change, telling us what fine fellows we are and that it is our institutions that are at fault. On the contrary. He makes it clear enough to his contemporaries that their institutions were all right, but their human weakness and ill-will misused them or made them helpless. 'Christianity has been tried and has failed.' 'It has not failed because it has not been tried.' Langland's one remedy for the troubles of his day was religion: he was therefore not a social reformer in the classical sense.

The efforts of moralists, especially Christian moralists, are less effective than they should be, and bring down dislike and contempt on their makers, because the impression is so often given that the moralist views with jealousy, or is trying improperly to narrow the bounds of, lawful human enjoyment. The notion is quite wrong and quite understandable. The average professional moralist has only average insight, energy, enthusiasm, and spirituality, and so he takes the easiest line, concentrates on the

more obviously disorderly actions and abuses of acts intrinsically good, and denounces and exhorts with a lamentable
lack of discrimination and finesse, meeting exaggeration with
exaggeration.

Not so Langland. 'Chastity without charity shall be chained
in Hell,' he says, and has done. Charity, that is, not a vague
benevolence, a 'universal embrace,' or even just refraining from
adverse speech and being kind (especially to those one likes), but
the habit or virtue which enables men to love God above all
things for His own sake and for His sake to love all their fellow
men; the *agape* of St Paul. It goes to the root of the matter,
psychologically, theologically, and spiritually. He does not exhort his hearers to fantastic penances, to heroic renunciations,
to revolutionary changes, to action against their proper state and
personal nature: the rich are not abused for being rich, but told to
have pity on the poor; the poor are to work and not over-reach
their neighbours; the monk is not told to leave his cloister and get
busy in the world, for prayer is work, and Christ ordained the
contemplative life; those who will not work shall be coerced by
Hunger, yet no beggar must be refused *quia incertum pro quo Deo
magis placeas*; trade is not condemned, but merchants must try
to be honest (Langland does not seem very hopeful about this);
neither is the law condemned, but lawyers must observe equity;
nothing shall be done out of measure. In a word, he preaches
on the text of St Augustine: *Dilige et quod vis fac*, Love, and do
what you will.

Joined with Charity as handmaidens of Truth (God the
Father) is Reason. Charity is not personified in the poem, but
Reason is, and the part he plays may be studied profitably both
by those who have old-fashioned ideas about the 'ages of faith'
and those who have new-fashioned and sub-human ideas about
the worthlessness of intellectual processes. To Reason Conscience appeals against his projected wedding to Meed ('Graft');
with Conscience he is made the perpetual counsellor of the King;
and his sermon moves the Deadly Sins to confess themselves to
Repentance. Then, and not till then, towards the end of Passus
V, does Piers himself appear on the scene, and he quickly develops
from the hard-working, God-fearing yeoman farmer, taught by
Truth through Conscience and Mother-Wit, into what is practically an incarnation of God the Son, embodying in himself
Reason, Conscience, Mother-Wit, and the rest. Christ, as man,
is the common man, Piers Plowman. To him God the Father

entrusts the dispensing of a bull of pardon surpassing all others, that supreme indulgence which is man's Redemption and the price of which is good deeds, both spiritual and corporal.

DONALD ATTWATER.

1930.

The second part of the poem, *The Vision of Do-well, Do-better, and Do-best,* is a broadening and deepening of the theme. The strictures on the life of the world, and especially on the ways of church dignitaries in relation to that world, are still there in abundance. But Langland is primarily examining the fundamental principles on which his strictures rest. What is in fact 'the good life'? What is it to do well, to do better, and to do best? His illustrations and parallels are many and varied, but they are finally all taken up into the life of our Lord, and especially His death and resurrection. The poem, however, does not end on any such devotional climax. In Passus XIX Langland returns, or rather goes forward, to the church of to-day, as it were, working, suffering, fighting the arrayed forces of evil and betrayals from within not always with conspicuous success. Finally Conscience, in great distress, sets out to seek Piers the Plowman—Langland's continued symbol of integrity, from the man working in the field to Christ Himself. The pilgrimage has only just begun.

In making a version of the B-text of *The Vision of Do-well, Do-better, and Do-best* I have followed the same principles as those which directed the version of *The Vision of Piers Plowman*; that is, making changes only as it was necessary for clarification for the modern reader. It has been attempted to preserve the style of Langland, his own peculiar 'flavour,' which includes not only variety but a lack of academic care (if we do not call it carelessness) which makes such treatment not only possible but rewarding.

RACHEL ATTWATER.

1957.

# SELECT BIBLIOGRAPHY

EDITIONS. W. W. Skeat: *The Vision of William concerning Piers the Plowman*. 2 vols. Oxford, 1886 (the standard edition of all three texts); *Publications of the Early English Text Society*, Nos. 28, 38, 54, 81 (separate editions of A, B, and C Texts, with notes and glosses).


TRANSLATIONS. W. W. Skeat: *The Vision of Piers Plowman*, London (1906); K. M. Warren: *The Vision of Piers the Plowman*, London (1913) (Prose. Prologue and Passus, B Text); H. W. Wells: *The Vision of Piers Plowman*, London (1935) (Verse. Whole poem); N. K. Coghill: *Visions from Piers Plowman*, London (1949) (Verse. Selections); J. F. Goodridge: *Piers the Ploughman*, Harmondsworth (1959) (Prose. Complete poem, B Text).


STUDIES. (*a*) *General*

D. Chadwick: *Social Life in the Days of Piers Plowman*, Cambridge (1922); R. W. Chambers: 'Long Will, Dante, and the Righteous Heathen,' *Essays and Studies*, 9; N. K. Coghill: 'The Character of Piers Plowman considered from the B Text,' in *Medium Aevum*, 2. 108–135, 1933; F. A. R. Carnegy: *The Relations between the Social and Divine Order in William Langland's Vision*, Breslau (1934); G. Hort: *Piers Plowman and Contemporary Religious Thought*, London (1938); R. W. Chambers: *Man's Unconquerable Mind*, chs. 4 and 5, London (1939); N. K. Coghill: *The Pardon of Piers Plowman*, London (1946).

(*b*) *Authorship, date, construction*

*The Piers Plowman Controversy.* Publications of the Early English Text Society, 139. Extra issue, 1910 (essays by Jusserand, Manly, Chambers, and Bradley); R. W. Chambers: 'Text of Piers Plowman: Critical Methods,' in *Modern Language Review* (Cambridge), *11*. 257–275 (1916); 'The Three Texts of Piers Plowman and their Grammatical Forms,' in *Modern Language Review*, *14*. 129–51 (1919); 'The Text of Piers Plowman' (with Grattan) in *Modern Language Review*, *26*. 1–51 (1926); A. H. Bright: *New Light on 'Piers Plowman*,' London (1928); J. A. W. Bennett: 'The Date of the B Text of Piers Plowman' in *Medium Aevum*, 11. 55–64 (1943); G. H. Gerould: 'The Structural Integrity of Piers Plowman' in *Studies in English Philology*, *45*. 60–75 (1948); J. R. Hulbert: 'Piers the Plowman after Forty Years' in *Modern Philology* (Chicago), *45*. 215–25 (1948); B. F. Huppé: 'Piers Plowman: the Date of the B Text Reconsidered' in *Studies in English Philology*, *46*. 6–13 (1949).

## PUBLISHER'S NOTE

The Donald Attwater translation of *The Vision*
is reproduced here by arrangement with Messrs
Cassell & Co. Ltd. *Do-well, Do-better and
Do-best* is based on Dr Skeat's edition (1886)
by permission of the Clarendon Press, Oxford.

# CONTENTS

The poem is written in the traditional long alliterative line which is divided in two by a caesura, each part being linked by alliteration or 'initial rhyme.' In the present rendering this pause is indicated by a space.

# INCIPIT LIBER
## DE PETRO PLOWMAN

## PROLOGUS

In a summer season    when soft was the sun,
I clothed myself in a cloak    as I shepherd were,
Habit like a hermit's    unholy in works,
And went wide in the world    wonders to hear.
But on a May morning    on Malvern hills,
A marvel befell me    of fairy, methought.
I was weary with wandering    and went me to rest
Under a broad bank    by a brook's side,
And as I lay and leaned over    and looked into the waters
I fell into a sleep    for it sounded so merry.

Then began I to dream    a marvellous dream,
That I was in a wilderness    wist I not where.
As I looked to the east    right into the sun,
I saw a tower on a toft    worthily built;
A deep dale beneath    a dungeon therein,
With deep ditches and dark    and dreadful of sight.
A fair field full of folk    found I in between,
Of all manner of men    the rich and the poor,
Working and wandering    as the world asketh.
Some put them to plow    and played little enough,
At setting and sowing    they sweated right hard
And won that which wasters    by gluttony destroy.

Some put them to pride    and apparelled themselves so
In a display of clothing    they came disguised.

To prayer and penance    put themselves many,
All for love of our Lord    living hard lives,
In hope for to have    heavenly bliss.
Such as anchorites and hermits    that kept them in their cells,
And desired not the country    around to roam;
Nor with luxurious living    their body to please.

And some chose trade    they fared the better,
As it seemeth to our sight    that such men thrive.

And some to make mirth    as minstrels know how,
And get gold with their glees    guiltlessly, I hold.
But jesters and janglers    children of Judas,
Feigning their fancies    and making folk fools,
They have wit at will    to work, if they would;
Paul preacheth of them    I'll not prove it here—
*Qui turpiloquium loquitur*    is Lucifer's hind.

 Tramps and beggars    went quickly about,
Their bellies and their bags    with bread well crammed;
Cadging for their food    fighting at ale;
In gluttony, God knows    going to bed,
And getting up with ribaldry    the thieving knaves!
Sleep and sorry sloth    ever pursue them.

 Pilgrims and palmers    pledged them together
To seek Saint James    and saints in Rome.
They went forth on their way    with many wise tales,
And had leave to lie    all their life after—
I saw some that said    they had sought saints:
Yet in each tale that they told    their tongue turned to lies
More than to tell truth    it seemed by their speech.

 Hermits, a heap of them    with hooked staves,
Were going to Walsingham    and their wenches too;
Big loafers and tall    that loth were to work,
Dressed up in capes    to be known from others;
And so clad as hermits    their ease to have.

 I found there friars [1]    of all the four orders,
Preaching to the people    for profit to themselves,
Explaining the Gospel    just as they liked,
To get clothes for themselves    they construed it as they would.
Many of these master friars    may dress as they will,
For money and their preaching    both go together.
For since charity hath been chapman    and chief to shrive lords,
Many miracles have happened    within a few years.
Except Holy Church and they    agree better together,
Great mischief on earth    is mounting up fast.

 There preached a pardoner [2]    as if he priest were:
He brought forth a brief    with bishops' seals thereon,
And said that himself might    absolve them all
From falseness in fasting    and of broken vows.
 Laymen believed him    welcomed his words,

   [1] See page 202.    [2] See page 202.

And came up on their knees    to kiss his seals;
He cozened them with his brevet    dimmed their eyes,
And with his parchment    got his rings and brooches:
Thus they gave their gold    gluttons to keep.
And lend it to such louts    as follow lechery.
If the bishop were holy    and worth both his ears,
His seal should not be sent    to deceive the people.
But a word 'gainst bishop    the knave never preacheth.
Parish priest and pardoner    share all the silver
That the parish poor would have    if he were not there.
   Parsons and parish priests    complained to the bishop
That their parishes were poor    since the pestilence time,
And asked leave and licence    in London to dwell
And sing *requiems* for stipends    for silver is sweet.
   Bishops and bachelors [1]    both masters and doctors,
That have charge under Christ    and the tonsure as token
And sign that they should    shrive their parishioners,
Preach and pray for them    and feed the poor,
These lodge in London in Lent    and at other times too.
Some serve the king    and his silver count
In Chequer and Chancery courts    making claim for his debts
Of wards and of wardmotes    waifs and estrays.
And some serve as servants    to lords and ladies,
And instead of stewards    sit in session to judge.
Their Mass and their matins    their canonical hours,
Are said undevoutly    I fear at the last
Lest Christ in his council    accurse will full many.
I perceived of the power    that Peter had to keep,
To bind and to unbind    as the Book telleth,
How he left it with love    as our Lord ordained,
Amongst four virtues    the best of all virtues,
That cardinal are called    for they hinge the gates
Where Christ is in glory    to close and to shut
And to open it to them    and show heavenly bliss.
But of cardinals at Rome    that received that name
And power presumed in them    a pope to make,
To have Peter's power    deny it I will not;
For to love and learning    that election belongeth,
Therefore I can, and yet cannot    of that court speak more.
   Then came there a king    with knighthood before him,

[1] See page 202.

The might of the commons     made him to reign;
Then came Mother-Wit     and he made wise clerks
For to counsel the king     and the commons save.

    The king and the knighthood     the clergy as well,
Planned that the commons     should provide for themselves.

    The commons contrived     of Mother-Wit, crafts,
And for profit of all     they plowmen ordained
To till and travail     as true life asketh.
The king and the commons     and Mother-Wit too
Cause by law and loyalty     each man to know his own.

    Then looked up a lunatic     a lean thing withal,
And kneeling before the king     well speaking said:
'Christ keep thee sir King     and thy kingdom,
And grant thee to rule the realm     so Loyalty may love thee,
And for thy rightful ruling     be rewarded in heaven.'

    Then in the air on high     an angel of heaven
Stooped and spoke in Latin     for simple men could not
Discuss nor judge     that which should justify them,
But should suffer and serve     therefore said the angel:

    *'Sum Rex, sum Princeps: neutram fortasse deinceps;*
     *O qui jura regis Christi specialia regis, hoc quod agas melius justus es,*
      *esto pius!*
     *Nudum jus a te vestiri vult pietate; qualia vis metere talia grana sere.*
     *Si jus nudatur nudo de jure metatur; si seritur pietas de pietate metas.'*

Then an angry buffoon     a glutton of words,
To the angel on high     answered after:

     *'Dum rex a regere dicatur nomen habere,*
     *Nomen habet sine re nisi studet jura tenere.'*

    Then began all the commons     to cry out in Latin,
For counsel of the king     construe how-so he would:

     *'Praecepta regis sunt nobis vincula legis.'*

[1] With that there ran a rout     of rats at once,
And small mice with them     more than a thousand,
And came to a council     for their common profit;
For a cat from the Court     came when he liked
And o'er leaped them lightly     and caught them at will,
Played with them perilously     and pushed them about.
'For dread of divers dangers     we dare not look about;
If we grumble at his game     he will attack us all,
Scratch us or clutch us     and in his claws hold us,

                [1] See page 202.

So that we loathe life     ere he lets us go.
Could we with any wit     his will withstand
We might be lords above him     and live at our ease.'
    A rat of renown     most ready of tongue
Said, as a sovereign     help to himself:
'I have seen men,' quoth he     'in the city of London
Bearing bright necklaces     about their necks,
Some with collars of skilful work     uncoupled they wander
Both in warrens and wastes     wherever they like;
And otherwhile they are elsewhere     as I tell you.
Were there a bell on their collars     by Jesus, I think
Men might know where they went     and get out of their way!
And right so,' quoth that rat     'reason me showeth
To buy a brass bell     or one of bright silver
Make it fast to a collar     for our common profit,
And hang it on the cat's neck     then we may hear
When he romps or rests     or runneth to play.
And if he wants play     then we may look out
And appear in his presence     the while he play liketh,
And if he gets angry, beware     and shun all his paths.'
All this rout of rats     to this plan assented.
But though the bell was bought     and on the collar hanged,
There was not a rat in the rout     for all the realm of France
That dare bind on the bell     about the cat's neck,
Nor hang it round her ears     all England to win;
They held themselves not bold     and their counsel feeble,
Esteemed their labour as lost     and all their long plotting.
    A mouse that knew much more     as it seemed to me,
Ran forth determined     and stood before them all,
And to the rout of rats     rehearsed these words:
'Though we killed the cat     yet there would come another,
To scratch us and all our kind     though we creep under benches.
Therefore I counsel all the commons     to let the cat be,
And be we never so bold     to show to him the bell;
For I heard my sire say     now seven years ago,
"When the cat is a kitten     the Court is right wretched,"
As witnesseth Holy Writ     whoso will it read:
    " *Vae tibi, terra, cujus rex puer est.* "
No man can have rest there     for the rats by night;
While the cat catcheth conies     he covets not our carrion,
But feeds himself on venison     may we never defame him!

For better is a little loss    than a long sorrow;
He's the fear among us all    whereby we miss worse things.
For many men's malt    we mice would destroy,
And the riot of rats    would rend men's clothes,
Were it not for that Court cat    that can leap in among you;
For had ye rats your will    ye could not rule yourselves.
As for me,' quoth the mouse    'I see so much to come
That cat nor kitten never shall    by my counsel be harmed,
Nor carping of this collar    that cost me nothing.
Though it had cost me full dear    I would not own to it
But suffer him to live    and do just as he liketh:
Coupled and uncoupled    to catch what they can.
Therefore each wise wight I warn    to watch well his own.'
    What this dream meaneth    ye men that be merry,
Divine ye, for I never dare    by dear God in heaven!
    There hovered an hundred    in caps of silk,
Serjeants they seemed    who practised at Bar,
Pleading the law    for pennies and pounds,
And never for love of our Lord    unloosing their lips.
You might better measure the mist    on the Malvern hills,
Than get a sound out of their mouth    unless money were showed.
    Barons and burgesses    and bondmen also
I saw in this crowd    as you shall hear later.
Bakers and brewers    and butchers a-many,
Woollen-websters    and weavers of linen,
Tailors and tinkers    toll-takers in markets,
Masons and miners    and men of all crafts.
Of all kinds of labourers    there stood forth some;
Ditchers and diggers    that do their work ill
And spend all the day singing    '*Dieu vous sauve, dame Emme!*'
Cooks and their knaves    cried 'Pies, hot pies!
Good pork and good goose!    Come, dine!    Come, dine!'
    Taverners unto them    told the same tale:
'White wine of Alsace    red wine of Gascony,
Wine of the Rhine, of Rochelle    to help settle your meat!'
All this I saw sleeping    and seven times more.

# PASSUS I

WHAT this mountain meaneth     and the dark dale
And the field full of folk     I fairly will show.
A lady, lovely of looks     in linen clothed,
Came down from a castle     and called me fairly
And said: 'Son, sleepest thou?     Seest thou this people,
How busy they be     about all the throng?
The most part of this people     that passeth on earth,
Have worship in this world     and wish for no better;
Of other heaven than here     they hold no account.'
    I was feared of her face     though she were so fair,
And said, 'Mercy, madam     what is this to mean?'
'The tower on the toft,' quoth she     'Truth is therein
And would have that ye do     as his word teacheth;
For he is Father of Faith     formed you all
Both with flesh and with face     and gave you fine wits
To worship him therewith     while that ye are here.
Therefore he hath bade the earth     to help you each one
With woollen, with linen     with food at your need,
In reasonable measure     to make you at ease.
    'And commanded of his courtesy     three things in common.
None are needful but those     and name them I will
And reckon them rightly     rehearse thou them after.
The first one is vesture     to save thee from chill;
And meat for meals     to save thee misease
And drink when thou art dry     but do naught out of reason
Lest thy worth be wanting     when thou shouldest work.
    'For Lot in his lifetime     for liking of drink
Did with his daughters     what the Devil liked.
He delighted in drink     as the Devil wished,
And Lechery was gainer     and lay with them both,
Putting blame on the wine     for that wicked deed:
> *Inebriamus eum vino, dormiamusque cum eo, ut servare possimus de patre nostro semen.*

Through wine and through women     there was Lot overcome,
Begetting in gluttony     boys that were blackguards.

Therefore dread delicious drink     and thou shalt do the better;
Measure is medicine     though thou yearn for much.
All is not good for the spirit     that the guts asketh,
Nor livelihood to thy body     that is life to the soul.
Believe not thy body     for him a liar teacheth:
That is, the wretched world     which would thee betray.
For the fiend and thy flesh     follow thee together;
This and that chaseth thy soul     and speak in thine heart;
That thou shouldest be ware     I teach thee the best.'
     'Madam, mercy,' quoth I     'I like well your words.
But the money of this earth     that men hold to so fast,
Tell me, madam, to whom     that treasure belongeth?'
     'Go to the Gospel,' quoth she     'that God spoke himself,
When the people posed him     with a penny in the Temple,
Whether they should therewith     worship king Caesar.
And God asked of them     of whom spake the writing
And likewise the image     that stood thereon?
"*Caesaris*," they said     "Each one sees him well."
     '"*Reddite Caesari*," quoth God     "that *Caesari* belongeth,
*Et quae sunt Dei, Deo*     or else ye do ill."
For rightful Reason     should rule you all,
And Mother-Wit be warden     your wealth to keep,
And tutor of your treasure     to give it you at need;
For husbandry and they     hold well together.'
Then I asked her plainly     by him that made her,
'That dungeon in the dale     that dreadful is to see,
What may it mean     *ma dame*, I beseech you?'
     'That is the castle of Care     whoso cometh therein
May curse he was born     in body or in soul.
Therein abideth a wight     that is called Wrong,
Father of Falsehood     who built it himself.
Adam and Eve     he egged on to ill;
Counselled Cain     to kill his brother;
Judas he jockeyed     with Jewish silver,
And then on an elder     hanged him after.
He is the letter of love     and lieth to all;
Those who trust in his treasure     betrayeth he soonest.'
     Then had I wonder in my wit     what woman it were
That such wise words     of Holy Writ showed,
And asked her in the high name     ere she thence went,
Who indeed she was     that taught me so fairly?

'Holy Church I am,' quoth she    'thou oughtest me to know.
I received thee first    and taught thee the faith,
And thou broughtest me sponsors    my bidding to fulfil
And to love me loyally    while thy life lasteth.'
   Then I fell on my knees    and cried of her grace,
And prayed her piteously    to pray for my sins,
And to teach me kindly    on Christ to believe,
That I might work his will    that made of me man.
'Show me no treasure    but tell me this only—
How may I save my soul    thou that holy art held?'
   'When all treasures are tried,' quoth she    'truth is the best;
I appeal to *Deus caritas*    to tell thee truth;
It is as dear a darling    as dear God himself.
   'Whoso is true of his tongue    and telleth none other,
And doth works therewith    and willeth no man ill:
He is a god, says the Gospel    on earth and in heaven,
And like to our Lord    by Saint Luke's own words.
The clergy that know this    should tell it about,
For Christian and heathen    alike claim the truth.
   'Kings and their knights all    should care for it rightly;
Ride to reach the oppressors    all round the realms,
And take *trangressores*    tying them tightly,
Till Truth had determined    the tale of their trespass.
That profession plainly    pertaineth to knights;
Not to fast on one Friday    in five score winters,
But hold with him and with her    that desireth all truth
And never leave them for love    nor for seizing of silver.
   'For David in his days    dubbed knights,
And swore them on their swords    to serve Truth ever;
And whoso passed that point    *apostata* was from the order.
   'But Christ, king of all kings    ten orders knighted,
Cherubim and Seraphim    seven such and one other,
And gave them might of his majesty    the merrier they thought it;
And over his common court    made them archangels,
Taught them by the Trinity    the truth to know
And to bow to his bidding    he bade them naught else.
   'Lucifer with his legions    learned it in Heaven,
But because he obeyed not    his bliss he did lose,
And fell from that fellowship    in a fiend's likeness
Into a deep dark hell    to dwell there for ever;
And more thousands with him    than man could number

Leapt out with Lucifer     in loathly form:
For they believed in him     that lied in this manner—
    *Ponam pedem in aquilone, et similis ero altissimo.*
    'And all that hoped it might be so     no Heaven might hold them;
They fell out in fiend's likeness     nine days together,
Till God of his goodness     steadied and stayed
Made the heavens to be shut     and stand so in quiet.
    'When these wicked went out     wonderwise they fell;
Some in air, some in earth     and some in deep hell;
But Lucifer lowest     lieth of them all.
For the pride he put on     his pain hath no end;
And all that work wrong     wander they shall
After their death day     and dwell with that wretch.
But those that work well     as holy writ telleth,
And end, as I have said     in truth, that is best,
May be sure that their soul     shall wend to Heaven,
Where Truth is in Trinity     and enthroneth them all.
Therefore I say, as I said     in sight of these texts,
When all treasures are tried     Truth is the best.
Learn these unlearned     for lettered men know it,
That Truth is treasure     the best tried on earth.'
    'Yet have I no natural knowing,' [1] quoth I     'ye must teach me better,
By what craft of my body     begins it, and where.'
    'Thou doting duffer,' quoth she     'dull are thy wits;
Too little Latin thou learnest     man, in thy youth;
    *Heu mihi, quod sterilem duxi vitam juvenilem!*
    'It is natural knowing,' quoth she     'that teacheth thine heart
For to love thy good Lord     liefer than thyself;
No deadly sin to do     die though thou shouldest:
This I trow to be Truth     who can teach thee better,
See you suffer him to say     and then teach it after.
For thus witnesseth his words     work thou thereafter;
For Truth telleth that Love     is the remedy of Heaven;
No sin may be seen in him     that useth that sort,
And all his works he wrought     with Love as he listed;
And taught it Moses for the best thing     and most like to Heaven
With the plant of peace     most precious of virtues.
    'For Heaven might not hold it     so heavy of itself,
Till it had of the earth     eaten its fill.
    'And when it had of this fold     flesh and blood taken,
                    [1] See page 202.

Never was leaf upon linden    lighter thereafter,
And pricking and piercing    as the point of a needle,
That no armour might stay it    nor any high walls.
  'Therefore is Love leader    of the Lord's folk of Heaven,
And a mean, as the mayor is    between king and commons;
Right so is Love a leader    and the law shapeth,
Upon man for his misdeeds    he fixeth the fine.
And for to know it by nature    it springeth in might,
In the heart is its head    and there its well-spring.
  'For in natural knowing    there might beginneth
That comes from the Father    that formed us all,
Looked on us with love    and let his Son die
Meekly for our misdeeds    to amend us all;
And yet would he them no woe    that wrought him that pain,
But meekly with his mouth    mercy he besought
To have pity of that people    that pained him to death.
  'Here might thou see examples    in himself alone,
That he was mightful and meek    and mercy did grant
To them that hanged him on high    and pierced his heart.
  'Therefore I rede you rich    to have pity on the poor;
Though ye be mighty at law    be meek in your works.
  'For the same measures that ye mete    amiss or aright,
Ye shall be weighed therewith    when ye wend hence;
    *Eadem mensura qua mensi fueritis, remetietur vobis.*
  'For though ye be true of your tongue    and honestly earn,
And as chaste as a child    that weepeth in church,
Unless ye love loyally    and give to the poor,
Such goods as God sends you    to them gladly giving,
Ye have no more merit    in Mass or in hours
Than Malkin of her maidenhood    that no man desireth.
  'For James the gentle    judged in his books
That faith without deed    is right nothing worth
And as dead as a door-post    unless actions follow;
    *Fides sine operibus mortua est, etc.*
  'Therefore chastity without charity    shall be chained in hell;
It is lacking as a lamp    that no light is in.
Many churchmen are chaste    but their charity is away;
Are no men more avaricious    when they be advanced:
Unkind to their kin    and to all Christian folk,
They chew up their charity    and chide after more.
Such chastity without charity    shall be chained in hell.

'Many pastors keep themselves    clean in their bodies
But are cumbered with covetousness    they can not drive it from them
So hardly hath avarice    hasped them together.
And that is no truth of the Trinity    but treachery of hell,
Lessoning the unlearned    to withhold their alms.
    'Therefore these words    are written in the Gospel,
*Date et dabitur vobis*    for I give to you all.
And that is the lock of Love    that letteth out my grace
To comfort the care-full    encumbered with sin.
    'Love is leech of life    and next our Lord's self,
And also the right road    that runneth unto Heaven;
Therefore I say as I said    before by the texts,
When all treasures be tried    Truth is the best.
Now have I told thee what Truth is    that no treasure is better;
I may linger no longer thee with    now look on thee our Lord!'

Yet I knelt on my knees    and cried of her grace,
And said: 'Mercy, Madame    for Mary's love of Heaven.
That bore that blissful Child    that bought us on the rood,
Teach me by some skilled way    Falsehood to know.'
   'Look upon thy left side    and lo! where he standeth,
Both Falsehood and Flattery    and their many fellows!'
   I looked on my left side    as the lady taught me,
And was ware of a woman    worthily clothed,
With fringes of fur    the finest on earth,
Crowned with a crown    the king hath no better
Featly her fingers    were framed with gold wire,
And thereon red rubies    as red as any coal,
And diamonds of dearest price    and two kinds of sapphires,
Orientals and beryls    poison banes to destroy.
   Her robe was full rich    of red scarlet dyed,
With ribands of red gold    and of richest stones;
Her array me ravished    such riches saw I never;
I had wonder what she was    and whose wife she were.
   'What is this woman,' quoth I    'so worthily attired?'
'That is Meed [1] the Maid,' quoth she    'who hath vexed me full oft,
And lied of my lover    that Loyalty is called,
And slandered him to lords    that have to guard laws;
In the pope's palace    familiar as myself,
Though truth would not so    for she is a bastard.
   'For Flattery was her father    that had a fickle tongue
And never said sooth    since he came to earth.
And Meed is mannered after him    right as nature requireth;
     *Qualis pater, talis filius bona arbor bonum fructum facit.*
   'I ought to be higher than she    my birth is the better.
My father the great God is    and ground of all graces,
One infinite God    and I his good daughter;
And he gave me Mercy    to marry with myself.
And what man be merciful    and loyally me love
Shall be my lord, I his lover    in highest Heaven.
   'And what man taketh Meed    mine head dare I lay
That he shall lose for her love    a lot of *caritatis.*
How construeth David the king    of men that take Meed

[1] See page 202.

13

And of men of this mould     that maintaineth Truth
And how ye shall save yourselves     the Psalter beareth witness:
    *Domine, quis habitabit in tabernaculo tuo, etc.*
  'And now will Meed be married     all to a cursed wretch,
To one False-Fickle-Tongue     offspring of a fiend.
Flattery through his fair speech     hath this folk enchanted,
And all is Liar's leading     that she is thus wedded.
  'To-morrow will be made     the maiden's bridal,
And there might thou know if thou wilt     which they be all
That belong to that lordship     the less and the more.
Know them there if thou canst     and keep thy tongue still,
Blame them not, but let be     till Loyalty be judge
And have power to punish them     then put forth thy plaint.
  'I commend thee to Christ,' quoth she     'and his clean mother,
And may no conscience cumber thee     for coveting of Meed.'
  Thus left me that lady     there lying asleep.
And how Meed was married     meseemed in a dream
That all the rich retinue     that with Falsehood reign
Were bidden to the bridal     on both the two sides
Of all manner of men     the mean and the rich.
To marry this maiden     was many man assembled,
As of knights and of clerks     and other common people,
Assessors and summoners [1]     sheriffs and their clerks,
Beadles and bailiffs     and brokers of wares,
Couriers and victuallers     advocates of the Arches—
I cannot reckon the rout     that ran about Meed.
  But Simony and Civil Law     and assessors of courts
Were most privy with Meed     of any man, methought.
But Flattery was the first     that fetched her out of bower,
And like a broker brought her     to be with Falsehood joined.
When Simony and Civil Law     saw the will of them both,
They assented, for silver     to say as both would.
Then leapt Liar forth and said     'Lo here! a charter
That Guile with his great oaths     gave them together,'
And prayed Civil Law see     and Simony read it.
Then Simony and Civil Law     stand they forth both
And unfold the enfeoffment     that Falsehood hath made,
And thus being these fellows     to read out full loud:
  '*Sciant praesentes et futuri, etc.*
  'Wit ye and witness ye     that wander on this earth,
                      [1] See page 202.

That Meed is married     more for her goods
Than for any virtue or fairness     or generous nature.
Falseness is fain of her     for he knows her riches;
And Flattery with fickle speech     invests them by charter
To be princes in pride     poverty to despise,
To backbite and to boast     and false witness to bear,
To scorn and to scold     and slander to make,
Disobedient, and bold     to break the Ten Laws.
  'And the earldom of Envy     and of Wrath together,
With the stronghold of Strife     and Chattering-out-of-Reason,
The county of Covetousness     and its coasts about,
That is, Usury and Avarice     all them I grant,
With bargains and brokerage     and the borough of Theft.
  'All the lordship of Lechery     in length and in breadth,
As in works and in wards     and watching with eyes,
And in clothes and in wishings     and with idle thoughts
Where the will gladly would     but the power is weak.'
  Gluttony he gave also     and great oaths together,
And all day to drink     at divers taverns,
There to jangle and jape     and judge their fellow Christians,
And on fast days to feed     before the full time
And then sit and sup     till sleep them assail,
And to breed like town swine     and repose at their ease,
Till sloth and sleep     make sleek their sides;
And Despair to awaken them so     with no will to amend;
They believe themselves lost     this is their last end.
  And they to have and to hold     and their heirs after,
Dwelling with the Devil     and damned be for ever,
With all that pertaining to purgatory     in the pain of hell,
Yielding for this thing     at one year's end
Their souls to Satan     to suffer with him pains
And with him to wander with woe     while God is in heaven.
  In witness of which thing     Wrong was the first,
And Piers the pardoner     of the Pauline order,
Bart the beadle     of Buckinghamshire,
Reynold the reeve     of Rutland soke,
Mund the miller     and many more other.
'On the date of the Devil     this deed I enseal,
In sight of Sir Simony     and by Civil Law's leave.'
  Then Theology was vexed     when this tale he heard,
And said to Civil Law     'Now sorrow mayest thou have,

Such weddings to wangle    to work against Truth;
And ere this wedding be wrought    woe thee betide!
  'For Meed is a woman    of Amends engendered,
And God granted to give    this Meed to Truth;
Thou hast given her a beguiler    now God give thee sorrow!
Thy text telleth thee not so    Truth knows the sooth,
For *dignus est operarius*    his hire to have;
Thou hast fastened her to Falsehood    fie on thy law!
For all by lying thou livest    and lecherous works;
Simony and thyself    shame Holy Church;
The notaries and thee    annoy the people.
Ye shall atone for it both    by God that me made!
Well wot ye, ye liars    unless your wit fails,
That Falsehood is faithless    and false in his works,
And was a bastard born    of Beelzebub's kin.
And Meed is a mistress    a maiden of wealth,
And might kiss the king    as his cousin, if she would.
  'Therefore, work ye by wisdom    and by wit also,
And lead her to London    there law is declared,
If any law will allow    of their lying together.
And though justices judge her    to be joined with Falsehood,
Yet beware of their wedding    for a wise one is Truth
And Conscience is of his council    and knoweth you each one;
And if he find you in default    and with Falsehood hold,
It shall beset your souls    full sour at the last!'
  Hereto assented Civil Law    but Simony would not
Till he had silver for his service    and also the notaries.
  Then fetched Flattery forth    florins enough,
And bade Guile to give    gold all about,
And notably to the notaries    that them none might fail,
And fee False-Witness    with florins enough:
'For he can manage Meed    and make her assent.'
  When this gold was given    great was the thanking
To Falsehood and Flattery    for their fair gifts;
And they came to comfort    from care this Falsehood
And said: 'Certes, sir    cease shall we never
Till Meed be thy wedded wife    through the wits of us all.
For we have Meed managed    with our merry speech,
That she granteth to go    with a very good will
To London to look    if that the law would
Adjudge you jointly    in joy for ever.'

Then was Falseness fain    and Flattery as blithe,
And caused all men to be summoned    from the shires about,
And bade them be bound    beggars and others,
To wend with them to Westminster    to witness this deed.
   But then looked they for horses    to carry them thither,
And Flattery fetched forth then    foals enough,
And set Meed on a sheriff    all newly shod;
Falsehood sat on an assessor    that softly trotted;
Flattery on a flatterer    finely attired.
   Then had notaries none    annoyed they were
That Simony and Civil Law    should on their feet go.
   But then swore Simony    and Civil Law both
That summoners should be saddled    and serve them each one,
And had provisors apparalled    in palfrey wise.
'Sir Simony himself    shall sit their backs.
   'Deans and subdeans    draw you together,
Archdeacons and officials    and all your registrars,
Saddle them with silver    our sin to sanction,
As adultery and divorces    and secret usury,
To bear bishops about    on visitations.
   'Partisans of the Paulines [1]    for plaints in consistory
Shall serve myself    that Civil Law is called;
And cart-saddle the commissary    our cart shall he draw
And fetch forth our victuals    from fornicators' fines.
   'And make of Liar a long cart    to draw all these others,
Such as friars and false fellows    that on their feet run.'
And thus Falsehood and Flattery    fared forth together,
And Meed in the midst    and all these men after.
I have no time to tell    the tail that them followed,
Of many manner of men    that on this mould live;
But Guile was foregoer    and guided them all.
   Truth saw them well    and said but a little,
But pricked his palfrey    and passed them all,
And came to the king's court    and Conscience it told.
And Conscience to the king    rehearsed it after.
'Now by Christ!' quoth the king    'if I might catch
Falsehood or Flattery    or any of his fellows,
I would wreak on those wretches    that work so ill,
Make them hang by the neck    and all that maintain them!
Shall no man on this mould    go bail for the least,

                    [1] See page 202.

But right as law shall allow     let it fall on them all.'
    And commanded a constable     the first one that came,
To, 'Arrest those tyrants     at any cost, I bid;
And fetter Falsehood fast     in spite of any gifts
And get off Guile's head     and let him go not.
And if ye light on Liar     let him not escape
Ere he be put in pillory     for any prayer, I bid;
And bring ye Meed to me     in spite of them all.'
    Dread at the door stood     and the doom heard,
And how the king commanded     constables and serjeants
Falseness and his fellowship     to fetter and to bind.
Then Dread went quickly     and warned Falsehood
And bade him flee for fear     and his fellows all.
    Falsehood for fear then     fled to the friars.
And Guile started to go     aghast for to die.
But merchants met with him     and made him abide
And shut him in their shops     to show their wares,
And apparelled him as a prentice     the people to serve.
    Lightly then Liar     leaped away,
Lurking through lanes     lugged about by many.
He was nowhere welcome     for his many tales,
Everywhere hooted     and hustled away;
Till pardoners had pity     and pulled him indoors.
They washed him and wiped him     and wound him in clouts;
And sent him with seals     on Sundays to churches,
To give pardons [1] for pence     by pounds at a time.
Then looked at him leeches     and letter they sent
That he should live with them     and look at men's water.
Spicers spoke with him     to inspect their wares,
For he kenned their craft     and knew many gums.
But minstrels and messengers     met with him once
And held him an half-year     and eleven days.
    Friars with fair speech     fetched him thence,
And lest others should know him     dressed him as a friar.
But he hath leave to leap out     as oft as him liketh,
And is welcome when he will     to stay with them oft.
    All fled for fear     and were hiding in holes;
Save Meed the Maid     no man durst abide.
But truly to tell     she trembled for dread,
Her hands wrung, and wept     when she was arrested.

[1] See page 202.

# PASSUS III

Now is Meed the Maid    and no more of them all,
With beadles and bailiffs    brought before the king.
The king called a clerk    (I know not his name)
To take Meed the Maid    and make her at ease.
'I shall try her myself    and truly inquire
What man of this earth    is dearest to her.
And if she works by my wisdom    and my will follows
I will forgive her this guilt    so me God help!'
    Courteously the clerk then    as the king ordered,
Took Meed by the middle    and brought her indoors,
And there was mirth and minstrelsy    Maid Meed to please.
They that harboured in Westminster    honoured her all;
And gently with joy    of the justices some,
Betook them to the bower    where the bride dwelled
To comfort her kindly    with Learning's leave;
And said: 'Mourn not thou Meed    nor make no sorrow,
For we will counsel the king    and thy way shape
To be wedded at thy will    and where thy love liketh,
For all Conscience's care    or craft, as I trow.'
    Mildly Meed then    thanked them all
For their great goodness    and gave them each one
Cups of clean gold    and cups of silver,
Rings also with rubies    and rich things many,
The least men of her train    money of gold.
Then took they their leave    these lords, of Meed.
    With that came clerks    to comfort her too
And bade her be blithe    'for we be thine own
For to work thy will    so long as thou last.'
Prettily she then    promised them the same,
To 'love you loyally    and lords to make,
And in consistory of the court    to call out your names;
Lack of wit shall not hinder    the man that I love
That he be well advanced    for I am known
Where learned clerks`    shall be left behind.'
    Then came there a confessor    clothed as a friar;
To Meed the Maid    he muttered these words
And said full softly    in shrift as it were:

19

'Though ignorant men and learned     had lain by thee both
And Falseness had followed thee     these fifty winters,
I shall absolve thee myself     for a horse-load of wheat,
Also be thy bedesman     and bear well thy message
Amongst knights and clerks     Conscience to turn.'
     Then Meed for her misdeeds     to that man kneeled,
And shrove her of her sinfulness     shamelessly, I trow,
Told him a tale     and tendered a noble
For to be her bedesman     and her broker too.
     Then soon he absolved her     and afterwards said:
'We have a window a-making     will mulct us in much;
Wouldst thou glaze that gable     and grave on it thy name,
Surer should thy soul be     heaven to have.'
'Wist I that,' quoth that woman     'I would not spare
For to be your friend, friar     and fail you never
All the while you love lords     that lechery haunt
And blame not the ladies     that love well the same.
'Tis but frailty of flesh     you find it in books—
In the course of nature     whereof we all come;
If you scandal escape     scathe is soon mended;
It's the sin of the seven     soonest forgiven.
     'Have you mercy,' quoth Meed     'on men that it haunt
And I shall cover your church     and your cloister make,
Your walls well whiten     and their windows glaze,
Do painting and picturing     and pay for the making,
That all seeing it shall say     'of your house I'm a sister.'
     But God to all good folk     such graving forbiddeth,
To write so in windows     of their worthy deeds,
Lest pride be painted there     and pomp of the world.
For Christ knoweth thy conscience     thy inmost intention,
The cost and thy covetousness     and whose was the wealth.
     Therefore I advise you, lords     leave ye such works,
To write up in windows     of your worthy deeds
Or call for God's men     when ye deal out doles,
Lest ye have your reward here     and your Heaven also.
          *Nesciat sinistra quid faciat dextra.*
Let not thy left half     later or sooner,
Know what thou workest     with thy right side;
For thus bids the Gospel     good men to do alms.
     Mayors and mace-bearers     the means are between
The king and the commons     to see the law kept,

To punish on pillories     and punishment stools
Brewers and bakers     butchers and cooks,
For these are this world's men     that work the most harm
To the poor people that     must buy piece-meal.
    For they poison the people     privily and oft,
Get rich by retailing     and buy themselves rents
With what the poor people     should put in their bellies;
For traded they truly     they'd have built not so high,
Nor bought any ground-rents     be full certain of that!
    But now Meed the Maid     the mayor hath besought
Of all such sellers     silver to take,
Or presents without pence     as goblets of silver,
Rings or other riches     trade's frauds to maintain.
    'For my love,' quoth that lady     'love them each one,
And suffer them to sell     somewhat against reason.'
    Solomon the sage     a sermon he made
For to amend mayors     and men that guard laws,
And told them this theme     that I think to tell:
    *Ignis devorabit tabernacula eorum qui libenter accipiunt munera, etc.*
    Among lettered men     this Latin is to mean
That fire shall fall and burn     all to blue ashes
The houses and the homes     of them that desire
Presents or briberies     because of their office.
    The king from council came     and called after Meed,
And sent for her quickly     with serjeants many,
That brought her to bower     with bliss and with joy.
    Courteously the king then     commenced to talk
To Meed the Maiden     speaking these words:
'Unwisely, woman     wrought hast thou oft;
But worse wroughtest thou never     than when Falsehood you took.
But I forgive thee that guilt     and grant thee my grace;
Hence on, to thy death day     do so no more!
    'I have a knight, Conscience     come of late from beyond.
If he willeth thee to wife     wilt thou him have?'
'Yea, lord,' quoth that lady     'the Lord forbid else!
If I be not wholly at your hest     let me hang soon!'
    And then was Conscience called     to come and appear
Before king and council     the clerks and the others.
Kneeling, then Conscience     to the king louted
To learn what his will were     and what he should do.
    'Wilt thou wed this woman,' quoth the king     'if I will assent?

For she is fain of my fellowship     for to be thy mate.'
    Quoth Conscience to the king     'Christ it me forbid!
Ere I wed such a wife     woe me betide!
For she is frail of her faith     fickle of her speech,
And maketh men misdo     many score times,
Trust in her treasure     betrayeth full many.
To wives and widows     wantonness she teacheth,
And learneth them lechery     that love her gifts.
Your father she felled     through her false behest,
And hath poisoned popes     and impaired Holy Church.
There is no better bawd     by him that me made!
Though me search through the earth     between heaven and hell.
For she is lecherous in her looks     and loose in her tongue,
Common as a cart-road     to each knave that walks,
To monks and to minstrels     and lepers in hedges.
Assessors and summoners     such men her praise;
Sheriffs of shires were ruined     if she were not.
For she makes men to lose     their land and life both.
She letteth pass prisoners     and pays for them often,
Giveth gold to gaolers     and great groats as well
To unfetter the false     to flee where they like;
And taketh the true man by the top-knot     and tieth him fast
And hangeth him for hatred     that harm never did.
To be cursed by a council     she counts not a rush,
For she clotheth the commissory     and covers his clerks;
She's absolved as soon     as herself liketh,
And may nigh as much do     in one single month
As your secret seal     in six score of days.
For she is privy with the pope     provisors it know
For Sir Simony and herself     seal all their bulls.
    'She blesseth the bishops     though they be unlearned
Provideth for parsons     and priests enableth
To have lemans and lovers     all through their lives
And beget them babies     though the law forbids.
Where she is well with the king     woe is the realm,
For she favoureth the false     and fouleth truth oft.
    'By Jesus! with her jewels     your judges she shames,
Lieth against Law     and gets in his way
That Faith may not pass by     her florins are so thick.
She leadeth the law as she list     and law-days maketh,
And makes men lose through her love     that the law may win;

A poor person's perplexed    though he plead for ever.
Law is so lordly    and loth to make end;
Without presents or pence    she pleaseth full few.
    'Barons and burghers she    brings into sorrows,
And the commons to care    that would live in truth;
For clerkship and coveting    she coupleth together.
This is the life of that lady    the Lord give her sorrow!
And all that maintaineth her men    mischance them betide!
For poor men have no power    to complain, though they smart,
Such a master is Meed    among men of wealth.'
    Then mourned Meed    and moaned to the king
To have space to speak    succeed if she might.
    The king granted her grace    with a good will:
'Excuse thee if thou canst    I can no more say,
For Conscience accuseth thee    to cast thee off for ever.'
    'Nay, lord,' quoth that lady    'believe him the less,
When ye understand truly    where the wrong lieth.
Where that mischief is great    Maid Meed may help.
And thou knowest, Conscience    I came not to chide
Nor deprave thy person    with a proud heart.
Well thou knowest, liar    unless thou wilt be,
How thou hast been with me    eleven times,
And griped at my gold    to give where thee liked;
And why thou art wrathful now    a wonder methinketh.
Yet I may, if I might    make to thee gifts
And maintain thy manhood    more than thou knowest.
    'But thou hast famed me foully    before the king here.
For killed I never no king    nor counselled thereafter
Nor did as thou deemest    I appeal to the king!
    'In Normandy was he not    annoyed for my sake.
But thou thyself soothly    shamedst him oft;
Crept into a cabin    for cold of thy nails,
Weening that winter    would have lasted for ever,
And didst dread to be dead    because of the downpour
And hiedest thou homeward    for hunger of guts.
    'Without pity, pillager    poor men thou didst spoil
And bore their brass on thy back    to Calais to sell.
While I lingered with my lord    his life for to save;
I made his men merry    and mended their mourning
I patted their backs and    emboldened their hearts
And made them hop for hope of    my help at their will.

Had I been marshal of his men     by Mary of heaven!
I durst have laid my life     and no less a pledge,
He should have been lord of that land     in length and in breadth,
And also bring of that country     his kin for to help—
The least brat of his blood     the peer of a baron.

'Cowardly thou, Conscience     counselled him thence
To leave all his lordship     for a little silver,
And that the richest realm     that rain hovereth over.

'It becometh a king     that keepeth a realm
To give meed to men     that meekly him serve,
To aliens and to all men     to honour them with gifts.
Meed maketh him loved     and for a man holden.
Emperors and earls     and all manner of lords
For gifts have young men     to run and to ride.
The pope and all prelates     presents accept
And fee men themselves     to maintain their laws.
Servants for their service     we see well the sooth,
Take meed of their masters     as they may agree.
Beggars for their begging     beg of men meed;
And minstrels for their mirth     meed do they ask.
The king hath meed of his men     to make peace in the land;
Men that teach children     crave of them meed.
Priests that preach to the people     for goodness, ask meed,
And mass-pence and their meat     at their meal times.
All kinds of craftsmen     crave meed for their prentice;
Merchants and meed     must needs go together.
No wight, as I ween     without me, Meed, may live.'

Quoth the king to Conscience     'By Christ! as methinketh
Meed is well worthy     the mastery to have.'

'Nay,' quoth Conscience to the king     and kneeled to the earth,
'There are two manner of meeds     my lord, with your leave.
The one, God of his grace     granteth, in his bliss,
To those that do good deeds     the while they are here.
The prophet preacheth thereof     and put it in the Psalter:
     *Domine, quis habitabit in tabernaculo tuo?*
"Lord, who shall dwell in thy dwellings     and with thy holy saints,
Or rest on thine holy hills?"     this asked David.

'And David answered himself     as the Psalter telleth:
     *Qui ingreditur sine macula, & operatur justitiam.*
"Those spotless that enter     and all of one will,
And have wrought their works     with right and with reason;

And he that useth not　　the life of usury,
And instructeth poor men　　and pursueth truth;

> *Qui pecuniam suam non dedit ad usuram, et munera super innocentem,*
> *etc.*

And all that helpeth the innocent　　and hold with the rightful,
And without meed do them good　　and the truth helpeth."
Such manner of men, lord　　shall have this first meed
Of God, at their great need　　when they go hence.

'There is another meed, measureless　　that masters desire.
To maintain misdoers　　meed they do take;
And thereof saith the psalter　　at a psalm's end,

> *In quorum manibus iniquitates sunt, dextra eorum repleta est mun-*
> *eribus;*

And he that graspeth her gold　　so me God help!
Shall abide it bitterly　　or the Book lieth!

'Priests and parsons　　that pleasure desire
And take meed and money　　for the masses they sing,
Receive their meed here　　as Matthew us teacheth:

> *Amen, amen, receperunt mercedem suam.*

That which labourers and low folk　　take of their masters
Is in no manner meed　　but a moderate hire.

'In merchandise is no meed　　I may well it avow:
It is clearly exchange　　one pennyworth for another.

'But readest thou never *Regum* [1]　　thou recreant Meed,
Why the vengeance fell　　on Saul and his children?
God sent to Saul　　by Samuel the prophet
That Agag of Amalek　　and all his people after
Should die for a deed　　that their elders had done.
"So," said Samuel to Saul　　"God himself biddeth
Thee be true at his bidding　　his will to fulfil.
Wend to Amalek with thine host　　and what thou findest there, slay it;
Both men and their beasts　　burn them to death;
Widows and wives　　women and children,
Chattels and fixtures　　and all that thou findest,
Burn, and bear not away　　be it never so rich,
For meed nor for money　　look thou destroy it,
Spill it and spare it not　　thou shalt speed the better."

'Because he coveted cattle　　and the king spared,
Spared both him and his beasts　　the Bible witnesseth,
Otherwise than he was　　warned by the prophet,

[1] See page 203.

God said then to Samuel     that Saul should die,
And his seed for that sin     shamefully end.
Such a mischief Meed     made King Saul to have
That God hated him for ever     and all his heirs after.
The conclusion of this case     I care not to show;
For fear that it vex men     no end will I make.
For so is this world's way     with them that have power,
That whoso saith sooth     is the soonest blamed.

'I, Conscience, know this     Mother-Wit me it taught,
That Reason shall reign     and the realms govern.
As it happened to Agag     shall happen to others.
Samuel shall slay him     and Saul shall be blamed,
And David shall be diademed     and subdue them all;
And one Christian king shall     care for them all.

'Meed shall no more be master     as she is now,
But Love and Lowliness     and Loyalty together,
These shall be masters on earth     Truth to save.

'And who trespasseth against Truth     or traverseth his will,
Loyalty shall judge him     no living man else.
Shall no serjeant for service     wear a silk hood
And no fur on his cloak     for pleading at bar.
Meed of many misdoers     maketh more lords,
And over the lords' laws     ruleth the realms.

'But man's Love shall come yet     and Conscience together,
And make Law a labourer     such love shall arise
And such peace among the people     and a perfect truth
That Jews shall ween in their wits     and wax wondrous glad,
That Moses or Messiah     be come into this earth,
And have wonder in their hearts     that men be so true.

'All that bear a dagger     broad sword or lance,
An axe or an hatchet     or any weapon else
Shall be doomed to the death     if he have it not smithed
Into sickle or scythe     into plow-share or coulter.

     *Conflabunt gladios suos in vomeres, etc.*

Each man to play with a plow     a pick-axe or spade,
Spin, or spread dung     or perish in sloth.

'All priests and parsons     shall hunt with *placebo* [1]
And cry upon David     each day until eve.
Hunting or hawking     if any of them use,
The boast of his benefice     shall be taken from him.

[1] See page 203.

Shall neither king nor knight     constable nor mayor,
Oppress the commons     nor summon to court
Not empanel them on juries     to make them plight truth
But according to the deed done     one judgment shall reward,
Mercy or no mercy     as Truth shall accord.
   'King's court and common court     consistory and chapter,
All shall be but one court     and one baron judge:
Namely True-Tongue, a tidy man     that troubled me never.
Battles shall not be     nor no man bear weapon,
And what smith that any maketh     be smitten therewith to death,
    *Non levabit gens contra gentem gladium, etc.*
   'And ere this fortune fall     men shall find the worst,
By six suns and a ship [1]     and an half sheaf of arrows;
And the full of the moon     shall turn Jews to the Faith,
And Saracens at that sight     shall sing *Gloria in excelsis, etc.*,
For Mahomet and Meed     shall mishap at that time;
    *For melius est bonum nomen quam divitiae multa.*'
  As wroth as the wind then     waxed Meed in a while.
'I know no Latin,' quoth she     'but clerks know the truth.
See what Solomon saith     in Wisdom book,
That they that giveth gifts     the victory win
And much worship have therewith     as holy writ telleth:
    *Honorem adquiret qui dat numera, etc.*'
  'I well believe, lady,' quoth Conscience     'that thy Latin be true;
But thou art like a lady     that once read a lesson:
It was, *Omnia probate*     and that pleased her heart
For that line was no longer     being at the leaf's end.
Had she looked the other side     and turned the leaf over,
She would have found many words     following thereafter:
*Quod bonum est tenete.*     Truth made that text!
And so fared ye, madam!     Ye couldst no more find,
Though ye looked on Wisdom     sitting in your study.
This text that ye have told     were good for the lords
But you lacked a cunning clerk     that could the leaf turn!
And if ye seek Wisdom again     find shall ye that followeth
A full troublesome text     to them that take meed;
And that is, *animam autem auferet accipientium, etc.*
That is the tail of the text     of that that ye shewed:
That, though we win worship     and with meed have victory.
The soul that bribes taketh     is by so much in bonds.'

             [1] See page 203.

# PASSUS IV

'CEASE now!' saith the king     'I suffer you no longer,
Ye shall agree, forsooth     and then serve me both.
Kiss her,' quoth the king     'Conscience, I bid thee.'
    'Nay, by Christ!' quoth Conscience     'dismiss me for ever!
Unless Reason rede me thereto     rather will I die.'
    'And I command thee,' quoth the king     to Conscience then,
'Be ready to ride     and Reason thou fetch;
Command him that he come     my counsel to hear.
For he shall rule my realm     and rede me the best,
And account with thee, Conscience     so me Christ help!
How thou lessonest the people     the learned and unlearned.'
    'I am glad of that charge'     said the man then,
And rode right to Reason     rehearsed in his ear,
And said as the king bade     and soon took his leave.
    'I shall array me to ride,' quoth Reason     'rest thee awhile;'
And called Cato his knave     courteous of speech,
And also Tom-true-tongue-     tell-me-no-tales-
Nor-lies-for-to-laugh-at-     for-I-loved-them-never;
'And set saddle upon Suffer-     till-I-see-my-time,
And girdle it well     with Wise-Word's girths,
Hang on the heavy bridle     to hold his head low,
For he will neigh more than once     ere that he be there.'
    Then Conscience on his courser     fareth forth fast
And Reason with him rode     rehearsing together
What masteries Meed     maketh on this earth.
    One Warren Wisdom     and Witty his fellow
Followed them fast     they had business to do,
In Exchequer and at Chancery     to be discharged:
And rode fast, for Reason     should advise them best
For to save them, for silver     from shame and from harm.
    And Conscience knew them well     they loved covetousness,
And bade Reason ride fast     and reck of them neither.
'There are wiles in their words     and with Meed they dwell;
Where wrath is and wrangling     there win they silver;
But where loyalty and love is     they will not come near.
    *Contritia & in felicitas in viis eorum, etc.*

28

They will give naught for God    not even one goose wing,
    *Non est timor Dei ante oculos eorum.*
For, God knows, they would do more    for a dozen chickens
Or as many capons    or for a sack of oats,
Than for the love of our Lord    or all his loyal saints.
Therefore, Reason, let those rich ones    ride by themselves,
For Conscience knows them not    nor does Christ, as I think.'
And then Reason rode fast    on the right highway,
As Conscience advised    till they came to the king.

    Courteously the king then    came to meet Reason,
And between himself and his son    set him on a bench,
And they talked most wisely    a great while together.

    Then came Peace into parliament    and put forth a bill—
How Wrong against his will    had his wife taken,
How he had ravished Rose    Reginald's love,
And Margaret her maidenhood    not minding her kicks.
Both my poultry and pigs    his purveyors fetch;
I dare not for fear of him    fight or complain.
He borrowed my bay horse    and brought him home never,
Nor no farthing there for    for aught I could plead.
He maintaineth his men    to murder my menials,
Fighteth in my markets    and forestalleth my fairs,
Breaketh up my barn door    beareth off my wheat,
And for ten quarters of oats    tenders a tally;
He beats me also    and lies with my maid—
I am not brave enough    to give him a look.'
The king knew he said sooth    for Conscience him told
Wrong was a wicked wretch    who wrought much sorrow.

    Wrong was afeared then    and Wisdom he sought
To make peace with his pence    and proffered him many,
And said: 'Had I the king's love    little would I reck,
Though Peace and his power    complained for ever.'

    Then went Wisdom    and Sir Warren the witty,
For that Wrong had wrought    so wicked a deed,
And warned Wrong then    with this wise tale:
'Whoso worketh wilfully    wrath maketh oft;
I say it of thyself    thou shalt it well find.
Except Meed it mend    thy mischief is certain,
For both thy life and thy land    lie in his grace.'

    Then wooed Wrong    Wisdom full hard
To make peace with his pence    paid out on the sly.

Wisdom and Wit then　　went they together
And took Meed along with them　　mercy to win.
　　Peace put forth his head　　and his bloody pate:
'Without guilt, God knoweth　　got I this harm;
Conscience and the Commons　　know I speak sooth.'
　　But Wisdom and Wit　　worked away fast
To come over the king　　with money, if they might.
　　The king swore, by Christ　　and by his crown both,
That Wrong for his works　　should woe endure,
And commanded a constable　　to cast him in irons,
'And let him not in seven years　　see his feet once.'
　　'God knows,' quoth Wisdom　　'that were not the best;
If he make amends　　let Surety have him
And be bail for his baseness　　and buy his well-being,
So amend what is misdone　　and evermore be better.'
Wit accorded therewith　　and said the same:
'Better it is that good　　evil down bring,
Than evil be beaten　　and good never the better.'
　　Then began Meed to moan　　and mercy besought,
And proffered Peace a present　　all of pure gold.
'Have this, man, of me,' quoth she　　'to amend thy scathe,
For I will wager for Wrong　　he will do so no more.'
　　Piteously Peace then　　prayed to the king
To have mercy on that man　　that misdid him so oft;
'For he hath pledged me well　　as Wisdom him taught,
And I forgive him that guilt　　with a good will,
So that the king assent　　I can say no better,
For Meed hath made me amends　　and I may no more ask.'
　　'Nay,' quoth the king then　　'so me Christ help!
Wrong mendeth not so away　　first will I know more;
For if let off so lightly　　laugh loud he would,
And afterwards bolder be　　to beat my subjects.
Unless Reason have ruth on him　　he shall rest in my stocks,
And that as long as he liveth　　except Lowliness him bail.'
　　Some men prompted Reason　　to have pity on that wretch,
And counselled the king　　and Conscience after;
And that Meed might be surety　　Reason besought.
　　'Tell me not,' quoth Reason　　'pity to have,
Till lords and ladies　　all love truth
And hate all wickedness　　to hear it or speak it;
Till Pernel puts her pretty things　　away in her drawer;

And cherishing of children   be by chastening with rods;
And holiness of rascals   be held not a marvel;
Till covetousness of clerks   the poor clothes and feeds;
And roaming religious sing   *Recordare* [1] in cloister,
As Saint Benet them bade   Bernard and Francis;
And till preachers' preaching   be proved on themselves;
And till the king's counsel   be common profit;
Till bishops' bay mares   buy shelter for beggars,
Their hawks and their hounds   help for poor religious.

   'And till Saint James be sought   where the poor sick be,
So none go to Galicia   but to stay there for ever;
And all the Rome-runners   to robbers beyond
Bear no silver over sea   that shows the king's sign,
Neither graven nor ungraven   golden nor silver,
Upon forfeiture of that fee   whoso finds him at Dover,
Except he be merchant or his man   or messenger with letters,
Provisor or priest   or penitent for his sins.
And yet,' quoth Reason, 'by the Rood   I shall no ruth have
While Meed hath the mastery   in this moot-hall.
But I may shew examples   as I see otherwiles.
I say for myself,' quoth he   'and it so were
That I were king with a crown   to care for a realm,
Should never wrong in this world   that I might know,
Be unpunished in my power   on peril of my soul!
Nor get my grace for gifts   so me God save!
Nor for no Meed have mercy   except she be meek.

   'For *nullum malum* the men   met with *impunitatem*
And bade *nullum bonum*   be *irremuneratum.*

   'Let your confessor, sir king   construe this without gloss;
And if ye put it to test   I pledge both my ears
That Law shall turn labourer   and spread dung afield,
And Love lead thy land   as thou likest best!'

   Clerks that were confessors   coupled them together
All to construe this clause   and for the king's profit,
Nor for comfort of the commons   nor for the king's soul.

   For I saw Meed in the moot-hall   on men of law wink,
And they laughing leaned to her   and many left Reason.

   Warren Wisdom   winked upon Meed
And said: 'Madam, I am your man   whatever my mouth say;
I fall in with florins,' quoth that fellow   'and then my speech fails.'

[1] See page 203.

All the righteous recorded     that Reason told truth,
Wit accorded therewith     and commended his words,
And most people in the hall     and many of the great
Held Meekness the master     and Meed a vile shrew.

Love held her lightly     and Loyalty still less,
And said it so loudly     that all the hall heard:
'Whoso wants her for wife     for the wealth of her goods,
If he be not a cuckold     then cut off my nose.'

Meed mourned then     and made heavy cheer,
For the commons in that court     called her an whore.
But a sizer and a summoner     pursued her fast,
And a sheriff's clerk     cursed all the rout,
'For often have I,' quoth he     'helped you at bar
And yet gave ye me never     the worth of a rush.'

The king called Conscience     and afterwards Reason
And recorded that Reason     had rightfully shown;
And moodily upon Meed     with might the king looked,
Waxed wroth with Law     Meed almost had fouled it,
And said: 'Through your law     I lose many escheats;
Meed over-mastereth Law     and Truth mightily hinders.
Reason shall reckon with you     if I reign any while,
And judge you, by this day     as you have deserved.
Meed shall not bail you     by Mary of heaven!
I will have loyalty in law     and stop all your jangling,
And as most folk witness well     Wrong shall be sentenced.'

Quoth Conscience to the king     'If the commons assent not
'Tis full hard, by mine head     thereto to bring it,
All of your liege-men     to lead thus aright.'

'By him racked on the wood'     quoth Reason to the king,
'If I rule not your realm     rend out my ribs!
If ye order Obedience     to be on my side.'

'And I assent,' saith the king     'by Saint Mary my lady!
When my council comes     of clerks and of earls.
But readily, Reason     thou shalt not ride from me,
For as long as I live     I will not let thee go.'

'I am ready,' quoth Reason     'to rest with you ever;
If Conscience will be of our council     I care for no better.
'And I grant,' quoth the king     'God forbid that it fail!
As long as our life lasteth     live we together.'

# PASSUS V

THE king and his knights    to the church went
To hear matins of the day    and the Mass after.
Then waked I of my winking    and was woeful withal
That I had not slept sounder    and so seen more.
But ere I fared a furlong    faintness me seized,
I might not go further a foot    for want of my sleep;
And sat softly adown    and said my Creed
And as I babbled on my beads    they brought me asleep.

   And then saw I much more    than I before told:
For I saw the field full of folk    that I before spoke of,
And how Reason got ready    to preach to the realm,
And with a cross before the king    began thus to teach.

   He proved that these pestilences [1]    were purely for sin,
And the south-west wind    on Saturday at even
Was plainly for pure pride    and for no point else.
Pear-trees and plum-trees    were puffed to the earth
For example, ye men    that ye should do better.
Beeches and broad oaks    were blown to the ground,
Turned upwards their tails    in token of dread
That deadly sin at doomsday    shall undo them all.

   Of this matter I might    mumble full long,
But I will say as I saw    so God me help!
How plainly before the people    Reason began to preach.

   He bade Waster go work    at what he best could
And win back his wasting    with some manner of craft.

   And prayed Pernel put off    her costly array
And keep it in her box    for money at her need.

   Tow Stowe he taught    to take two staves
And from women's punishment [2]    bring Phyllis home.

   He warned Wat    his wife was to blame,
That her hat was worth half a mark    his hood cost not a groat.
And bade Batt cut down    a bough or even two
And beat Betty therewith    unless she should work.
And then he charged chapmen    to chasten their children:

[1] See page 203.        [2] See page 203.

'Let no wish for wealth spoil them     while they be young,
Nor for power of the pestilence     please them out of reason.
    My sire said so to me     and so did my dame,
That the more loved the child     the more teaching it needs,
And Solomon said the same     that Wisdom made,
        *Qui parcit virgae, odit filium.*
The English of this Latin is     whoso will it know,
Whoso spareth the sprig     spoileth the children.'
    And then he prayed prelates     and priests together,
'What ye preach to the people     prove it on yourselves
And do it in deeds     it shall draw you to good;
If ye live as ye teach us     we'll believe you the better.'
    And then he counselled religious     their rule to uphold,
'Lest the king and his council     your commons curtail
And be stewards of your steads     till ye be better ruled.'
    Then he counselled the king     the commons to love,
'They're thy treasure in treason     and help at thy need.'
And then he prayed the pope     to pity Holy Church,
And ere he give any grace     to govern first himself.
    'And ye that have laws to guard     let truth be your desire
More than gold or other gifts     if ye will God please;
For whoso contrarieth truth     he telleth in the gospel,
That God knoweth him not     nor doth no saint in Heaven:
        *Amen dico vobis, nescio vos.*
    'And ye that seek Saint James     and the Saints of Rome,
Seek ye Saint Truth     for he may save you all,
*Qui cum Patre & Filio*     may fair them befall
That list to my sermon'     And thus said Reason.
Then ran Repentance     and rehearsed his theme
And made Will to weep     water with his eyes.

### SUPERBIA

    Pernel Proud-heart     leaned her to the earth
And lay long ere she looked     and 'Lord, mercy!' cried,
And vowed to him     that us all made
She should unsew her shift     and wear a hairshirt
To enfeeble her flesh     that fierce was to sin.
'Shall never high heart have me     but hold myself lowly
And suffer myself slighted     and so did I never.
But now will I be meek     and mercy beseech,
For all this I have     hated in mine heart.'

## LUXURIA

Then Lecher said: 'Alas!'     and on our Lady he cried,
To make mercy for his misdeeds     between God and his soul,
If he should every Saturday     for seven year thereafter
Drink but with the duck     and dine only once.

## INVIDIA

Envy with heavy heart     asked them for shrift,
And sadly *mea culpa*     began to repeat.
He was pale as a stone     in a palsy he seemed,
And clothed in coarse cloth     which I could not describe;
In a kilt and a coat     and a knife by his side;
Of a friar's frock     were the fore-sleeves.
Like a leek that had lain     too long in the sun,
So looked he with lean cheeks     lowering foully.
His body bursting with wrath     so that he bit his lips,
And went wringing with his fists     to wreak himself he thought
With works or with words     when he saw his time.
Each sentence he said     was of an adder's tongue,
Chiding and challenge     was his chief livelihood
With backbiting and blackguarding     and bearing false witness
This was all his courtesy     wherever he showed him.
'I'd be shriven,' quoth this wretch     'and I for shame dare not;
I'd be gladder, by God     that Gib had mischance
Than if I'd this week won     weight of Essex cheese.
I've a neighbour nigh me     whom I've annoyed oft,
And lied on him to lords     to make him lose his silver.
And made his friends be his foes     through my false tongue;
His grace and his good haps     grieve me full sore.
Between family and family     I make debate oft,
That both life and limb     is lost through my speech.
And when I meet him in market     that I most hate,
I hail him heartily     as I his friend were;
For he is braver than I     and I dare do no other;
But had I mastery and might     God wot my will!
'And when I come to the church     and should kneel to the rood
And pray for the people     as the priest teacheth,
For pilgrims and palmers     and for all people after,
Then I cry on my knees     that Christ give them sorrow
Who bare away my bowl     and my ragged sheet.

'Away from the altar then      turn I mine eyes,
And behold how Helen      hath a new coat:
I wish then it were mine      and all the webb as well.
At men's losses I laugh      that liketh mine heart.
For their winnings I weep      and wail all the time;
Deem that they do ill      where I do far worse;
Whoso chides me therefore      I hate him deadly after.
I would that each wight      were mine own knave,
For whoso hath more than I      angereth me sore.
And thus I live loveless      like a lousy dog,
So that my body bursts      for bitterness of my gall.
I might not eat many years      as a man ought,
For envy and ill will      is bad to digest.
Can no sugar nor sweet thing      assuage my swelling,
Nor no *diapenidion* [1]      drive it from mine heart,
Nor neither shrift nor sham      if my maw be not scraped?'
     'Yes, readily,' quoth Repentance      and ruled him from the best.
'Sorrow for sins      is salvation of souls.'
     'I am sorry,' quoth the man      'I am but seldom other,
And that maketh me thus meagre      for I cannot revenge.
Among burgesses have I been      dwelling at London,
And got Backbiting by a broker      to blame men's wares.
When one sold and I not      then was I ready
To lie and lower on my neighbour      and slander his goods.
I will amend this if I may      by the Almighty's might.'


IRA

     Now awaketh Wrath      with two white eyes
And snivelling at the nose      and his neck hanging.
     'I am Wrath,' quoth he      'I was some time a friar
And the convent's gardener      for to graft shoots.
On limiters and lectors [2]      lyings I grafted,
Till they bare leaves of lowly speech      the lords to please;
And then they blossomed abroad      in bowers to hear shrifts.
And now is fallen a fruit      that folk much prefer
To show their sins to them      than be shriven by their parsons.
     'And now parsons have perceived      that they must share with friars,
The beneficed ones preach      and the friars defame;
The friars find them at fault      as folk bear witness,

----

<sup></sup>[1] See page 203.          [2] See page 203.

That when they preach to the people     in any place about
I, Wrath, walk with them     and guide them from my looks.
Thus they speak of the spirit     but either despiseth other
Till they be both beggars     and by my ministering live,
Or else all are rich     and ride horses about.
I, Wrath, rest never     but that I must follow
This wicked folk     for such is my grace.

 'I have an aunt a nun     and an abbess as well;
Her were liefer swoon or die     than suffer pain.

 'I've been cook in her kitchen     in the convent served
Many months with them     and with monks as well.
I was prioresses' pottager     and for other poor ladies,
And made them pottage of prattling     that Dame Joan was a bastard;
Dame Clarice a knight's daughter     and a cuckold her sire;
And Dame Pernel a priest's wench     prioress to be never,
For she childed in cherry-time     as the whole chapter knew.

 'Of wicked words, I, Wrath     their salads made,
Till "Thou liest!" and "Thou liest!"     leaped out at once
And either hit other     under the cheek;
Had they had knives, by Christ     each had killed other.

 'Saint Gregory was a good pope     and had good forewit,
That no prioress should be priest [1]     so he ordained.
They had else incurred infamy     the very first day
That they took up their office     they're so ill to keep counsel.

 'Among monks I might be     but oft times I shun them,
For there be many strict ones     mine affairs to espy,
Both prior and subprior     and our *pater abbas*.
If I tell any tales     they counsel together
And make me fast Fridays     on bread and water;
I'm charged in the chapter-house     as if I a child were
And beaten on my backside     no breeches between,
So have I no liking     with those men to dwell.
I eat there stale stockfish     and feeble ale drink.
At other time, when wine cometh     when I drink wine at eve
I have a flux of a foul mouth     a good five days after.
All the wickedness I know of     by any of our brethren,
I tell it in the cloister     till the whole convent knows.'

 'Now repent ye,' quoth Repentance     'and rehearse thou never
Counsel that thou knowest     by favour or by right.
And drink not over delicately     nor too deep neither,

<hr />

[1] See page 203.

Lest thy will because thereof    to wrath might be turned.
*Esto sobrius*,' he said    and absolved me after
And bade me wish to weep    my wickedness to amend.


## AVARICIA

And then came Covetousness    I can him not describe,
So hungry and hollow    Sir Harvey him looked.
He was beetle-browed    and blubber-lipped too,
With two bleared eyes    as a blind hog;
And as a leather purse    lolled his cheeks
Yet lower than his chin    trembling with age;
And as a bondman's with bacon    his beard was bedraggled.
With an hood on his head    a lousy hat above,
And in a tawny tabard    of twelve winters' age,
All tattered and dirty    and full of lice creeping—
But if a louse could not    have leaped with the best
She could not have walked there    so threadbare the stuff.
   'I have been covetous,' quoth this caitiff    'I acknowledge it here.
For some time I served    Sim-at-the-stile
And was his prentice pledged    his profit to serve.
First I learned to lie    for a leaf or two;
Wickedly to weigh    was my first lesson.
To Weyhill and Winchester    I went to the fair,
With many manner of merchandise    as my master me bade;
And had not grace of Guile    gone in with my wares
They had been unsold this seven years    so help me God!
   'Then tarried I amongst drapers    my grammar to learn;
To draw the selvedge along    the longer it seemed;
Among the rich ranged cloths    I rendered a lesson,
To pierce them with a pack-needle    and plait them together,
Put them in a press    and pin them therein
Till ten yards or twelve    had tolled out to thirteen.
   'My wife was a weaver    and woollen cloth made.
She spoke to the spinsters    to spin it all out,
But the pound that she paid by    poised a quartern more
Than did mine own balance    whoso weighed true.
   'I bought her barley malt    she brewed it to sell.
Penny-ale and pudding-ale    she poured together
For labourers and for low folk    that was kept by itself.
   'The best ale lay in my bower    or in my bedchamber,

And whoso tasted thereof    bought it thereafter
A gallon for a groat    no less, God knows:
And 'twas measure in cupfuls    this craft my wife used.
Rose the Retailer    was her right name;
She hath holden huckstering    all through her lifetime.

   'But I swear now, may I thrive!    that sin will I stop,
And never wickedly weigh    nor wicked chaffer use.
But wend to Walsingham    and my wife also
And pray the Rood of Bromholm [1]    bring me out of debt.'

   'Repentedest thou ever,' quoth Repentance    'or restitution madest?'

   'Yes, once I was harboured    with an heap of chapmen;
I rose when they were at rest    and rifled their bags.'

   'That was no restitution    but a robber's theft.
Thou haddest be better worthy    to be hanged there for
Than for all that    that thou hast here showed.'

   'I weened rifling were restitution    for I've not learned in books
And I know no French, i'faith    but of furthest end of Norfolk.'

   'Usedest thou every usury    in all thy life-time?'

   'Nay, soothly,' he said    'save in my youth.
I learned a lesson    among Jews and Lombards,
To weigh pence with a weight    and pare down the heaviest;
And lend it for love of the Cross    for a pledge, to be lost;
Such deeds I did write    lest he due day miss.
I have more money through arrears    than through *miseretur et commodat.*
I have lent lords    and ladies my goods,
And been their broker after    and bought it myself.
Exchanges and contracts    with much chaffer I deal;
Lend to folk that will lose    of every noble a part.
And with Lombard's letters    I lend gold to Rome,
Here took it by tally    and told it there less.'

   'Lentest ever to lords    for love of protection?'

   'Yea, I have lent to lords    who loved me never after,
And have made many a knight    both mercer and draper
That paid for his prenticehood    not a pair of gloves even.'

   'Hast thou pity on poor men    that must needs borrow?'

   'I have as much pity of poor men    as hath pedlar of cats
He would kill if he could    for the sake of their skins.'

   'Art thou generous to thy neighbours    with thy meat and drink?'

   'I am holden as kind    as a hound in the kitchen;
Among my neighbours especially    I have such a name.'

               [1] See page 203.

'Now God never grant thee     but thou soon repent,
His grace on this ground     thy goods well to bestow,
Nor thine heirs after thee     to have joy of thy winnings,
Nor executors spend well     the silver thou leavest;
That which by wrong was won     by wicked men to be spent.
For were I friar of that house     where is good faith and charity,
I'd not clothe us with thy cash     nor our church amend,
Nor have for our pittance     a penn'orth of thine
For the best book in our house     though bright gold were leaves,
If I knew indeed     thou wert such as thou tellest,
Or if I could know it     in any sure way.

> *Servus es alterius cum fercula pinguia quaeris,*
> *Pane tuo potius vescere, liber eris.*

'Thou art an unkindly creature     I cannot absolve thee
Till thou make restitution     reckon up with them all;
And till Reason enrol     in the register of Heaven
That thou hast made each man good     I may not absolve thee—

> *Non dimittitur peccatum, donec restituatur oblatum, etc.*

'For all that have aught of thy goods     so God have my truth!
Will be held at the high Day of Doom     to help thee to restore.
And whoso believeth not this     let him look in the Psalter,
In *Miserere mei Deus*     whether I speak truth;

> *Ecce enim veritatem dilexisti, etc.*

'Shall never workman in this world     thrive with what thou winnest;
*Cum sancto sanctus eris*     construe me that in English.'

Then drooped the scamp in despair     and would have himself hanged,
Had not Repentance the rather     recomforted him in this manner,
'Have mercy in thy mind     and with thy mouth ask it,
For God his mercy is more     than all his other works;

> *Misericordia ejus super omnia opera ejus, etc.*

'And all the wickedness in this world     that man might work or think
Is no more to the mercy of God     than a live coal in the sea;

> *Omnis iniquitas quantum ad misericordiam Dei, est quasi scintilla in*
> *medio maris.*

'Therefore have mercy in mind     and in merchandise, trust it:
For thou hast no good ground     to get thee a cake with,
Unless it were with thy tongue     or else with thy two hands.
For the goods thou hast gotten     began all with falsehood,
And whilst thou livest therewith     thou payest not, but borrowest.
And if thou know never to which     nor to whom to restore,
Bear it to the bishop     and bid him of his grace

Bestow it himself     as is best for thy soul.
For for thee shall be answer     at the high Day of Doom;
For thee and many more     shall that man give a reckoning.
What he taught you in Lent     believe thou none other,
What he gave of our Lord's goods     to lead you from sin.'


### GULA

Now beginneth Glutton     for to go to shrift
And carries him to kirk-ward     his fault there to show.
But Betty the brewster     bade him good-morrow
And asked of him with that     whitherward he would.
'To holy church,' quoth he     'for to hear Mass,
And after will be shriven     and then sin no more.'
'Gossip, I've good ale,' quoth she     'Glutton, wilt thou try it?'
'Hast thou aught in thy bag?     Any hot spices?'
'I have pepper and peony     and a pound too of garlic,
And a farthing's worth of fennel-seed     for fasting days.'
Then goeth Glutton in     and great oaths come after.
Cis the shoe-seller     sat on the bench,
Wat the game-keeper     and his wife too,
Tim the tinker     and two of his prentices,
Hick the horsedealer     and Hugh the needle-seller,
Clarice of Cock lane     and the clerk of the church,
Davy the ditcher     and a dozen other;
Sir Piers the priest     and Pernel of Flanders,
A fiddler, a rat-catcher     the street sweeper of Cheapside,
A roper, a riding-man     and Rose the dish-seller,
Godfrey of Garlickhithe     and Griffith the Welshman,
And old-clothesmen a heap     early in the morning
Give Glutton with glad cheer     good ale for himself.
Clement the cobbler     cast off his cloak
And named it for sale     at the 'new fair' game.[1]
Hick the horse dealer     heaved his hood after
And bade Bart the butcher     be on his side.
There were chapmen chosen     the goods to appraise;
Whoso hath the hood     should have amends for the cloak.
Two rose up quickly     and whispered together
And priced these pennyworths     apart by themselves.
They could not in their conscience     agree on a value,

[1] See page 203.

Till Robin the roper      arose for the truth
And named himself umpire      to avoid a debate
And to settle this business      betwixt them three.
   Hickey the hostler      he had the cloak,
In covenant that Clement      should the cup fill
And have Hick hostler's hood      and hold himself served;
And whoso sooner repented      should arise after
And give to Sir Glutton      a gallon of ale.
   There was laughing and lowering      and 'Let go the cup!'
They sat so till evensong      singing now and then,
Till Glutton had gulped down      a gallon and a gill.
His guts 'gan to grumble      like two greedy sows;
He pissed a pot-full      in a paternoster-while;
And blew with the bugle      at his backbone's end,
That all hearing that horn      held their nose after
And wished it were stopped up      with a wisp of furze.
   He could neither step nor stand      before he had his staff;
Then began he to go      like a gleeman's bitch,
Sometimes aside      sometimes astern
As whoso layeth lines      for to snare fowl.
   And when he drew to the door      then dimmed his eyes;
He stumbled on threshold      and fell to the earth.
Clement the cobbler      caught him by the middle
For to lift him aloft      and laid him on his knees;
Glutton was a great lout      and lumpish to lift
And coughed up a caudle      in Clement's lap:
No hound is so hungry      in Hertfordshire
Dare lap up those leavings      so unlovely they smelt.
   With all the woe of this world      his wife and his wench
Bare him home to his bed      and brought him therein.
And after all his excess      he had such a head
He slept Saturday and Sunday      till the sun went to rest.
Then waked he of his winking      and wiped his eyes;
The first word that he said      was: 'Where is the bowl?'
His wife began to reproach him      for how wickedly he lived,
And Repentance right so      rebuked him that time:
'As thou with words and works      hast wrought evil in thy life,
Shrive thee and be shamed therefore      and show it with thy mouth.'
   'I, Glutton,' quoth the wretch      'confess me guilty,
That I have trespassed with my tongue      I can not tell how oft:
Sworn "by God's soul" and      "so help me, God and his saints,"

Where there was no need     over nine hundred times.
And surfeited me at supper     and sometimes at noon,
That I, Glutton, threw it up     ere I'd gone a mile
And spilt what might be spared     and spent on some hungry one.
Over-delicately on fasting-days     drunken and eaten,
And sometimes sat so long I     slept and ate together.
For love of tales dined I     in taverns to drink more,
And hurried to meat ere noon     when fasting-days were.'
   'This shewing of shrift,' quoth Repentance     'shall merit to thee.'
   Began Glutton to cry     and great dole to make
For his evil life     that he had so lived;
And vowed to fast     'for hunger as for thirst
Shall never fish on Friday     digest in my womb,
Till Abstinence mine aunt     hath given me leave;
And yet have I hated her     all my life long.'


## ACCIDIA

   Then came Sloth all beslobbered     with two slimy eyes.
'I must sit,' said the fellow     'or else should I nap.
I cannot stand nor stoop     nor without a stool kneel.
But were I put to bed     unless my tail made me,
Should no ringing make me rise     ere I were ripe to dine.'
He began *Benedicite* [1] with a belch     and knocked on his breast
And stretched and snored     and slumbered at last.
'Awake, wretch!' quoth Repentance     'and run thee to shrift.'
'Should I die on this day     I'd not trouble to look.
I know not *Paternoster*     as the priest it singeth,
But I know rhymes of Robin Hood     and Earl Randolph of Chester,
But of our Lord or our Lady     not the least ever made.
I have made forty vows     and forgot them at morning;
I performed never penance     as the priest me bade,
Nor right sorry for my sins     yet was I never.
If I pray any prayers     except it be in wrath,
What I tell with my tongue     is two miles from mine heart.
I am occupied each day     holidays and other,
With idle tales in the alehouse     and sometimes in churches.
God's pain and his passion     seldom think I thereon.
I visited never feeble men     nor fettered folk in jail;
I had liefer hear an harlotry     or cobbler's summer games,

---

[1] See page 203.

Or lyings to laugh at     and belying my neighbour,
Than all that ever Mark made     Matthew, John and Luke.
And vigils and fasting days     all these I let pass,
And lie abed in Lent     my wench in my arms,
Till matins and Mass be done     then I go to the friars;
Come I to *Ite, missa est*     I hold myself served.
I'm not shriven for a long time     unless sickness make me,
Not twice in two years     and then confession is a guess.

　'I have been priest and a parson     passing thirty winters,
Yet can I not sing *sol-fa*     nor read the saints' lives;
But I can find in a field     or a furrow an hare,
Better than in *Beatus vir*     or *Beati omnes*
Construe one clause well     and teach my parishioners.
I can hold love-days [1]     and hear a reeve's reckoning,
But in the canon or decretals     I can not read a line.
If I buy on tick     unless it be tallied
I forget it as soon     and if men me it ask,
Six times or seven     I deny it with oaths,
And thus trouble I true men     ten hundred times.

　'And my servants' salary     a long time is behind;
Rueful is the reckoning     when we render account.
So with wicked will and wrath     my workmer I pay.

　'If man doth me a benefit     or helpeth me at need,
I am unkind to his courtesy     and can not understand it;
For I have, and have had     something of a hawk's manner:
I am not lured with love     unless there lie aught under the thumb.

　'Kindness my fellow Christians     accorded me formerly,
Sixty times I, Sloth     have forgot it since.
In speech, and in sparing speech     I waste many a time
Both flesh and fish     and much other victual;
Both bread and ale     butter, milk and cheese,
I spoiled in my service     so it might serve no man.

　'I ran about in my youth     nor set me to learn,
And ever since have been beggared     for my foul sloth:
　　　*Heu mihi, quod sterilem vitam duxi juvenilem.*'
　'Repentest thou not?' quoth Repentance     and right with that he
　　　　　　　　　　　　　　　　　　　　　　swooned,

Till *Vigilate* the vigilant     fetched water from his eyes
And flooded his face     and fast on him cried
And said, 'Beware of Despair     who would thee betray.
　　　　　　　　[1] See page 203.

"I am sorry for my sins,"     say so to thyself,
Beat thyself on the breast     and beseech of him grace:
For is no guilt there so great     that his goodness is not more.'
   Then sat Sloth up     and crossed himself
And made a vow to God     'gainst his foul sloth:
'Shall no Sunday be for seven year     unless sickness me stop,
That I go not before dawn     to the dear church
And matins hear and Mass     as though I were a monk.
No ale after meat     shall hold me thence
Till evensong I've heard     I vow it to the rood.
Moreover will I pay back     if I it have,
All I've wickedly won     since I had wit.
   'Though I lack livelihood     stop will I not
Till each man shall have his     ere that I go hence;
And with the residue and remnant     by the Rood of Chester!
I shall seek Truth first     before I see Rome.'
   Robert the Robber     on *Reddite* looked;
He'd naught to pay with     and wept full sore.
But yet the sinful wretch     said to himself,
'Christ, that on Calvary     upon the cross died,
When Dismas [1] my brother     besought you of grace,
Thou haddest mercy on that man     for *memento's* sake
Have pity on this robber     that cannot repay
And may never hope to win     with work what I owe.
But for thy much mercy     mitigation I beseech;
Damn me not at doomsday     for that I did ill.'
   What fell to this felon     I can not fairly show;
Well I wot he wept water     fast with both eyes,
And acknowledged his guilt     right soon after to Christ,
That his pike of penitence     he should polish anew
And use it on pilgrimage     all his life-time,
For he had lain with *Latro*     Lucifer's aunt.
   Then had Repentance ruth     and bade them all kneel:
'For I shall beseech for all sinners     our Saviour of grace
To amend us of misdeeds     and do mercy to all.
   'Now God,' quoth he, 'that of thy goodness     didst the world make
And of naught madest aught     and man most like to thyself,
And since suffered him to sin     a sickness to us all,
Yet for the best—as I hold     whatever the Book telleth,
    *O felix culpa! O necessarium peccatum Adae! etc.*

[1] See page 203.

'For through that sin thy son    sent was to this earth,
And became man of a maid    mankind to save,
And thyself with thy son    was made like to us sinners:

> *Faciamus hominen ad imaginem et similitudinem nostram;*
> *Et alibi:*
> *Qui manet in caritate, in Dea manet, & Deus in eo.*

'And then with thy Son's self    in our suit [1] died
On Good Friday for man's sake    at full time of day,
Where thyself nor thy Son    no sorrow felt in death,
But in ourselves was the sorrow    and thy Son it led—

> *Captivam duxit captivitatem.*

'The sun thereof for sorrow    lost sight for a time
About midday, when most light is    the meal time of saints,
When thou didst feed with thy fresh blood    our forefathers in darkness:

> *Populus qui ambulabat in tenebris, vidit lucem magnam;*

Through the light that leaped from thee    Lucifer was blinded,
And all thy Blessed blown    into Paradise bliss.
The third day after    thou goest in our guise;
A sinful Mary saw thee    before Saint Mary thy mother,
And all to solace the sinful    thou sufferedest it so:

> *Non veni vocare justos, sed peccatores ad poenitentiam.*

'And all that Mark hath written    Matthew, John and Luke,
Of thy doughtiest deeds    were done beneath our arms:

> *Verbum caro factum est, et habitavit in nobis.*

'And by so much, meseemeth    the more surely we may
Pray and beseech    if it be thy will,
That art our father and brother    to be merciful to us;
And to have pity on those ribalds    that repent them here sore
That they wrathed thee in this world    in word, thought or deeds.'

Then grasped Hope an horn    of *Deus, tu conversus vivificabis nos,*
And blew it with *Beati quorum    remissae sunt iniquitates,*
So that all saints in Heaven    sang loudly together:

> *Homines & jumenta salvabis, quemadmodum multiplicasti miseri-*
> *cordiam tuam, Deus, etc.*

A thousand men then    came thronging together,
Who cried upward to Christ    and to his clean Mother
To have grace to go with them    Truth for to seek.

But there was no wight so wise    that he knew the way thither
But blundered like beasts    over banks and on hills
A long time, till 'twas late    that they a man met

---

[1] See page 203.

Apparelled as a Paynim     in a pilgrim's wise.
He bare a staff bound     with a broad strip
In bindweed wise     wound about.
A bowl and a bag     he bare by his side;
An hundred ampullas     on his hat set,
Signs of Sinai     and shells of Galicia,
Many a cross on his cloak     keys also of Rome
And the vernicle in front     so that men should know
And see by his signs     what shrines he had sought.[1]
    This folk asked him first     from whence he did come.
    'From Sinai,' he said     'and from our Lord's sepulchre;
Bethlehem and Babylon     I have been in both;
In Armenia, in Alexandria     and many other places.
Ye may see by my signs     that sit on my hat
That I've walked full wide     in wet and in dry,
And have sought good saints     for my soul's health.'
    'Knowest thou aught of a saint     that men call Truth?
Could'st thou show us the way     where that wight dwelleth?'
    'Nay, so help me God!'     said the man then,
'I saw never palmer     with pike nor with scrip
Ask after him, till     now in this place.'
    'Peter!' quoth a plowman     and put forth his head,
'I know him as well     as a clerk doth his books.
Conscience and Mother-Wit     made known his place
And made me swear surely     to serve him for ever
Both in sowing and setting     so long as I work.
I have been his follower     all these fifty winters,
Both sown his seed     and driven his beasts,
And watched over his profit     within and without.
I dike and I delve     and do what Truth biddeth:
Sometimes I sow     and sometimes I thresh;
In tailor's and tinker's craft     what Truth can devise;
I weave and I wind     and do what Truth biddeth.
For though I say it myself     I serve him to his pleasure;
I have good hire of him     and oftentimes more.
He is the readiest payer     that a poor man knoweth;
He withholds not his hire     from his servants at even.
He is lowly as a lamb     and lovely of speech,
And if ye are wishful to know     where that he dwelleth,
I shall show you surely     the way to his place.'

[1] See page 203.

'Yea, dear Piers,' quoth these pilgrims     and proffered him hire
For to wend with them     to Truth's dwelling-place.
     'Nay, by my soul's health!' quoth Piers     and began for to swear,
'I would not take a farthing     for Saint Thomas's shrine!
Truth would love me the less     a long time thereafter!
     'But if ye will to wend well     this is the way thither,
That I shall say to you     and set you in the path.
Ye must go through Meekness     both men and their wives,
Till ye come into Conscience     let Christ know the truth
That ye love our lord God     the best of all things;
And then your neighbours next     in no wise use
Otherwise than thou wouldest     be wrought to thyself.
     'And so bend round by a brook     Be-humble-of-speech,
Till ye find a ford called     Honour-your-fathers:
          *Honora patrem et matrem, etc.*
Wade in that water     and wash you well there,
And you shall leap the lighter     all your lifetime.
And so shalt thou see Swear-not-     but-it-be-for-need-
Especially-not-idly-     by-God-Almighty's-name.
     'Then shalt thou come by a croft     but come not therein;
That croft is called Covet-not-     men's-cattle-nor-their-wives-
Nor-none-of-their-servants-     that-might-them-annoy.
Look ye break no boughs there     unless it be your own.
     'Two stocks there standeth     but stay ye not there;
They're called Steal-not and Slay-not     strike forth by both
And leave them on thy left hand     and look not thereafter
But hold well thine holiday     holy till even.
     'Then shalt thou turn at a tump     Bear-no-false-witness
He is fenced with florins     and other fees many;
Look that thou pluck no plant there     for peril of thy soul;
     'Then shall ye see Say-sooth-     as-it-is-to-be-done-
And-in-no-manner-else-     for-any-man's-bidding.
     'Then shalt thou come to a court     as clear as the sun;
The moat is of Mercy     the manor about,
And its walls are of Wit     to hold the Will out,
Crenellated with Christendom     mankind to save,
Buttressed with Believe-so-     or-thou-beest-not-saved.
And all the houses are covered     the halls and the chambers,
With no lead but with Love     and Low-speech-of-brethren.
The bridge is of Pray-well-     the-better-mayest-thou-speed;
Each pillar is of Penance     and of Prayers to saints;

Of alms-deeds are the hooks     whereon the gates hang.
    'Grace is the gateward     a good man forsooth;
His man is Amend-you     many men him know:
Tell him this token     that Truth may know sooth:
"I performed the penance     the priest me enjoined,
And full sorry for my sins     and so shall be ever
When I think thereon     though I were a pope."
    'Bid Amend-you full meekly     his master to ask
To draw up the wicket     that the woman shut
When Adam and Eve     ate apples unroasted:

   *Per Evam cunctis clausa est, & per Mariam virginem iterum patefacta est.*

For he hath key and catch     though the king sleep.
    'And if Grace grant thee     to go in this wise,
Thou shalt see in thyself     Truth sit in thine heart
In a chain of charity     as thou a child were
To suffer him and say naught     against thy Sire's will.
    'But beware then of Wrath-thee     that is a wicked wretch;
He hath envy for him     that in thine heart sitteth,
And putteth forth Pride     for praise of thyself.
Boldness of thy benefactions     then maketh thee blind
And thou'lt be driven out as dew     and the door closed,
Keyed and clamped up     to keep thee without;
And hundred winters haply     ere ever thou enter.
So thus might thou lose his love     by uplifting thyself,
And never enter haply again     unless thou have grace.
    'But there are seven sisters     that ever serve Truth
And are porters of the posterns     that belong to the place;
One is called Abstinence     and Humility another;
Charity and Chastity     be his chief maidens;
Patience and Peace     much people they help;
The lady Largesse     hath let in full many:
She hath helped thousands out     from the Devil's pinfold.
He who is kin to this seven     so help me God!
He is wondrously welcome     and fairly received;
And unless ye be kin     to some of these seven,
'Tis full hard, by my head!     for any of you all
To get in at any gate     unless grace be given.'
    'Now, by Christ!' quoth a cutpurse     'I have no kin here!'
'Nor I,' quoth an apeward     'for aught that I know!'
'God knows,' quoth a waferer [1]     'knew I this for sooth

      [1] See page 204.

I'd go no foot further     for any friar's preaching.'
    'Yes,' quoth Piers the Plowman     and pushed them towards good,
'Mercy is a maiden there     hath might over all;
She is cousin to all sinners     and her Son also;
Through help of them two     (hope not in none other)
Thou might get grace there     if thou go betimes.'
    'By Saint Paul,' quoth a pardoner     'perchance I'm not known there.
I'll fetch my box with my briefs     bishop's letters and a bull!' [1]
'By Christ!' quoth a common woman     'thy company I'll follow,
Thou shalt say I'm thy sister     I know not where they've gone!'

[1] See page 204.

'This were a wicked way    unless we had a guide
That would show us each step'    thus these folk complained.
Quoth Perkin the plowman    'By Saint Peter of Rome!
I've an half acre to plow    hard by the highway.
Had I plowed this half acre    and sown it after,
I would wend then with you    and show you the way.'
  'This were long delay'    quoth a dame in a veil,
'What should we women    work at meanwhile?'
  'Some shall sew sacks,' quoth Piers    'for sheltering the wheat;
And ye, lovely ladies    with your long fingers,
Have silk and sendal    to sew, while there's time,
Chasubles for chaplains    churches to honour.
Wives and widows    wool and flax spin;
Make cloth, I counsel you    and so teach your daughters.
The needy and naked    take heed how they lie
And contrive for them clothes    for so commands Truth.
I shall get them livelihood    unless the land fails,
Flesh and bread both    to rich and to poor,
As long as I live    for the Lord's love of Heaven.
And all manner of men    that by meat and drink live,
Help ye them to work well    that win you your food.'
  'By Christ!' quoth a knight then    'he teaches the best;
But on this theme truly    taught was I never.
Teach me,' quoth the knight    'and, by Christ, I will try!'
  'By Saint Paul!' quoth Perkin    'ye proffer so fairly
That I'll swink and sweat    and sow for us both,
And other labours do for thy love    all my lifetime,
In covenant that thou keep    Holy Church and myself
From wasters and wicked men    that this world destroy.
And go and hunt hardily    for hares and for foxes,
For boars and for badgers    that break down mine hedges;
And go train thy falcons    wildfowl to kill,
For such come to my croft    and crop off my wheat.'
  Courteously the knight then    answered these words:
'By my powers, Piers,' quoth he    'I plight thee my troth

That pact to fulfil     though for it I fight;
As long as I live     I shall thee maintain.'

   'Yea; yet one point,' quoth Piers     'I pray of you more.
Look ye sue no tenant     unless Truth assent.
Though he may amerce them     let Mercy be taxer
And Meekness thy master     in spite of Meed's checks.
And though poor men proffer you     presents and gifts,
Take it not; for perchance     ye may not deserve it,
And then must repay it     again at a year's end
In a full perilous place     purgatory called.
Mishandle not bondmen     the better may thou speed.
Though he be underling here     well may happen in heaven
That he'll be worthier set     more blissful than thou,
Unless thou do better     and live as thou shouldest:
     *Amice, ascende superius.*

   'In the charnel at church     churls are hard to pick out,
Or a knight from a knave     know this in thine heart.
See thou'rt true of thy tongue     and tales that thou hate,
Unless they have wisdom     to chasten thy workmen.
Hold with no rascals     and hear not their tales,
Especially at meat     such men eschew;
They're the devil's minstrels     I bid thee to know.'

   'I assent, by St James!'     said the knight then,
'For to work by thy words     while my life endures.'

   'And I shall apparel me,' quoth Perkyn     'in pilgrim's wise,
And wend with you I will     till we find Truth;
Put on me my clothes     patched-up and ragged,
My leggings and mittens     'gainst cold of my nails,
Hang my seed basket at my neck     instead of a scrip,
And a bushel of breadcorn     bring me therein;
For I will sow it myself     and then will I wend
To pilgrimage as palmers do     pardon for to have.
Who will help me to plow     or to sow ere I wend
Shall have leave, by our Lord!     to glean here in harvest
And with it make himself merry     spite of who may begrudge it.
And all kinds of craftsmen     who will honestly live,
I shall find them food     that faithfully work.
Save Jack the juggler     and Janet of the stews,
Daniel the dicer     and Denot the bawd,
All lying friars     and folk of their order,
And Robin the ribald     for his smutty words——

Truth told me once and    bade me repeat it:
*Deleantur de libro viventium*    I'll not deal with them,
For Holy Church of their like    is told no tithe to take:
    *Qui cum justis non scribantur;*
By good luck they've escaped    now God them amend!'
    Dame Work-while-time-is    Pier's wife was called;
His daughter, Do-right-so-    or-thy-dame-shall-thee-beat;
His son, Suffer-thy-sovereigns-    to-have-their-will-
Judge-them-not-for-if-thou-dost-    thou-shalt-it-dearly-rue.
'May God be with all    for so his word teacheth.
For now I am hoary and old    and have goods of mine own
To penance and pilgrimage    I will pass with these others.
Wherefore ere I wend    I'll write out my bequest.
    '*In Dei nomine. Amen*    I make it myself.
He shall have my soul    that best hath deserved it
And if from the fiend will defend    for so I believe,
Till I come to his account    as my *Credo* me telleth,
To have release and remission    on that rental, I hope.
The church shall have my corpse    and keep all my bones,
For of my corn and cattle    she gathered the tithe.
I paid parson promptly    for peril of my soul;
So is he holden, I hope    to name me in his mass
And make a *memento* [1]    among other Christians.
    'My wife shall have my    honest gains and no more,
To share with my daughters    and my dear children.
For should I today die    all my debts are quit;
I bore back what I borrowed    ere I to bed went.
And with the residue and remnant    by the Rood of Lucca!
I will worship therewith    Truth, while I live,
And be his pilgrim at plow    for all poor men's sake.
My plow-foot shall be my pike-staff    and pick apart the roots
And help my coulter to carve    and clean up the furrows.'
    Now is Perkin and his pilgrims    to the plow gone;
To plow his half acre    helped him many.
Ditchers and delvers    digged up the balks;
Therewith Perkin was pleased    and praised them soon.
Other workmen there were    that worked eagerly;
Each man in his manner    made himself busy,
And some to please Perkin    piked up the weeds.
    At high prime-tide Piers    let the plow stand,

[1] See page 204.

To oversee them himself    and whoso worked best
Should be hired thereafter    when harvest time came.
   Then sat down some    and sang over the ale
And helped plow his half acre    with 'Ho, trollo-lolli!'
   'On peril of my soul!' quoth Piers    out of pure anger,
'Unless ye rise swiftly    and speed you to work,
Shall no grain that groweth    gladden you at need,
And though ye die for dole    devil take him who cares.'
   The false fellows were afeared    and feigned themselves blind;
Some laid their legs awry    in the way such louts know,
And made their moan to Piers    and prayed of him grace;
'For we have no limbs to labour with    Lord, thanked be thee!
But we pray for you, Piers    and for your plow too,
That God of his grace    your grain multiply
And yield to you for your alms    that ye give us here;
For we can not swink nor sweat    such sickness us aileth.'
   'If it be sooth,' quoth Piers, 'that ye say    I shall soon it espy.
Ye be wasters, I wot well    and Truth wots the sooth!
I am his old hind    and am bidden by him to warn
Those in this world    who have harmed his workmen.
Ye waste what men win    with travail and trouble,
But Truth shall teach you    · his plow-team to drive,
Or ye shall eat barley bread    and of the brook drink.
But if one be blind, broken-legged    or bolted with irons,
He shall eat wheat bread    and drink with myself,
Till God of his goodness    amendment him send.
But ye might travail as Truth wills    and take meat and hire
To keep kine in the field    the corn from the beasts,
To dike or to delve    or thresh out the sheaves,
Or help to make mortar    or bear muck afield.
In lechery and in lying    ye live, and in sloth,
And it is on sufferance    that vengeance is not taken.
But anchorites and hermits    that eat not but at noon,
And no more ere the morrow    mine alms shall they have,
And my goods shall clothe those    that have cloisters and churches.
But Robert the runabout    shall have naught of mine,
Nor friars; unless they preach well    and have leave of the bishop—
These shall have bread and pottage    and make themselves at ease:
'Tis an unreasonable religion [1]    hath right naught to depend on.'
Then a waster was wrath    and so would have fought,

                    [1] See page 204.

And to Piers the Plowman      he proffered his glove.
A Breton, a braggart      at Piers boasted too;
Bade him piss with his plow      for a starveling wretch!
'Willy or nilly      we will have our will;
Of thy flour and thy flesh      fetch when us like
And make merry therewith      despite thy accounts.'
   Then Piers the Plowman      complained to the knight
To keep him, as covenant was      from cursed wretches
And from these wolfish wasters      that do the world harm:
'For they waste and win naught      and meanwhile there'll be
No plenty for the people      while my plow be idle.'
   Courteously the knight then      as his nature was,
Warned the waster      and told him to mend:
'Or, by the order I bear      thou shalt suffer the law!'
   'I was not wont to work,' quoth Waster      'and now will not begin'—
And made light of the law      and less of the knight,
Set Piers and his plow      at the price of a pea
And menaced Pier's men      if they met again soon.
   'Now by peril of my soul      I shall punish you all!'
Piers whooped after Hunger      who heard him at once.
'Avenge me,' quoth he, 'on these wasters      who worry the world!'
   Hunger in haste then      seized Waste by the maw
And wrung him so by the belly      that both his eyes watered;
The Breton he buffeted      about the cheeks
That he looked lantern-jawed      all his life after.
He beat them so both      that he near burst their ribs;
Had not Piers with a pease-loaf      prayed Hunger to cease
They had been buried both      believe thou none other!
'Suffer them to live,' he said      'let them eat with the hogs
Or else beans and bran      baked up together,
Or else milk and mean ale'      thus prayed Piers for them.
   Loungers for fear thereof      fled into barns
And flapped on with flails      from morning till eve,
So that Hunger less hardily      looked upon them,
For a potful of pease      that Piers had made.
A heap of hermits      hung on to spades
And cut up their capes      to make themselves coats,
And went out as workmen      with spades and with shovels
To dig and to delve      to drive away hunger.
   The blind and bedridden      were bettered by thousands;
Those that sat to beg silver      soon were they healed;

For what was baked for a horse     was a boon for the hungry,
And many a beggar for beans     glad was to sweat,
And each poor man was well pleased     to have pease for his hire;
And what Piers prayed them to do     they did swift as a sparhawk.
Thereof was Piers proud     and put them to work,
Gave them meat as he might     and a moderate hire.
    Then had Piers pity     and prayed Hunger to wend
Home into his own place     and holden him there.
'For I am well avenged now     of wasters, through thy might.
But I pray thee, ere thou pass'     quoth Piers to Hunger,
'With beggars and bidders     what's best to be done?
For I wot well, when thou'rt gone     they will work full ill;
For misfortune makes them     to be so meek now
And for default of their food     this folk is at my will.
They're my brethren by blood     for God bought us all.
Truth taught me once     to love them each one
And to help them in all things     always, as they need.
And now would I know of thee     what were the best,
How I might master them     and make them to work.'
    'Hear now,' quoth Hunger     'and hold it for wisdom:
Bold beggars and big     that might earn bread by work,
With hounds' bread and horse bread     hold up their hearts,
Abate them with beans     to keep down their bellies;
And if grumblers grouse     bid them go work,
And they shall sup sweeter     when they've it deserved.
    'And if thou find any fellow     that any false man
Or fortune hath injured     find how such to know!
Comfort him with thy goods     for Christ's love of Heaven,
Love them and lend to them     so God's law teacheth:
    *Alter alterius onera portate.*
And all manner of man     that thou mayest espy
That be needy and have naught     help them with thy goods;
Love them and loathe them not     let God take the vengeance;
If they've done thee evil     let thou God alone;
    *Mihi vindicta, & ego retribuam.*
If thou wilt be gracious before God     do as the gospel teacheth,
And be loved among lowly men     so shalt thou have grace,
    *Facite vobis amicos de mamona iniquitatis.*'
    'I would not grieve God     for all the goods on ground.
Might I do as thou sayest and be sinless?'     said Piers then.
    'Yea, I promise thee,' quoth Hunger     'or else the Bible lieth.

Go to Genesis the giant      engenderer of us all:
"*In sudore* and swink      thou shalt earn thy meat
And labour for livelihood"      and so our Lord bade.
And Wisdom saith the same      I saw it in the Bible:
"*Piger prae frigore*      no field would till,
Therefore shall he beg and bid      and no man cure his hunger."
  'Matthew-with-man's-face      mouthed these words,
That *servus nequam* had a coin      and as he would not chaffer
Had rebuke of his master      for evermore after;
Who because he would not work      took away his coin
And gave that coin to him      that ten others had;
And with that he said so      that Holy Church heard:
"He that hath shall have      and be helped when he needeth,
And he that naught hath shall naught have      and no man him help;
And of that he weeneth to have      I will him bereave."
  'Mother-Wit wisheth      that each wight should work
In diking or in delving      or travailing in prayers;
At contemplative or active life      Christ would that men work,
The psalter saith in the psalm      of *Beati omnes*,
He that feedeth himself      with his faithful labour
He is blessed by the Book      in body and in soul:
    *Labores manuum tuarum, etc.*'
  'Yet I pray you,' quoth Piers      '*par charité*, if ye know
Any line of leechcraft      teach it me, my dear.
For some of my servants      and myself also
For all a week work not      so our belly acheth.'
  'I wot well,' quoth Hunger      'what sickness you aileth;
You have munched overmuch      and that maketh you groan.
But I bid thee,' quoth Hunger      'as thou thine health willest,
That thou drink not each day      ere thou dine somewhat.
Eat naught, I command thee      ere hunger thee take
And send thee of his sauce      to savour thy lips;
And keep some till supper-time      and sit not too long,
Rise up ere appetite      have eaten his fill.
Let not Sir Surfeit      sit at thy board;
Listen not, for he is lecherous      and lickerish of tongue,
After many manner of meats      his maw is anhungered.
  'And if thou diet thee thus      I dare lay mine ears
That Physic his furred hoods      for his food shall sell,
And his Calabrian cloak      with the knots of gold,
And be fain, by my faith      his physic to leave

And learn to labour on land      for livelihood's sweet.
For murderers are many leeches      the Lord them amend!
Making men die through their drinks      ere destiny wills.'
      'By St Paul,' quoth Piers      'these are profitable words!
Wend thou, Hunger, when thou wilt      and well be thou ever.
For this lovely lesson      may the Lord requite thee.'
      'I swear to God,' quoth Hunger      'hence will I not wend
Till I have dined this day      and drunken also.'
      'I have no penny,' quoth Piers      'pullets for to buy,
Nor neither geese nor pigs      but two green cheeses,
A few curds and cream      and an oaten cake,
And two loaves of beans and bran      baked for my youngsters.
And yet I say, by my soul      I have no salt bacon;
Nor no hen's eggs, by Christ      collops [1] for to make.
But I have parsley and leeks      with many cabbages,
And a cow and a calf      a cart-mare also
To draw dung afield      while the drought lasteth.
With this for our living we must live      until Lammas time come,
And by that I hope I have      harvest in my croft;
Then may I make thee thy dinner      as I'd like to dearly.'
All the poor people then      their peascods fetched,
Beans and baked apples      they brought in their laps,
Onions and chervils      and many ripe cherries,
And proffered Piers this present      wherewith to please Hunger.
      Hunger ate all in haste      and asked after more.
Then poor folk for fear      fed Hunger quickly;
With green leeks and pease      to poison him they sought.
By that it nighed near harvest      new corn came to market;
Then were folk fain      and fed Hunger with the best,
With good ale, as Glutton taught      and made Hunger go sleep.
      Then would Waster not work      but wandered about,
Nor no beggar eat bread      that had beans therein
But asked for the best      white, made of clean wheat;
Nor none halfpenny ale      in no wise would drink,
But of the best and the brownest      for sale in the borough.
      Labourers that have no land      to live on but their hands
Deigned not to dine at day      on worts a night old.
May no penny ale please them      nor no piece of bacon,
Only fresh flesh or fish      fried, roast, or baked,
And that *chaud* or *plus chaud*      'gainst chilling their maw.

[1] See page 204.

He must be hired at a high rate    else will he chide,
And wail at the time    when he was workman made;
And against Cato's counsel    begins he to rail:
    *Paupertatis onus patienter ferre memento.*
He has grievances against God    and grumbles against Reason;
Then curseth he the king    and all his counsel after
For licensing laws that    labourers grieve.
But while Hunger was their master    then would none of them chide
Nor strive against his statute    so sternly he looked.
    But I warn you, workmen    earn while ye may,
For Hunger hitherward    hasteth him fast,
He shall awake with water    wasters to chasten.
Ere five years be fulfilled    such famine shall arise,
Through floods and foul weather    all fruits shall fail.
So said planet Saturn [1]    and sent to warn you:
When ye see the sun gone amiss    and heads of two monks,
And a Maid have the mastery    and multiply by eight,
Then shall Death withdraw him    and Dearth be the judge,
And Davy the ditcher    shall die of hunger,
Unless God of his goodness    do grant us a truce.

[1] See page 204.

# PASSUS VII

T RUTH hereof heard tell    and to Piers he sent,
To take him his team    and to till the earth;
And provided a pardon    *a poena et a culpa* [1]
For him, and for his heirs    for evermore after.
And bade him hold him at home    and plow up his fields,
And all that helped him to plow    to set or to sow,
Or any other work    that might Piers avail,
Pardon with Piers Plowman    Truth them hath granted.

    Kings and knights    that keep Holy Church
And rightfully in realms    rule over the people
Have pardon through purgatory    to pass full lightly,
With patriarchs and prophets    in paradise to be fellows.

    Bishops most blessed    if they be as they should,
Legists of both the laws    to preach to the lawless,
And inasmuch as they may    amend all sinners,
Are peers with the apostles    (this pardon Piers showeth),
And at the day of doom    at the high dais to sit.

    Merchants to the good    had many years,
But none *a poena et a culpa*    would the pope them grant,
For they hold not her holy days    as Holy Church teacheth,
And they swear 'by their souls'    and 'so God must them help'
Clean against conscience    merchandise to sell.

    But under his secret seal    Truth sent them a letter
That they should buy boldly    what they liked best,
And afterwards sell again    and save their profits
Therewith to amend *maisons Dieu*    and miserable folk help;
To repair rotten roads    where plainly required;
And to build up bridges    that were broken down;
Help maidens to marry    or make of them nuns;
Poor people and prisoners    to find them their food;
And set scholars to school    or to some other craft;
Relieve poor religious    and lower their rents—
'And I shall send you myself    Michael mine archangel,
That no devil shall you daunt    nor fright you at death,

[1] See page 204.

60

And keep you from despair      if ye will thus work,
And send your souls safely      to my saints in joy.'
     Then were merchants merry      many wept for joy,
And praised Piers the Plowman      that provided this bull.
Men of law less pardon had      that pleaded for Meed;
For the psalter saveth not them      such as taketh gifts,
And especially from innocents      that no evil know:
        *Super innocentem munera non accipies.*
Pleaders should take much pains      to plead and help such;
Princes and prelates should      pay for their travail:
        *A regibus & principibus erit merces eorum.*
     But many justices and jurors      would do more for fees
Than *pro Dei pietate*      believe thou none other.
But he that spendeth his speech      and speaketh for the poor
That is innocent and needy      and no man oppresseth,
Comforteth them in that case      without coveting gifts,
And sheweth law for our Lord's love      as it hath learned,
Shall no devil at his death-day      daunt him with fear
That his soul is not safe      as witness the psalms:
        *Domine, quis habitabit in tabernaculo tuo, etc.*
     But to buy water, wind, wit      or fire, the fourth—
These four the Father of Heaven      made for his fold in common;
And these be Truth's treasures      true folk to help,
And shall never wax nor wane      without God himself.
     Those that pence of poor men      for their pleading take
Find their pardon full small      at their parting hence,
When they draw on to die      and indulgences would have.
Ye legists and lawyers      hold this for the truth,
That if that I lie      Matthew is to blame,
For he bade me write this      and this proverb told:
        *Quodcumque vultis ut faciant vobis homines, facite eis.*
     All living labourers      that live by their hands
And take the just wages      they honestly earn,
And live in love and in law      for their lowly hearts
Have the same absolution      that was sent to Piers.
     Beggars and bidders      are not in the bull,
Unless the occasion be honest      that makes them to beg.
He that beggeth or cadgeth      unless he have need
Is as false as the fiend      and defraudeth the needy;
He beguileth the giver      all against his will
For if he wist he were not needy      he would give to another

That were more needy than he    so the neediest would be helped.
Cato teacheth men thus    and the Clerk of the Stories;
*Cui des, videto*    is Cato's teaching
And in the stories he teacheth    to bestow thine alms well:
    *Sit elemosina tua in manu tua, donec studes cui des.*

    But Gregory was a good man    and bade give to all
That asketh for his love    that giveth to us all:
*Non eligas cui misererais, ne forte praetereas illum qui meretur accipere.*
*Quia incertum est pro quo Deo magis placeas.*

    For wit ye never who is worthy    but God wot who hath need.
In him that taketh is the treachery    if treason there be;
For he that giveth, parteth    and prepareth him to rest,
But he that beggeth, borroweth    and bringeth himself in debt.
For beggars borrow evermore    and their bail is God
To repay those that give to them    with interest added:
*Quare non dedisti pecuniam meam ad mensam,*
*Ut ego veniens cum usuris exegissem illam?*

    Therefore beg not, ye beggars    unless ye've great need.
For whoso must buy him bread    the Book beareth witness,
Hath enough that hath bread enough    though he have naught else.
    *Satis dives est, qui non indiget pane.*

    Find habit and solace    in reading saints' lines;
The Book banneth begging    and blameth them thus:
    *Junior fui, et jam senui: et non vidi justum derelictum, nec semen ejus*
      *quaerens panem.*

For ye live not in love    and hold to no law.
Many of you wed not    the women you go with,
But like whinnying beasts    mount them and tread them,
And so bring forth children    that bastards men call.
If the back or some bone    is broken in youth,
Ye will exploit that child    for evermore after.
There is more misshaped people    among all these beggars
Than of other manner of men    that on this mould move.
And they that live thus their life    may well loathe the time
That ever he was born    when he shall hence fare.

    But old men and hoary    without help or strength,
And all women with child    that can work no more,
The blind and bedridden    and broken in limb,
That bear mischief meekly    as lepers and others,
Have as plenary a pardon    as the plowman himself;
For love of their lowly hearts    our Lord hath them granted

Their penance and purgatory     here on this earth.

'Piers,' quoth a priest then     'thy pardon must I read,
For I will construe each clause     and tell it in English.'

And Piers at his prayer     the pardon unfoldeth,
And I behind both     beheld all the bull.
All in two lines it lay     and not a leaf more,
And was written right thus     in witness of Truth:

> *Et qui bona egerunt, ibunt in vitam aeternam; qui vero mala, in ignem
> aeternum.*

'Peter!' quoth the priest then     'I can no pardon find
But "Do well and have well     and God shall have thy soul;
But do evil and have evil     and after thy death-day
The Devil have thy soul     hope thou none other."'

And Piers in vexation     tore it in twain,
And said: '*Si ambulavero in medio umbrae mortis non timebo mala: quoniam
tu mecum es.*

'I shall cease from my sowing     and swink not so hard,
Nor about my belly-joy     so busy be more.
Of prayers and of penance     shall my plow be hereafter,
And I'll weep when I should sleep     though my wheat-bread fail.
The prophet his bread ate     in penance and sorrow,
And by what psalter saith     so did many others;
Whoso loveth God loyally     can live upon little:

> *Fuerunt mihi lacrimae meae panes die ac nocte.*

'And, unless Saint Luke lie     he shows by the birds
We should not be too busy     about the world's bliss.
*Ne solliciti sitis*     he saith in the gospel,
And sheweth us by examples     our own selves to guide.
The fowls in the fields     who feeds them in winter?
They've no garner to go to     God finds for them all.'

'What!' quoth priest to Perkin     'Peter! as methinketh,
Thou art lettered a little     who learned thee thy book?'

'Abstinence the abbess,' quoth Piers     'mine A B C taught me,
And Conscience came after     and taught me much more.'

'Wert thou priest, Piers,' quoth he     'thou mightest preach where thou
                                                      wouldest,
As a divine in divinity     with *dixit insipiens* for theme.'

'Ignorant fool!' quoth Piers     'little lookest thou on the Bible,
And the saws of Solomon     seldom thou seest:

> *Ejice derisores et jurgia cum eis, ne crescant, etc.*'

Thus the priest and Perkin     opposed one to the other.

Through their words I awoke     and looked about
And saw the sun in the south     set at that time,
Meatless and moneyless     on Malvern hills
And musing on this vision     I went on my way.

   Many times this vision     hath made me study
Of that I saw sleeping     if so it might be;
And also of Piers Plowman     full pensive in heart;
And what pardon he had     all the people to comfort,
And how the priest had impugned it     with just two words.
I've no savour in soothsaying     I see it oft fail;
And the canonists and Cato     counsel us not
To put faith in divining     fo *somnia ne cures.*
But the book of the Bible     clearly bears witness
How Daniel divined     the dreams of a king,
That was Nebuchadnezzar     named by the clerks.
To whom Daniel said: 'Sir King     thy dream betokeneth
That unknown knights shall come     thy kingdom to cleave;
Amongst lower lords thy lands     shall be divided.'
And as Daniel divined     indeed it fell out,
The king lost his lordship     and lower men had it.
And Joseph dreamed marvellously     how the moon and sun
And the eleven stars of heaven     saluted him all.
Then Jacob judged     of Joseph's dream:
'*Beau fils*,' then quoth his father     'for our lack we shall,
I myself and my sons     seek you in our need.'

   As his father said it befell     in Pharaoh's time,
That Joseph was justice     Egypt to govern;
It befell as his father told     his friends there him sought.
And all this maketh me     on this dream to think:
And how the priest proved     no pardon like Do-well,
And deemed that good deeds     an indulgence surpassed,
And biennials and triennials [1]     and letters of bishops.
And how Do-well at Doomsday     is honourable held,
Surpassing the pardon     of Saint Peter's church.

   Now hath the pope power     to grant the people
Remission of penance     to pass into Heaven:
This is our belief     as lettered men teach us:

   *Quodcumque ligaveris super terram, erit ligatum et in coelis, etc.*

So I believe loyally     (the Lord forbid else!)
That pardon, penance, and prayers     cause to be saved

   [1] See page 204.

Souls that have sinned     seven times deadly.
But to trust to indulgences     truly methinketh,
Is not so safe for the soul     as it is to do well.
     Therefore I advise all you     the rich on this earth
That on trust of your treasure     triennials can have,
Be ye never the bolder     to break the ten laws
And especially ye, masters     mayors, and judges,
Who for wise men are held     and have this world's wealth
To purchase your pardons     and the pope's bulls.
At the dreadful Doom when     the dead shall arise
And come all before Christ     their account to yield,
How thou leddest thy life     and here his laws kept,
And how thou didst day by day     the doom will declare:
Then a poke full of pardons     as provincials' letters,
Though found in the fraternity     of all the friars' orders
With doublefold indulgence     unless good deeds help you,
I put your patents and pardons     at one pea-pod's value!
Therefore I counsel Christians     to cry God mercy,
And Mary his mother     be our mediatress,
That God give us grace here     ere that we go hence
That we may work such works     while we are here
That after our death-day     Do-well will declare
At the day of Doom that     we did as he bade.

## PASSUS VIII

Thus robed in russet      I roamed about
All a summer season      for to seek Do-well,
And inquired full oft      of folk that I met,
If any wight wist      where Do-well was at in,
And what man he might be      of many men I asked.

Was never wight as I went      that could show me the way
Where this man dwelled      less nor more;
Till it befell on a Friday      two friars I met,
Masters of the Minors      men of great wit.[1]
I hailed them politely      as I had learned,
And prayed them, for charity      ere they passed further,
If they knew any country      or coasts, as they went,
Where that Do-well dwelleth      grant me to know.

For they be men of this mould      that most widely walk,
And know countries, and courts      and poor men's cots,
And Do-well and Do-evil      where they dwell both.

'Amongst us,' quoth the Minors      'that man is dwelling,
And ever hath, as I hope      and ever shall hereafter.'

'Contra,' quoth I like a clerk      and began to dispute,
And told them truly, '*septies      in die cadit justus;*
Seven times, saith the Book      sinneth the righteous.
And whoso sinneth,' I said      'doth evil, as methinketh,
And Do-well and Do-evil      may not dwell together.
*Ergo*, he is not always      among you friars;
He is sometimes elsewhere      teaching the people.'

'I shall tell thee, my son'      said the friar then,
'How seven times the upright      in a day sinneth;
By a picture,' quoth the friar      'I shall thee fair show.

'Put a man in a boat      on a broad water,
The wind and the water      and the boat rocking
Make the man many a time      to fall and recover;
For stand he never so firm      he stumbleth if he move;
And yet is he safe and sound      and so it behoves him,
For if he did not rise quickly      and reach for the helm,

[1] See page 204.

66

The wind would with the water     the boat overthrow;
And then were his life lost     through his own neglect.
And thus it falleth,' quoth the friar     'to folk here on earth;
The water is likened to the world     that waneth and waxeth,
The goods of this earth are like     to the great waves,
That as winds and weather     toss about.
The boat is likened to our body     that brittle is by nature,
So through the fiend and the flesh     and the fickle world,
Sinneth the upright     a day, seven times.
    'But deadly sin doth he not     for Do-well him keepeth,
And that Christ the champion     chief help against sin;
For he strengtheneth man to stand     and steareth man's soul,
And though thy body waver     as boat doth in water,
Ever is thy soul safe     unless thyself will
Do a deadly sin     and drown so thy soul;
God will suffer well thy sloth     if thyself liketh.
For he gave thee a new year's gift [1]     to care well for thyself,
And that is wit and free will     to every wight a portion,
To flying fowls     to fishes and to beasts.
But man hath most thereof     and most is to blame
Unless he work well therewith     as Do-well him teacheth.'
    'I have no natural knowing,' quoth I     'to conceive all your words,
But if I may live and look     I shall go to learn better.'
'I commit thee to Christ,' quoth he     'that on the cross died.'
And I said, 'The same     save you from mischance,
And give you grace on this ground     good men to become.'
    And thus I went widely     walking alone,
By a wild wilderness     and by a wood side.
Bliss of the birds     made me abide,
And under a linden in a glade     leaned I awhile,
To listen to the lays     the lovely fowls made.
Mirth of their mouths     made me there to sleep;
The most marvellous dream     met me then
That ever dreamed wight     in world as I ween.
    A tall man, as methought     and like to myself,
Came and called me     by my own name.
'What art thou?' quoth I then     'that thou my name knowest?'
'That thou knowest well,' quoth he     'and no wight better.'
    'Know I what thou art?'     'Thought,' said he then,
'I have attended thee these seven years     sawest thou me no sooner?'

[1] See page 204.

'Art thou Thought?' quoth I then      'canst thou me show
Where that Do-well dwelleth      and let me know?'
      'Do-well and Do-better      and Do-best the third,' quoth he,
'Are three fair virtues      and be not far to find.
Whoso is true of his tongue      and of his two hands,
And through his labour or through his land      his livelihood winneth.
And is trusty of his tallying      taketh but his own,
And is not a drunkard nor disdainful      Do-well is with him.
      'Do-better doth right thus      but he doth much more;
He is as lowly as a lamb and gentle of speech,
And helpeth all men      as they are in need;
The bags and the purses      he hath burst them all
That the earl Avaricious      held, and his heirs;
And thus with Mammon's money      he hath made him friends,
And hath hurried into religion      and hath translated the Bible,
And preacheth to the people      St Paul's words.
      *Libenter suffertis insipientes, cum sitis ipsi sapientes.*
"And suffer the unwise      with you for to live."
And with glad will do them good      for so God you bids.
      'Do-best is above both      and beareth a bishop's crozier;
It is hooked at one end      to hale men from hell.
A spike is on that staff      to strike down the wicked
That watch for any wickedness      Do-well to vex.
And Do-well and Do-better      amongst them ordained
To crown one to be king      to rule them both;
But if Do-well or Do-better      act against Do-best,
Then shall the king come      and cast them in irons,
And unless Do-best plead for them      they to be there for ever.
      'Thus Do-well and Do-better      and Do-best the third,
Crowned one to be king      to watch over them all,
And to rule the Realm      by their three wits,
And none otherwise      but as they three assented.'
      I thanked Thought then      that he me thus taught;
'But yet satisfies me not thy saying      I long to learn
How Do-well, Do-better and Do-best      do amongst the people.'
      'But Wit can teach thee,' quoth Thought      'where those three dwell;
Else know I none that can      that now is alive.'
      Thought and I thus      three days we went,
Discussing Do-well      day after other,
And ere we were aware      with Wit did we meet.
He was long and lean      like to no other,

Was no pomp in his apparel    nor poverty neither,
Sober in his semblance    and of mild mien.
I dared move no matter    to make him dispute,
But I begged Thought then    to be intermediary,
And put forth some proposition    to test his wits,
What was Do-well from Do-better    and Do-best from them both.
  Then Thought at that time    said these words,
'Where Do-well, Do-better    and Do-best be in the land,
Here is Will would know    if Wit can teach him,
And whether he be man or no man    this man fain would discover,
And act as they three would have    this is his purpose.'

# PASSUS IX

'Sir Do-well dwelleth,' quoth Wit    'not a day hence,
In a castle that Kind [1] made    of four kinds of things;
Of earth and air is it made    mingled together,
With wind and with water    certainly joined.
Nature hath closed therein    craftily withal,
A beloved that he loveth    as himself,
*Anima* [2] she is called    but Envy her hateth,
A proud pricker of France    *princeps hujus mundi*,
And would win her away    with wiles, if he might.
But Kind knoweth this well    and keepeth her the better,
And hath placed her with Sir Do-well    who is duke of these marches.
Do-better is her damsel    Sir Do-well's daughter,
To serve this lady truly    both early and late.
Do-best is above both    a bishop's peer;
What he bids must be done    he ruleth them all;
*Anima* that lady    is led by his teaching.
    'But the constable of that castle    who keepeth all the watch,
Is a wise knight withal    Sir Conscience he is called,
And hath five fair sons    by his first wife;
Sir See-well and Say-well    and Hear-well the kind,
Sir Work-well-with-thine-hand    an active man of strength,
And Sir Godfrey Go-well    great lords in truth.
These five are set    to save this lady *Anima*,
Till Kind come or send    to save her for ever.'
    'What kind of thing is Kind,' quoth I    'canst thou me tell?'
    'Kind,' quoth Wit 'is a being    of all kinds of things;
Father and former    of all that ever was made;
And that is the great God    that beginning had never,
Lord of life and of light    of joy and of pain.
Angels and all things    are at his will.
But man is him most like    in mark and in form;
For through the word that he spake    came forth beasts,
    *Dixit, et facta sunt;*
And made man likest    to himself, one,

[1] See page 204.                [2] See page 204.

70

And Eve of his rib-bone     without any mediary.
For he was sole of himself     and said *faciamus*,
As who saith, "more must be here     than my word one;
My might must help     now with my speech."
Right as a lord should make letters     and he lacked parchment,
Though he knew how to write never so well     if he had no pen,
The letters for all the lordship     I believe, were never made.
  'And so it seemeth by him     as the Bible telleth,
      There he said, *dixit, et facta sunt*;
He must work with his word     and his wit show.
And in this manner was man made     through might of God almighty,
With his word and workmanship     and with life to endure.
And thus God gave him a soul     of the Godhead of heaven,
And of his great grace     granted him bliss,
And that is life that aye shall last     to all his lineage after.
And that is the castle that Kind made     *Caro* it is called,
And is as much as to say     man with a soul;
And that he wrought with work     and with word both;
Through might of the majesty     man was made.
  'Conscience and all wits     closed be therein,
For love of the lady *Anima*     who Life is named;
Over all in man's body     she walketh and wandereth,
And in the heart is her home     and her chief rest.
But Conscience is in the head     and to the heart he looketh,
What *Anima* loves or loathes     he allows her at his will;
For after the grace of God     the greatest is Conscience.
  'Much woe to that man     that misruleth his Conscience,
And that be greedy gluttons     their god is their belly;
      *Quorum deus venter est.*
For they serve Satan     their soul shall he have;
That liveth sinful life here     their soul is like the devil.
And all that live good life     are like God almighty,
      *Qui manet in caritate, in Deo manet, etc.*
  'Alas! that drink shall undo     what God bought dear,
And makes God forsake them     that he shaped to his likeness;
      *Amen dico vobis, nescio vos; et alibi: et dimisi eos secundum desideria
      eorum.*
  'Simpletons that lack Conscience     I find that holy church
Should provide for them that fail     and fatherless children;
And widows that have naught wherewith     to win them their food,
Mad men, and maidens     that helpless were;

All these lack Conscience      and should be taught.
    'Of this matter I might      make a long tale,
And find many witnesses      amongst the four Doctors,
And that I lie not in that I teach thee      Luke beareth witness.
    'Godfather and godmother      that see their godchildren
In grief and misfortune      and may them comfort,
Shall have penance in purgatory      unless they them help.
For more is due to the little child      ere he the law knows,
Than naming of name      and he never the wiser!
Would no Christian creature      cry at the gate,
Nor lack bread nor soup      if prelates did as they should.
A Jew would not see a Jew      go begging for need,
For all the goods on this earth      if he amend it might.
    'Alas! that a Christian creature      shall be unkind to another,
Since Jews that we judge      Judas' fellows,
Each of them helpeth the other      in that that he needeth.
Why will not we Christians      of Christ's goods be as generous
As Jews, that be our teachers?      shame to us all!
The commons for their uncharity      I fear me, shall pay.
    'Bishops shall be blamed      for beggars' sake;
He is worse than Judas      that giveth a jester silver,
And biddeth the beggar go      for his torn clothes:
        *Proditor est prelatus cum Juda, qui patrimonium Christi minus distri-*
            *buit; et alibi:*
        *Pernitiosus dispensator est, qui res pauperum Christi inutiliter consumit.*
He doth not well that doth thus      nor dreadeth not God almighty,
Nor loveth not Solomon's sayings      that Wisdom taught;
        *Initium sapientiae, timor Domini:*
That dreadeth God, he doth well;      that dreadeth him for love,
And not for dread of punishment      doth in that the better;
He doth best, that withdraweth him      by day and by night
From wasting any speech      or any space of time;
        *Qui offendit in uno, in omnibus est reus.*
    'Squandering of time      as true as true!
Is most hated upon earth      by them that be in heaven,
And to waste speech      that germ is of grace,
And God's glee-man      and a game of heaven;
Would never the faithful Father      his fiddle were un-tuned,
Nor his gleeman a vagabond      a goer to taverns!
    'To all true upright men      that work desire,
Our Lord loveth them and lends      in calm or storm,

Grace to go to them    and gain their livelihood;
> *Inquirentes autem dominum non minuentur omni bono.*

'True wedded living folk    in this world is Do-well;
For they must work and earn    and the world sustain.
For of their kind they come    that confessors are called,
Kings and knights    caesars and serfs,
Maidens and martyrs    out of one man come.
The wife was made the way    for to help the work,
And thus was wedlock wrought    with a middle person;
First by the father's will    and the friends' council,
And then by assent of themselves    as they two might accord.
And thus was wedlock wrought    and God himself it made;
In earth its heaven is    himself was the witness.

'But false folk faithless    thieves and liars,
Wasters and wretches    out of wedlock, I trow,
Conceived be in evil time    as Cain was by Eve.[1]
Of such sinful wretches    the psalter maketh mention,
> *Concepit in dolore, et peperit iniquitatem,* etc.:

And all that came of that Cain    came to evil end.
For God sent to Seth    and said by an angel,
"Thine issue with thine issue    I will that they be wedded,
And not thy kind with Cain's    coupled nor espoused."

'Yet some, against the sending    of our Saviour of heaven,
Cain's kind and his kind    coupled together,
Till God was wrath for their works    and such a word said,
"That I made man    now it me repenteth";
> *Poenitet me fecisse hominem.*

And came to Noah anon    and bade not stay:
"Quickly go shape a ship    of planks and of boards.
Thyself and thy sons three    and then your wives,
Hurry you to that boat    and bideth ye therein,
Till forty days be fulfilled    that the flood have washed
Clean away the cursed blood    that Cain made.
Beasts that now be    shall blame the time,
That ever that cursed Cain    came on this earth;
All shall die for his deeds    by dales and by hills,
And the fowls that fly    forth with other beasts,
Except only    of each kind a couple,
That in thy shingled ship    shall be saved."

'In this the child    for the grandsire's guilt,

[1] See page 204.

And all for their forefathers    they fared the worse.
The gospel is against this    in one degree, I find,

> *Filius non portabit iniquitatem patris, et pater non portabit iniquitatem*
> *filii, etc.*

'But I find, if the father    be false and a rascal,
That somewhat the son    shall have the sire's splotches.
Graft on an elder    and if thine apple be sweet,
Much marvel methinketh    and more, of a rascal
That bringeth forth any child    unless he be the same,
And have a savour of the sire    seldom seest thou other;

> *Numquam colligimus de spinis uvas, nec de tribulis ficus.*

And thus through cursed Cain    came care upon earth;
And all for they wrought wedlock    against God's will.
Therefore have they punishment for their marriages    that marry so their
                                                        children;
For some, as I see now    truly to tell,
For covetousness of wealth    unnaturally be wedded.
As unhappy conception    cometh of such marriages,
As befell of the folk    that I before told.
For good should wed good    though they no goods have;
"I am *via et veritas*," saith Christ    "I may prosper all."
'It is an uncomely coupling    by Christ, as methinketh,
To give a young wench    to an old dotard,
Or wed any widow    for wealth of her goods,
That never shall child bear    except in her arms!
Many a pair since the pestilence    have plight them together;
The fruit that they bring forth    are foul words,
In jealousy joyless    and scolding in bed.
Have they no children but strife    and abusing each other.
'And though they betake them to Dunmow [1]    unless the devil help
To try for the flitch    fetch they it never;
And unless they both be forsworn    that bacon they lose.
'Therefore I council all Christians    covet not to be wed
For covetousness of wealth    nor of kindred rich.
But young men and maidens    match you together,
Widows and widowers    do the same.
For no lands, but for love    look ye to be wedded,
And then get ye the grace of God    and goods enough to live with.
'And every manner layman    that may not continue,
Wisely go wed    and beware him of sin;

                    [1] See page 204.

For lechery in desire    is a limed snare of hell.
Whilst thou art young    and thy weapon keen,
Content thee with wiving    if though wilt be exempt.
*Dum sis vir fortis    ne des tua robora scortis,*
*Scribitur in portis    meretrix est janua mortis.*
    'When ye have wived, beware    and act in due time;
Not as Adam and Eve    when Cain was engendered.
For unseasonably, truely    between man and woman,
Should no play in bed be    unless they both be clean
Both of life and of soul    and in perfect charity,
That same private deed    do no man should.
And if they lead thus their life    it pleaseth God almighty;
For he made wedlock first    and himself it said;
    *Bonum est ut unusquisque uxorem suam habeat, propter fornicationem.*
    'And they that otherwise be got    for vagabonds be held,
As false folk, foundlings    cheaters and liars;
Ungracious in getting goods    or love of the people,
Wandering and wasting    what they may gain.
Against Do-well they do evil    and the devil serve,
And after their death-day    shall dwell with the same,
But God give them grace here    themselves to amend.
    'Do-well, my friend, is    to do as law teacheth;
To love thy friend and thy foe    believe me, that is Do-better.
To give and to cherish    both young and old,
To heal and to help    is Do-best of all.
And Do-well is to dread God    and Do-better to suffer,
And so cometh Do-best of both    and bringeth down the proud,
And that is wicked will    that many a work ruins,
And driveth away Do-well    through deadly sins.'

# PASSUS X

THEN had Wit a wife     was called Dame Study,
That lean was of face     and of body both.
She was wondrously wrath     that Wit me thus taught,
And all staring Dame Study     sternly said,
'Well art thou wise,' quoth she to Wit     'any wisdom to tell
To flatterers or to fools     that frantic be of wit!'
And blamed him and scolded him     and bade him be still,
With such wise words     from teaching any sots;
And said '*noli mittere*, man     margery pearls [1]
Amongst hogs, that have     haws at will.
They do but drivel there-on     draff is dearer to them
Than all the precious stones     that in Paradise grow.
I say it·of such,' quoth she     'that showeth by their works,
That they would rather land     and lordship on earth,
Of riches or rents     and rest at their will,
Than all the true sayings     that Solomon said ever.
   'Wisdom and wit now     is not worth a cress,
Unless it be carded with covetousness     as clothiers comb their wool.
Whoso can contrive deceits     and conspire wrongs,
And conduct a law-day     to hinder truth,
He that such crafts knows     to council is called;
They lead lords with lies     and belie truth.
   'Job the gentle     in his tales witnesseth,
That wicked men they wield     the wealth of this world,
And that they be lords of each a land     that out of law live;
    *Quare impii vivunt? bene est omnibus, qui praevaricantur et inique agunt.*
The psalter saith the same     of such that do ill,
    *Ecce ipsi peccatores abundantes; in saeculo obtinuerunt divitias.*
"Lo!" saith Holy Scripture     "these lords be rascals!"
Those to whom God most giveth     least goods they dealeth,
And most unkind to the commons     that most wealth wieldeth;
    *Quae perfecisti, destruxerunt; justus autem quid fecit?*
Ribalds for their ribaldry     may have of their goods,
And jesters and jugglers     and tellers of tales.

[1] See page 204.

76

'But he that hath holy writ     ever in his mouth,
And can tell of Tobit     and of the twelve apostles,
Or preach of the punishment     that Pilate wrought
On Jesus the gentle     that Jews tortured:
Little is he loved     that such a lesson showeth,
Or cherished for advancement     I call on God himself!
　'But those that fain them fools     and with falsehood live,
Against the law of our Lord     and lie in themselves,
Spit and spew     and speak foul words,
Drink and drivel     and make men gape,
Mimic and lie against them     that give them no gifts,
They know no more minstrelsy     nor music,
Than Mund the miller     of *multa fecit Deus*!
Nor were their vile ribaldry     have God my troth,
If never king nor knight     nor canon of Saint Paul's
Gave them for the new year     the gift of a groat!
But mirth and minstrelsy     amongst men is now
Lechery, lying     and vagabonds' tales;
Gluttony and great oaths     this mirth they loveth.
　'But if they chatter of Christ     these ignorant clerks
At meat in their pleasures     when minstrels be still,
Then telleth they of the Trinity     a tale or two,
And bring forth a bald reason     and take Bernard [1] to witness,
And put forth an assumption     to prove the truth.
Thus they drivel at their dais     the deity to know,
And gnaw God with their gorge     when their guts are full.
　'But the miserable may cry     and call at the gate,
Both a-hungered and a-thirst     and for chill a-quake;
Is none to receive near     his anguish to heal,
But shout at him as a hound     and bid him go thence.
Little loveth he that lord     that gave him all that bliss,
That thus shares with the poor man     a portion when he is in need.
Unless mercy were in common men     more than in rich,
Mendicants meat-less     might go to bed.
God is much in the mouth     of these great masters,
But amongst poor men     his mercy and his works;
And so saith the psalter     I have seen it oft,
　　　*Ecce audivimus eam in Ephrata, invenimus eam in campis silvae.*
　'Clerks and other kinds of men     talk of God in plenty,
And have him much on their lips     but mean men at heart.

---

[1] See page 204.

Friars and deceivers     have found such questions
To please with proud men     since the pestilence time,
And preach at Saint Paul's [1]     for pure envy of clerks,
So that folk are not confirmed in the faith     nor free of their goods,
Nor sorry for their sins     so is pride waxed
In religion and in all the realm     amongst rich and poor,
That prayers have no power     the pestilence to stay.
And yet the wretches of this world     is none warned by the other,
Nor for dread of the Death     withdrawn not their pride,
Nor be plenteous to the poor     as pure charity wills,
But in gayness and gluttony     devour their goods themselves,
And give not to the beggar     as the Book teacheth,

>    *Frange esurienti panem tuum, etc.*

And the more he winneth and wields     wealth and riches,
And lordeth it in lands     the less goods he distributes.
     'Tobit telleth you not so     take heed, ye rich,
How the book Bible     of him beareth witness:

>    *Si tibi sit copia, abundanter tribue; si autem exiguum, illud impertiri stude
>        libenter:*

Whoso hath much, expend it humanely     so meaneth Tobit,
And whoso little wieldeth     rule himself accordingly;
For we have no compact of our life     how long it shall last.
Such lessons lords should     love to hear,
And how they might the most of the poor     humanely succour.
     'Not to fare as a fiddler or a friar     for to seek feasts,
At home in other men's houses     and hating their own.
Wretched is the hall     each day in the week,
Where the lord nor the lady     liketh not to sit.
Now hath each rich man a rule     to eat by himself
In a private parlour     because of poor men,
Or in a chamber with a chimney     and leave the chief hall,
That was made for meals     men to eat in;
And all to spare from spilling     what spend shall another.
     'I have heard high men     eating at table,
Talk as they clerks were     of Christ and of his powers,
And lay faults upon the Father     that formed us all,
And carp against clerks     crabbed words;
"Why would our Saviour suffer     such a worm [2] into his paradise,
That beguiled the woman     and the man after,
Through whose wiles and words     they went to hell,

And all their seed for their sin    the same death suffered?
Here lieth your lore"    these lords begin to dispute,
"Of that ye clerks us teacheth    of Christ by the gospel;
    *Filius non portabit iniquitatem patris, etc.*
Why should we that now be    for the works of Adam
Perish and be destroyed?    reason warrants it never;
    *Unusquisque portabit onus suum, etc.*"
   'Such motions they move    these masters in their vainglory,
And make men disbelieve    that muse much on their words;
Imaginative hereafter    shall answer to your purpose.
Augustine to such arguers    he telleth them this text,
    *Non plus sapere quam oportet.*
Wish never to know    why that God would
Suffer Satan    his seed to beguile,
But believe loyally    in the lore of holy church,
And pray him for pardon    and penance in thy life,
And in his great mercy    to amend you here.
For all that wish to know    the ways of God almighty,
I would his eye were in his arse    and his finger after,
That ever wisheth to know    why that God would
Suffer Satan    his seed to beguile,
Or Judas to the Jews    Jesu betray.
All was as thou would'st    Lord, worshipped be thou,
And all shall be as thou wishest    whatever we dispute!
   'And he that uses these mazes    to blind men's wits,
What is Do-well from Do-better    now deaf must he be,
(Since he wisheth to know    what they be both),
Unless he live in the life    that belongs to Do-well;
For I dare go bail    that Do-better will he never,
Though Do-best draw him    day after other.'
   And when that Wit was aware    what Dame Study told,
He became so confused    he could not look,
And as dumb as death    and withdrew him back;
And for no speaking I could after    nor kneeling to the ground,
I might get no grain    of his great wits,
But all laughing be bowed    and looked upon Study,
In sign that I should    beseech her of grace.
   And when I was aware of his will    to his wife began I bow,
And said, 'Your pardon, madame    your man shall I become,
As long as I live    both late and soon,
For to work your will    the while my life lasteth,

With that ye teach me of your kindness     to know what is Do-well.'
    'For thy meekness, man,' quoth she     'and for thy mild speech,
I shall bring thee to my cousin     that Clergy is called.
He hath wedded a wife     within these six months,
Is kin to the seven arts [1]     Scripture is her name.
They two, as I hope     after my teaching,
Shall guide thee to Do-well     I dare it undertake.'

    Then was I also joyful     as bird on fair morning,
And gladder than the gleeman     that gold has been given,
And asked her the highway     where that Clergy dwelt,
'And tell me some token,' quoth I     'for time is that I went.'
    'Ask the highway,' quoth she     'hence of Suffer-
Both-well-and woe     if that thou wilt learn,
And ride forth by Riches     but rest thou not therein,
For if thou couplest thee therewith     to Clergy comest thou never.
And also the lickerish land     that Lechery is called,
Leave him on thy left hand     a large mile or more,
Till thou come to a court     Keep-well-thy-tongue
From-lies-and-vicious-speech     and-lickerish-drinks.

    'Then shalt thou see Sobriety     and Simplicity-of-speech.
That each wight be willing     his wit thee to show,
And thus shalt thou come to Clergy     that knows many things.
Say to him this sign     I set him to school,
And that I greet well his wife     for I wrote her many books,
And set her to Wisdom     and to the psalter to gloss.

    'Logic I taught her     and many other laws,
And all the measures in music     I made her to know.
Plato the poet     I put him first to books,
Aristotle and others more     to argue I taught.
Grammar for children     I caused first to be written,
And beat them with a birch     unless they would learn.
Of all kinds of crafts     I contrived tools,
Of carpentry, of carvers     and masons with compasses,
And taught them level and line     though I look dull.

    'But Theology hath troubled me     ten score times,
The more I muse therein     the mistier it seemeth,
And the deeper I search     the darker me it thinketh;
It is no science forsooth     to be too subtle in;
A full idle thing it were     if it were not for love.
But because it puts Love first     I love it the better;
                    [1] See page 204.

For there that Love is leader     never lacked grace.
Look thou love loyally     if thou wouldst please Do-well;
For Do-better and Do-best     be of Love's kin.
In another science it saith     I saw it in Cato,
*Qui simulat verbis, nec corde est fidus amicus,*
*Tu quoque fac simile, sic ars deluditur arte.*
Whoso speaks fair as flatterers do     let each do the same,
And so shalt thou false folk     and faithless beguile,
This is Cato's saying     to clerks that he teacheth,
But Theology teacheth not so     whoso taketh heed,
He instructs us the contrary     against Cato's words;
For he bids us be as brethren     and pray for our enemies,
And love them that lie to us     and give to them when they need,
And do good against evil     God himself it commands,

> *Dum tempus habemus, operemur bonum ad omnes, maxime autem ad*
> *domesticos fidei.*

  'Paul preached to the people     that perfection loved,
To do good for God's love     and give to men that asked,
And especially to such     that follow our faith.
And all that speak ill or lie to us     our Lord teacheth us to love,
And not to grieve them that grieve us     God himself has forbidden it,
> *Mihi vindictam, et ego retribuam.*
Therefore look thou love     as long as thou livest,
For there is no science under the sun     so sovereign for the soul.
  'But astronomy is a hard thing     and evil for to know,
Geometry and divination     are guileful of speech;
Whoso thinketh to work with those two     thriveth full late.
For sorcery is the sovereign book     that to these sciences belongeth.
And there are tricks in coffers     of many men's making,
Experiments in alchemy     the people to deceive,
If thou think on Do-well     deal therewith never.
All these sciences I myself     devised and ordained,
And founded them first     folk to deceive.
Tell Clergy these tokens     and Scripture after,
To counsel thee kindly     to know what is Do-well.'
  I said, 'Great thanks, madame'     and meekly saluted her,
And went quickly away     without more delay.
And till I came to Clergy     I knew no stop;
And saluted the good man     as Study me taught,
And afterwards the wife     and paid them both reverence,
And told them the tokens     that me taught were.

Was never man on this earth      since God made the world,
Fairer received      nor more at ease among friends,
Than myself truly      soon as he knew
That I was of Wit's house      and with his wife Dame Study.
I told him truly      that sent was I thither,
Do-well and Do-better      and Do-best to learn.

   'Do-well is a common life,' quoth Clergy      'on Holy Church to believe,
With all the articles of the faith      that should be known.
And that is to believe loyally      both the learned and unlearned,
On the great God      that beginning had never,
And on the true Son      that saved mankind
From the deadly death      and the devil's power,
Through the help of the Holy Ghost      the which Spirit is of both;
Three real persons      but not in plural number,
For all is but one God      and each is God himself;
      *Deus Pater, Deus Filius, Deus Spiritus Sanctus;*
God the Father, God the Son      God the Holy Ghost of both,
Maker of mankind      and of beasts both.
   'Austin [1] the old      hereof he made books,
And himself applied      to confirm us in faith.
Who was his authority?      all the four evangelists;
And Christ called himself so      the evangelists beareth witness:
      *Ego in Patre et Pater in me est; et, qui videt me, videt et Patrem meum.*
All the clerks under Christ      can not this explain,
But thus they should believe      the unlearned that wish to Do-well.
For had never man fine wit      the faith to dispute,
No man had any merit      could it all be proved:
      *Fides non habet meritum, ubi humana ratio praebet experimentum.*
   'Then it is Do-better to suffer      for thy soul's health,
All that the Book bids      by Holy Church's teaching;
And that is—"man, with thy might      for mercy's sake,
Look thou do the deed      that thy word declareth;
Such as thou seemest at sight      be, in the trial, found;
      *Appare quod es, vel esto quod appares:*
And let nobody be      by thy bearing beguiled,
But be such in thy soul      as thou seemest without."
   'Then is Do-best to be bold      to blame the guilty,
When thou seest thyself      as in soul clean;
But blame thou nobody      if thou be blameworthy:
*Si culpare velis      culpabilis esse cavebis,*

                    [1] See page 205.

*Dogma tuum sordet     cum te tua culpa remordet.*
God in the gospel     grimly reproveth
All that blame anyone     and faults have themselves:
> *Quid consideras festucam in oculo fratris tui, trabem in oculo tuo non vides?*

Why movest thou thy wrath     for a mote in thy brother's eye,
Since a beam in thine own     blindeth thyself?
> *Ejice primum trabem de oculo tuo, etc.,*

Which stops thee from seeing     less or more.
  'I counsel every blind buzzard     to remedy himself;
For abbots and for priors     and for all manner of prelates,
As parsons and parish priests     that preach should and teach,
All manner of men     to amend with their might;
This text was told you     to be warned, ere ye taught,
That ye were such as ye spoke of     with which to save others.
For God's word would not be lost     for that worketh ever,
If it availed not the people     it might avail yourselves.
  'But it seemeth now truly     to the world's sight,
That God's word worketh not     on learned or unlearned,
Except in such a manner as Mark     meaneth in the gospel,
> *Dum caecus ducit caecum, ambo in foveam cadunt.*

Unlearned men may compare you thus     that the beam lieth in your eyes,
And the mote is fallen     by your fault,
Into all manner of men     through cursed priests.
The Bible beareth witness     that all the folk of Israel
Bitterly paid for the guilt     of two bad priests,
Hophni and Phineas;     for their avarice,
*Archa dei* [1] came to grief     and Eli broke his neck.
  'Therefore, ye correctors, grasp this     and correct first yourselves,
And then may ye safely say     as David made the psalter:
> *Existimasti inique quod ero tui similis: arguam te, et statuam contra faciem tuam.*

  'And then shall lay clerks be abashed     to blame you or to grieve,
And carp not as they carp now     and call you dumb dogs,
> *Canes non valentes latrare,*

And dread to anger you by any word     your work to hinder,
And be readier at your prayer     than for a pound of gold;
And all for your holiness     have ye this at heart.
Amongst true religious     this rule should be held;
Gregory the great clerk     and the good pope

[1] See page 205.

Of religion the rule     rehearseth in his "Morals,"
And saith it by illustration     what they should do thereafter,
"When fishes lack the flood     or the fresh water,
They die for drought     when they stay dry;
Right so," quoth Gregory     "religion wandereth,
Perisheth and stinketh     and stealeth lords' alms,
That out of convent and cloister     coveteth to live."
For if heaven be on this earth     and ease to any soul,
It is in cloister or in learning     by many proofs I find;
For in cloister cometh no man     to chide nor to fight,
But all is courtesy there and books     to read and to learn.
    'In school there is scorn     unless a clerk will learn,
And great love and liking     for each of them loveth the other.
But now is Religion a rider     a roamer of the streets,
A conductor of law-days     and a buyer of land,
A pricker on a palfrey     from manor to manor,
A heap of hounds at his arse     as he a lord were.
And unless his page kneel     that shall his cup bring,
He lowereth on him and asketh him     who taught him courtesy?
Little use for lords     to give land away from their heirs
To religious, who have no care     though it rain on their altars!
    'In many places where parsons be     by themselves at ease,
Of the poor have they no pity     and that is their charity;
But they hold themselves as lords     their land reacheth so far.
    'But there shall come a king     and confess you of religion,
And beat you, as the Bible telleth     for breaking of your rule,
And amend nuns     monks and canons,
And put them to their penance     *ad pristinum statum ire*;
And barons and earls beat them     through *beatus vir*'s teaching,
And their children make claims     and blame you terribly:
    *Hi in curribus et hi in equis; ipsi obligati sunt, etc.,*
    'And then friars in the refectory     shall find a key
Of Constantine's [1] coffers     in which is the wealth
That Gregory's god-children     have spent so ill.
And then shall the abbot of Abingdon     and all his issue for ever
Have a knock from a king     and incurable the wound.
    'That this is true, seek ye     that often study the Bible:
    *Quomodo cessavit exactor, quievit tributum; contrivit Dominus baculum
        impiorum,*
    *et virgam dominantium caedentium plaga insanabili, etc.*
                    [1] See page 205.

But ere that king come    Cain shall awake.
But Do-well shall smite him down    and destroy his might.'
'Then is Do-well and Do-better,' quoth I    '*dominus* and knighthood.'
    'I will not be scornful,' quoth Scripture    'unless scribes lie;
Kinghood nor knighthood    by naught I can abide,
Helpeth not to heavenward    one hair's length,
Nor riches right not    nor pomp of lords.
Paul preacheth it impossible    rich men to have heaven,
Solomon saith also    that silver is worst to love;
    *Nihil iniquius quam amare peccuniam.*
And Cato teacheth us to covet it    not but as governed by need,
*Diligere denarium, sed parce dilige formam.*
And patriarchs and prophets    and poets both
Write to instruct us    to long for no riches,
And they praise poverty with patience;    the apostles bear witness,
That they have inheritance in heaven    and by true right,
Where rich men no right may claim    but of mercy and grace.'
    '*Contra*,' quoth I, 'by Christ    that I can disprove,
And prove it by Peter    and by Paul both,
That the baptized be safe    be he rich or poor.'
    'That is *in extremis*,' quoth Scripture    'amongst Saracens and Jews;
They must be saved so    and that is our belief,
That an un-Christian in that case    may christen a heathen,
And for his true belief    when his life fails,
Have the heritage of heaven    as any Christian man.
But Christians without more    may not come to heaven,
For Christ for Christian men died    and confirmed the law,
That whoso would and wisheth    with Christ to arise,
    *Si cum Christo surrexistis, etc.,*
He should love and believe    and the law fulfil.
That is—"love thy lord God    most dearly above all,
And after, all Christian creatures    in common, each man the other";
And thus they should love    that look to be saved.
And unless we do thus indeed    ere the day of doom,
It shall oppress us full bitterly    the silver that we hoard,
And our clothes that moth-eaten have become    and seen beggars go naked,
Or delight in wine and wild fowl    and know any in need.
    'For every Christian creature    should be kind to another,
And then the heathen to help    in hope of amendment.
God commandeth both high and low    that no man hurt other,
And saith, "slay not what resembles    mine own likeness,

Unless I send thee some token";     and saith, *non necabis*,
That is, slay not, but suffer     and all for the best.

    'For, *Mihi vindictam, et ego retribuam.*
"For I shall punish them in purgatory     or in the pit of hell,
Each man for his misdeeds     save mercy it hinders."'

    'This is a long lesson,' quoth I     'and little am I the wiser;
Where Do-well is, or Do-better     darkly ye show;
Many tales ye tell     that Theology teacheth;
And that I, man, made was     and my name entered
In the book of life     long ere I were,
Or else unwritten for some wickedness     as holy writ witnesseth,
      *Nemo ascendit ad caelum, nisi qui de caelo descendit.*
    'I believe it well,' quoth I, 'by our Lord     and on no doctrine better.
For Solomon the sage     that Wisdom taught,
God gave him grace of wit     and all his goods after,
To rule the realm     and rich to make;
He judged well and wisely     as holy writ telleth.
Aristotle and he     who taught men better?
Masters that of God's mercy     teach men and preach,
Of their words they tell us     for wisest in their time,
And all holy church     holdeth them damned!
And if I should go by their works     to win me heaven,
That for their works and wit     now live in pain,
Then did I unwisely     whatsoever ye preach.

    'But of many wise, in faith     little wonder I have,
Though their spirit be ungracious     God for to please.
For many men on this earth     more set their hearts
On goods than on God     therefore them grace faileth,
To their great mischief     when they shall life end.
As Solomon did, and such other     that showed great wits;
But their works, as holy writ saith     was ever the contrary.
Therefore wise witted men     and well lettered clerks,
As they say themselves     seldom do thereafter,
      *Super cathedram Moysi, etc.,*
    'But I think it be of many     as was in Noah's time,
When he shaped his ship     of planks and boards;
Was never wight saved that wrought thereon     nor other workman either,
But birds and beasts     and the blessed Noah,
And his wife with his sons     and also their wives;
Of wrights that it wrought     was none of them saved.
God grant it fare not so with folk     that the faith teach

Of holy church, that harbour is    and God's house to save,
And shield us from shame therein    as Noah's ship did beasts;
And men that made it    amid the flood drowned.
The *culorum* of this clause    pastors is to mean,
That be carpenters, holy church to make    for Christ's own beasts,
 *Homines et jumenta salvabis, Domine, etc.*
At doomsday the deluge be    of death and fire at once;
Therefore I counsel you clerks    of holy church the wrights,
Do your work as ye see written    lest ye be worth naught therein.
 'On Good Friday I find    a felon was saved,
That had lived all his life    with falsehood and theft;
And for he acknowledged on the cross    and to Christ confessed him,
He was saved before    Saint John the Baptist,
And either Adam or Isaiah    or any of the prophets,
That had lain with Lucifer    many long years.
A robber was ransomed    rather than them all,
Without any penance of purgatory    to perpetual bliss.
 'Then Mary Magdalen    what woman did worse?
Or who worse than David    that Uriah's death conspired?
Or Paul the apostle    that no pity had,
Many Christians    to kill to death?
And now be these as sovereigns    with saints in heaven,
Those that wrought most wickedly    in the world when they were.
And those that wisely spoke    and wrote many books
Of wit and wisdom    with damned souls live.
What Solomon saith, I trow be true    and certain of us all,
 *Sunt justi atque sapientes; et opera eorum in manu Dei sunt, etc.;*
 'They are wise and well-living    but their works be hid
In the hands of almighty God    and he knows the truth
Whether for love a man be valued there    and his true deeds,
Or else for his evil will    and envy of heart,
According as he lived    for by evil men know the good;
And whereby know men which is white    if all things black were,
And who was a good man    unless there were some rogue?
Therefore live we still with evil men    I think few be good.
For *quand oportet vient en place    il n'y a que pati*,
And he that can all amend    have mercy on us all!
For truest word that ever God said    was when he said, *nemo bonus.*
 'Clergy of Christ's mouth    commended was little,
For he said to Saint Peter    and to such as he loved,
 *Dum steteritis ante reges et praesides, etc.;*

"Though ye come before kings     and clerks of the law,
Be not abashed     for I shall be in your mouths,
And give you wit at will     and skill to refute
Them all that against you     about Christendom dispute."

   'David is an example     he spake amongst kings,
And might no king overcome him     in skill of speech.
But wit nor wisdom     won never the mastery,
When man was at mischief     without the more grace.

   'The doughtiest doctor     and interpreter of the Trinity,
Was Augustine the old     and highest of the four,
He said thus in a sermon     I saw it written once,
   *Ecce ipsi idiotae rapiunt caelum, ubi nos sapientes in inferno mergimur:*
And it means to English man     neither more nor less,
"Are none sooner ravished     from the right belief
Than are these clever clerks     that know many books;
Nor none sooner saved     nor firmer of belief,
Than plowmen and herdsmen     and poor common labourers."
Cobblers and shepherds     such ignorant fellows
Pierce with a *pater noster*     the palace of heaven,
And pass purgatory penance-less     at their parting hence,
Into the bliss of paradise     for their pure faith,
That imperfectly here     knew and indeed lived.
Yea, men know clerks     that have cursed the time,
That ever they knew more     than *credo in Deum Patrem*;
And above all their *pater noster*     many a person hath wished.

   'I see examples myself     and so may many another,
That servants that serve lords     seldom fall in debt,
But those that keep the lords' property     clerks and reeves.
Right so unlearned men     and of little knowledge,
Seldom fall they so foul     and so far in sin,
As clerks of holy church     that keep Christ's treasure,
The which is man's soul to save     as God saith in the gospel:
   *Ite vos in vineam meam.*'

# PASSUS XI

THEN Scripture poured scorn on me      and a reason gave,
And rated me in Latin      and light by me she set,
   And said, '*multi multa sciunt, et seipsos nesciunt.*'
Then wept I for woe      and wrath of her speech,
And in a drowsy wrath      went I to sleep.
A marvellous dream      met me then,
So I was ravished on the spot      and Fortune me fetched,
And into the land of Longing      alone she me brought,
And in a mirror called Middle-Earth      she made me to behold.
Then she said to me      'Here may'st thou see wonders,
And know what thou covetest      and come thereto, by good luck.'

   Then had Fortune following her      two fair damsels,
*Concupiscentia-carnis*      men called the elder maid,
And Covetousness-of-eyes      called was that other;
Pride-of-perfect-living      followed them both,
And bade me, for my favour      account Clergy lightly.

   *Concupiscentia-carnis*      clasped me around the neck,
And said, 'Thou art young and alive      and hast years enough,
For to live long      and ladies to love;
And in this mirror thou might see      joys full many,
That lead thee will to loving      all thy life time.'

   The second said the same      'I shall attend thy wish;
Till thou be a lord and have land      leave thee I will not,
While I shall follow thy fellowship      if Fortune it like.'
'He shall find me his friend'      quoth Fortune thereupon;
'The man that followed my will      lacked never bliss.'

   Then was there one called Age      that heavy was of cheer,
'Man,' quoth he, 'if I meet with thee      by Mary of heaven,
Thou shalt find Fortune thee fail      at thy most need,
And *Concupiscentia-carnis*      clean thee forsake.
Bitterly shall thou curse then      both days and nights
Covetousness-of-eyes      that ever thou her knew,
And Pride-of-perfect-living      to much peril thee bring.'

   'Yea, reck thee not,' quoth Recklessness      stood forth in ragged clothes,
'Follow forth as Fortune wills      thou hast a long way till old age;
A man may stoop times enough      when he has gone bald.

"*Homo proponit*," quoth a poet     and Plato he is called,
"And *Deus disponit*," quoth he     "let God do his will."
If Truth will witness it be well done     Fortune to follow,
*Concupiscentia-carnis*     nor Covetousness-of-eyes
Shall not grieve thee greatly     nor beguile thee, unless thou will it.'
     'Yea, farewell, Philip sparrow!' quoth Childishness     and began to
                                                          lead me on,
Till *Concupiscentia-carnis*     accorded with all my works.
     'Alas, indeed!' quoth Age     and Holiness both,
'That wit shall turn to wretchedness     for Will to have his liking!'
     Covetousness-of-eyes     comforted me anon after,
And followed me forty winters     and five more,
So that Do-well nor Do-better     of no value I thought;
I had no liking, believe me if you will     of them aught to know.
     Covetousness-of-eyes     came more often to mind
Than Do-well or Do-better     amongst all my deeds.
Covetousness-of-eyes     comforted me often,
And said, 'Have no conscience     how thou come by thy goods
Go confess thee to some friar     and show him thy sins.
For whilst Fortune is thy friend     friars will thee love,
And fetch thee to their fraternity     and for thee beseech
Their prior provincial     a pardon for to have,
And pray for thee, each of them     if thou be *pecuniosus*.'
          *Sed poena pecuniaria non sufficit pro spiritualibus delictis.*
     By the teaching of this wench I went     the words were so sweet,
Till I forgot youth     and hurried into age.
And then was Fortune my foe     for all her fair promises,
And Poverty pursued me     and brought me low,
And then found I the friars afraid     and flitting both,
Against our first bargain     for I said I would not
Be buried at their house     but at my parish church.
For I heard once     how Conscience it told,
That where a man was christened     by rights he should be buried,
Or where he was a parishioner     right there he should be interred.
And because I said thus to the friars     a fool they me held,
And loved me the less     for my true speech.
But yet I cried at my confessor     that held himself so learned,
'By my faith, friar,' quoth I     'ye behave like these wooers,
That wed no widows     except to wield their goods;
Right so, by the rood     recked ye never
Where my body were buried     so long as ye had my silver.

I have much wondered at you    and so hath many another,
Why your convent coveteth    to confess and to bury,
Rather than to baptize children    that be catechumens.
Baptizing and burying    both be full needful,
But much more meritorious    methinketh it is to baptize.
For a baptized man may    as masters tell,
Through contrition come    to the high heaven;
    *Sola contritio delet peccatum.*
But a child without baptism    may not so be saved;
    *Nisi quis renatus fuerit ex aqua, etc.;*
Look, ye lettered men    whether I lie or do not.'
And Loyalty looked on me    and I lowered after.
'Wherefore lowerest thou?' quoth Loyalty    and looked at me hard,
'If I durst,' quoth I, 'amongst men    this dream avow!'
'Yea, by Peter and by Paul,' quoth he    'and take them both to witness,
    *Non oderis fratres secrete in corde tuo, sed publice argue illos.*'
'They will declare also,' quoth I    'and by the gospel prove,
    *Nolite judicare quemquam.*'
    'And wherefore serveth law,' quoth Loyalty    'if no man reproved it,
Falsehood nor fraud?    for some purpose the apostle said,
    *Non oderis fratrem.*
And in the psalter also    saith David the prophet,
    *Existimasti inique quod ero tui similis, etc.*
It is *licitum* for laymen    to declare the truth,
If it pleaseth them    to each a law it granteth,
Except parsons and priests    and prelates of holy church,
It falleth not to those folk    any tales to tell,
Though the tale were true    if it touched on sin.[1]
A thing that all the world knows    wherefore shouldst thou spare
To counsel on with rhetoric    to rate deadly sin?
But be never the first    the fault to blame;
Though thou see evil, speak of it not first    but be sorry it was not
                                    amended.
Nothing that is private    publish thou it never,
Neither for love laud it not    nor attack it not for envy;
    *Parum lauda, vitupera parcius.*'
    'He speaketh true, quoth Scripture then    and skipped on high and
                                      preached;
But the matter that she dealt with    if unlearned men it knew,
The less, I believe    love it they would.

                     [1] See page 205.

This was her theme and her text      I took full good heed;
'*Multi* to a feast      and to the meat were summoned,
And when the people were come in plenty      the porter unlocked the gate,
And plucked in *pauci* privately      and let the rest go hang!'
    All for pain of her text      trembled mine heart,
And into a doubt I fell      and with myself began to dispute,
Whether I were chosen or not chosen      on Holy Church I thought,
That received me at the font      as one of God's chosen;
For Christ called us all      to come if we willed,
Saracens and schismatics      and so he did the Jews,
    *O vos omnes sitientes, venite, etc.;*
And bade them suck for sin      safely at his breast,
And drink cure for evil      receive it whoso will.
    'Then may all Christians come,' quoth I      'and claim their entry
By the blood that he bought us with      and through baptism after,
    *Qui crediderit et baptizatus fuerit, etc.*
For though a Christian man coveted      his Christianity to reject,
To reject it with probity      no reason will allow.
    'For may no churl charter make      nor his goods sell
Without leave of his lord      no law will it grant.
But he may run into arrears      and roam then from home,
And as a renegade rascal      recklessly go about;
But Reason shall reckon with him      and rebuke him at the last,
And Conscience account with him      and cast him into debt,
And put him after in a prison      in purgatory to burn,
And for his debts reward him there      to the day of judgment,
Unless Contrition will come      and cry, by his life,
Mercy for his misdeeds      with mouth or with heart.'
    'That is true,' said Scripture      'can no sin stop
Mercy from amending all      if meekness goes with her,
For they be as our books tell      the highest of God's works,
    *Misericordia ejus super omnia opera ejus.*'
    'Yea, bah for books!' quoth one      was broken out of hell,
Called Trajan,[1] had been a true knight      as a pope bore witness,
How he was dead and damned      to dwell in pain,
As an unchristened creature;      —'clerks know the truth,
That all the clergy under Christ      could not snatch me from hell,
But only love and loyalty      and my rightful judgement.
Gregory knew this well      and wished well for my soul
Unbeliever, for the virtue      that he saw in my works.

    [1] See page 205.

And, after that he wept      and longed I be granted
Grace, without any bead-bidding      his boon was accepted,
And I saved, as ye may see      without singing of masses;
By love, and by learning      of my living in truth,
Brought me from bitter pain      when no praying might.'
 Lo, ye lords, what faithfulness did      for an emperor of Rome,
That was an unchristian creature      as clerks find in books.
Not through prayer of a pope      but for his pure truth
Was that infidel saved      as Saint Gregory beareth witness.
Well ought ye lords, that laws keep      this lesson to have in mind,
And on Trajan's truth to think      and give truth to the people.
 This matter is murky for many of you      but, men of holy church,
The *Legenda Sanctorum* you teacheth      better than I you tell!
But thus loyal love      and living in truth
Pulled out of pain      a pagan of Rome.
Blessed be truth      that so broke hell-gates,
And saved this infidel      from Satan and his power,
Where no clergy could      nor knowledge of laws.
Love and loyalty      is a true science;
For that is the Book blessed      of bliss and of joy:
God wrought it and wrote it      with his finger alone,
And gave it to Moses upon the mount      all men to teach.
 'Law without love,' quoth Trajan      'count it a bean,
Or any science under sun      the seven arts and all,
Unless they be learned in our Lord's love      lost is all the time'—
'For no cause to catch silver thereby      nor to be called master,
But all for love of our Lord      and the better to love the people.
For Saint John said it      and soth are his words,

  *Qui non diligit, manet in morte*—

Whoso loveth not, believe me      he liveth in death-dying—
And that all manner of men      enemies and friends,
Love each other      and give as to themselves.
Whoso giveth not, he loveth not      God knows the truth,
And commandeth each creature      to conform him to love,
And above all poor people      their enemies next.
For them that hate us      it is our merit to love,
And poor people to please      their prayers may us help.
For our joy and our health      Jesu Christ of heaven,
In a poor man's apparel      pursueth us ever,
And looketh on us in their likeness      and that with lovely face,
To know us by our kind heart      and casting of our eyes,

Whether we love the lords here    before our Lord of bliss;
And exciteth us by the evangelist    that, when we make feasts,
We should not ask our kin thereto    nor no rich men;
    "*Cum facitis convivia, nolite invitare amicos:*
But call the unhappy thereto    the bent, and the poor,
For your friends will feed you    and foster you, to repay
Your feasting and your fair gift    each friend repayeth so the other.
But for the poor I shall pay    and well requite their toil,
That giveth them meat or money    and loveth them for my sake."
For of the best be some rich    and some beggars and some poor.
For all are we Christ's creatures    and of his coffers rich,
And brethren as of one blood    as well beggars as earls.
For on Calvary of Christ's blood    Christendom first sprang,
And brethren in blood we became there    by one body won,
As *quasi modo geniti*    and gentle men each one,
Nor beggar nor knave amongst us    unless it sin made;
    *Qui facit peccatum, servus est peccati, etc.*
   'In the old law    as holy scripture telleth,
Men's sons    men called us each one,
Of Adam's issue and Eve    ever till God-man died;
And after his resurrection    *Redemptor* was his name,
And we his brethren, through him bought    both rich and poor.
Therefore love we as true brethren shall    and each man laugh on the
                                        other,
And of that each man can spare    give aid where it is needed,
And every man help the other    for go hence shall we all;
    *Alter alterius onera portate.*
And be we not ungenerous with our goods    nor of our skill either,
For knows not man how nigh he is    to be taken from both.
Therefore blame no man another    though he more Latin knows,
Nor rebuke not foully    for is none without fault.
For whatever clerks prate    of Christianity or otherwise,
Christ to a common woman said    in public at a feast,
That *fides sua* should save her    and heal her of all sins.
   'Then is belief a true help    above logic or law;
For of logic or of law    in *Legenda Sanctorum*
Is little allowance made    unless belief them help.
For it is long ere logic    any lesson reveal,
And law is loth to love    unless he get silver,
Both logic and law    that loveth not to lie,
I counsel all Christians    cleave not thereon too closely.

For some words I find written     were of faith's teaching,
That saved sinful men     as Saint John beareth witness;

*Eadem mensura qua mensi fueritis, remetietur vobis.*

Therefore learn we the law of love     as our Lord taught,
And as Saint Gregory said     for man's soul's health,

*Melius est scrutari scelera nostra, quam naturas rerum.*

'Why I move this matter     is most for the poor,
For in their likeness our Lord     oft hath been known.
Witness in Pasch week     when he went to Emmaus;
Cleophas knew him not     that he Christ were,
For his poor apparel     and pilgrim's weeds,
Till he blessed and brake     the bread that they eat,
So by his works they wist     that he was Jesus;
But by clothing they knew him not     nor by speaking of tongue.

'And all was in example     to us sinful here,
That we should be humble     and courteous of speech,
And apparel us not over proudly     for pilgrims are we all;
And in the apparel of a poor man     and pilgrim's likeness
Many time God hath been met     among needy people,
When never man him saw     in company of the rich.

'Saint John and other saints     were seen in poor clothing,
And as poor pilgrims     begged men's charity.
Jesus Christ from a Jew's daughter was born     gentle woman though she
were,
Was a pure poor maid     and to a poor man wedded.

'Martha about Mary Magdalen     a huge plaint made,
And to our Saviour himself     said these words,

*Domine, non est tibi curae quod soror mea reliquit me solam ministrare,
etc.?*

And quickly God answered     and both their ways allowed,
Both Martha's and Mary's     as Matthew beareth witness,
But poverty God put first     and praised it the better;

*Maria optimam partem elegit, quae non auferetur ab ea.*

'And all the wise that ever were     by aught I can discover,
Praise poverty for best life     if patience go with it,
And both better and more blessed     by many times than riches.
Even though it be sour to suffer     there cometh sweet after;
As on a walnut without     is a bitter bark,
And after that bitter bark     (be the shell away),
Is a kernel of comfort     life to restore;
So it is, after poverty or penance     patiently taken.

For it maketh man to have mind of God     and a great will
To weep and to well pray     whereof groweth mercy,
Of which Christ is a kernel     to comfort the soul.
And much more peacefully he sleepeth     the man that is poor,
And less he dreadeth death     and in dark to be robbed,
Than he that is right rich     reason beareth witness;
*Pauper ego ludo, dum tu dives meditaris.*
    'Although Solomon said     as folk see in the Bible,
      *Divitias nec paupertates, etc.,*
A wiser than Solomon was     beareth witness and taught,
That perfect poverty was     no possession to have,
And life most pleasing to God     as Luke beareth witness,
      *Si vis perfectus esse, vade et vende, etc.;*
And means to men     that on this earth live,
Whoso will be pure perfect     must possession forsake,
Or sell it, as saith the Book     and the silver give
To beggars that wander and beg     and ask goods for God's love.
    'For failed never man meat     that mighty God served;
      *Non vidi justum derelictum, nec semen ejus quaerens panem;*
As David saith in the psalter     to such that be willing
To serve God in a godly way     nor grieveth him no penance,
      *Nihil impossibile volenti,*
Nor lacketh never livelihood     linen nor wool,
      *Inquirentes autem dominum non minuentur omni bono.*
If priests were perfect     they would no silver take
For masses nor for matins     and not their meat of usurers,
Nor neither their kirtle nor coat     though they for cold should die,
If they their duty did     as David saith in the psalter,
      *Judica me, Deus, et discerne causam meam.*
*Spera-in-deo* speaketh of priests     that have no spending-silver,
That if they travail truly     and trust in God almighty,
They should lack no livelihood     neither woollen nor linen.
And the title that ye take your orders by     telleth ye are in authority;
Then needeth not you to take silver     for masses that ye sing.
For he that gave you your title     should give you your wages,
Or the bishop that blesseth you     if that ye be worthy.
    'For never king nor knight     but he had money to spend,
As became a knight     or provided him for his strength;
It is an unhappy knight     and of a caitif king's making,
That hath no land nor lineage rich     nor good fame of his deeds.
The same I say for sooth     of all such priests,

That have neither learning nor kin    but a tonsure one,
And a title, a tale of naught    for his livelihood, meaning mischief,
He hath more hope, I believe    of gaining through his tonsure
A cure of souls, than through learning    or—"fame for clean conduct."
I have wondered why    and wherefore the bishop
Maketh such priests    that unlearned men betray.

'A charter is challengeable    before a chief justice;
If false Latin be in the writing    the law it impugneth,
Or writing between the lines    or parts over-skipped;
The man that makes such charters    for a gawk is held.
So it is a gawk, by God    that in his gospel faileth,
Or in mass or in matins    maketh any fault,

> *Qui offendit in uno, in omnibus est reus, etc.*

And also in the psalter    saith David to over-skippers,

> *Psallite deo nostro, psallite; quoniam rex terrae Deus Israel; psallite*
> *sapienter.*

The bishop shall be blamed    before God, as I believe,
That tonsures such of God's servants    that can not *sapienter*
Sing nor psalms read    nor say a mass of the day.
But never neither is blameless    the bishop nor the chaplain,
For either of them is indicted    and that by "*ignorantia*
*Non excusat episcopos    nec* ignorant priests."

'This concern with unlearned priests    hath made me stray from poverty,
The which I praise, where patience is    more perfect than riches.'
And much more in dreaming thus    with me did one dispute,
And in sleeping I saw all this    and then came Kind,
And named me by my name    and bade me take heed,
And through the wonders of this world    wisdom take.
And on a mountain that Middle-Earth is called    as me then thought,
I was led forth    by examples to know,
Through each creature and Kind    my Creator to love.
I saw the sun and the sea    and the sand after,
And where that birds and beasts    by their mates they went,
Wild worms in woods    and wonderful birds,
With flecked feathers    and of many colours.
Man and his mate    I might both behold;
Poverty and plenty    both peace and war,
Bliss and bale    both I saw at once,
And how men took rewards    and mercy refused.

Reason I saw truly    attending all beasts
In eating, in drinking    and in engendering of kind;

H 57¹

And after course of conception     none took heed of the other,
As when they had met in rutting-time     anon right thereafter,
Males drew them to males     in mornings by themselves,
And in evenings also     went males from females.
There was not cow nor such creature     that conceived had,
That would bellow after bulls     nor boar after sow;
Both horse and hounds     and all other beasts
Meddled not with their mates     that with foal were.

   Birds I beheld     that in bushes made nests;
Had never man wit     to make in the least.
I had wonder from whom     and where the magpie learned
To lay the twigs     in which she lieth and breedeth;
There is no wright as I think     could make a nest would please him;
If any mason made a model thereof     much wonder it were.

   And yet me marvelled more     how many other birds
Hid and covered     their eggs full secretly
In marshes and moors     that men should them not find,
And hid their eggs     when they therefrom went,
For fear of other birds     and for wild beasts.
And some met their mates     and on trees bred,
And brought forth their birds so     all above the ground;
And some birds at the bill     through breathing conceived;
And some engendered thus     I took note how peacocks bred.
Much marvelled me     what master they had,
And who taught them on trees     to build so high,
Where neither man nor beast     may their birds reach.

   And then I looked upon the sea     thence forth upon the stars,
Many wonders I saw     which I say not now.
I saw flowers in the wood     and their fair colours,
And how among the green grass     grew so many hues,
And some sour and some sweet     wonder me thought;
Of their kind and their colour     to speak it were too long.

   But what most moved me     and impressed my mind,
Was that Reason regarded     and ruled all beasts,
Save man and his mate     many time and oft
No reason them followed     and then I rebuked
Reason, and right     to himself I said,
'I have wonder of thee,' quoth I     'that wise art held,
Why thou followest not man and his mate     that no mishap them attend?'

   And Reason rated me     and said, 'Reck thee never,
Why I allow or do not allow     thyself hast naught do with it;

Amend thou it, if thou might     for my time is to abide.
Patience is a sovereign virtue     and a swift vengeance.
Who is more long-suffering than God?' quoth he     'No man, as I believe!
He might amend in a minute's time     all that amiss standeth,
But he suffers it for some man's good     and so is it better for us.
   'Holy writ,' quoth that wight     'teacheth men patience;
      *Propter Deum subjecti estote omni creaturae.*

Frenchmen and free men     train thus their children,
*Belle vertue est suffrance     mal dire est petit veniance,*
*Bien dire et bien soufrir     fait lui suffrant a bien venir.*
Therefore I counsel,' quoth Reason     'rule thy tongue better,
And ere thou blame any man     look if thou be praiseworthy!
For is no creature under Christ     can form himself;
And if a man might make     himself good among the people,
Each life would be blameless     believe thou none other!
Nor shalt thou find but few     willing for to hear
Of their faults foul     before them rehearsed.
   'The wise and the clever     wrote thus in the Bible,
      *De re quae te non molestat, noli certare.*
For be a man fair or foul     it falleth not for to blame
The shape nor the form     that God shaped himself;
For all that he did was well done     as holy writ witnesseth.
      *Et vidit Deus cuncta quae fecerat, et erant valde bona;*
And bade every creature     in his kind increase,
All for mirth for man     that must woe suffer
In temptation of the flesh     and of the fiend both.
For man was made of such matter     he may not well avoid
That sometimes he is bid     to follow his kind;
Cato accordeth therewith     *nemo sine crimine vivit.*'
   Then caught I colour anon     and came to be ashamed,
And awoke therewith     woe was me then
That I in dreams might not     more have known.
And then spoke I to myself     and blamed that time:
'Now I know what Do-well is,' quoth I     'by dear God, as methinketh!'
And as I cast up mine eyes     one looked on me, and asked
Of me, what thing it were?     'Indeed, sir,' I said,
'To see much and suffer more     truly,' quoth I, 'is Do-well!'
   'Haddest thou been patient,' he said     'sleeping though thou were,
Thou shouldest have known what Clergy knows     and conceived more
                                        through Reason:
For Reason would have rehearsed thee     right as Clergy said,

But for thine intermeddling     here art thou forsook;
   *Philosophus esses, si tacuisses.*
Adam, while he spake not     had paradise at will,
But when he chattered about meat     and meddled to know
The wisdom and the knowledge of God     he was put from bliss;
And right so did Reason by thee     thou with rude speech
Blamed, and praised things     that belonged not to be done;
Then had he no wish     for to teach thee more.
   'Pride and Presumption     perchance, will thee call,
So that Clergy thy company     cares not to follow.
Shall never challenging nor chiding     chasten a man so soon
As shall Shame, and humble him     and shape him to amend.
For let a drunken dolt     in a ditch fall,
Let him lie, look not on him     till it pleases him to rise;
For though Reason rebuked him then     recketh he never,
Of Clergy nor of his council     he counteth not a rush;
To blame or for to beat him then     it were but pure sin.
But when Need pulleth him up     for doubt lest he die,
And Shame scrapes his clothes     and his shins washeth,
Then knows the drunken dolt     wherefore he is to blame.'
   'Ye say sooth,' quoth I     'I have seen it often,
There smites no thing so smart     nor smelleth so sour,
As Shame, where he showeth himself     for every man him shuns!
Why ye show me thus,' quoth I     'was for I rebuked Reason.'
   'Truly,' quoth he, 'that is so'     and prepared him to walk:
And I arose up right with that     and followed him after,
And prayed him of his courtesy     to tell me his name.

## PASSUS XII

' I ᴀᴍ Imaginative,' quoth he     'idle was I never,
Though I sit by myself     in sickness or in health.
I have followed thee in faith     this five and forty winters,
And many times have moved thee     to think on thine end,
And how many old years are gone     and so few to come,
And of thy wild wantonness     when thou young were,
To amend it in thy middle age     lest strength thee failed
In thine old age     when hard it is to bear
Poverty or penance     or prayers make;
     *Si non in prima vigilia, nec in secunda, etc.*
Amend thee while thou might     thou hast been warned oft
With attacks of pestilences     with poverty and with troubles;
And with these bitter rods     God beateth his dear children,
     *Quem diligo, castigo.*
And David in the psalter saith     of such that loveth Jesus,
     *Virga tua et baculus tuus, ipsa me consolata sunt, etc.*
Although thou strike me with thy staff     with stick or with rod,
It is but joy as for me     to amend my soul.
And thou meddlest thee with verse-making     and mightest go say
                                   thy psalter,
And pray for them that giveth thee bread     for there are books
                                   enough
To tell men what Do-well is     Do-better, and Do-best both,
And preachers to prove what it is     of many a pair of friars.'
   I saw well he told me true     and, somewhat me to excuse,
Said, 'Cato comforted his son     clerk though he were,
To solace him sometimes     as I do when I make verse;
*Interpone tuis interdum gaudia curis, etc.*
And of holy men I heard,' quoth I     'how they at times
Played, the more perfect to be     in many places.
But if there were any wight     that would me tell
What were Do-well and Do-better     and Do-best finally,
Would I never do work     but go to holy church,
And there say my beads     except when I eat or sleep.'

'Paul in his epistle,' quoth he        'proveth what is Do-well;
        *Fides, spes, caritas; et major horum, etc.*
Faith, hope, and charity        and all be good,
And save men sundry times        but none so soon as charity.
For he doth well without doubt        that doth as loyalty teacheth;
That is, if thou be man married        thy mate thou love,
And live forth as law wills        while ye live both.
        'Right so, if thou be a religious        run thou never further
To Rome nor to Roquemadour [1]        but as thy rule teacheth;
And hold thee under obedience        that highway is to heaven.
        'And if thou be maiden as to marriage        and may well continue so,
Seek thou never saint afar        for soul's health.
For what made Lucifer        to lose the high heaven,
Or Solomon his wisdom        or Sampson his strength?
Job the Jew his joy        dearly he it bought.
Aristotle and others more        Hippocrates, and Virgil;
Alexander that all won        miserably ended.
Wealth and their own wit        was cumbrance to them all.
Felicia's [2] fairness        brought her all to shame;
And Rosamund right so        unhappily used herself,
The beauty of her body        in badness she dispensed.
Of many such I may read        of men and of women,
That wise words would show        and do the contrary,
*Sunt homines nequam bene de virtute loquentes.*
        'And the rich right so        gather and save,
And then men that they most hate        spend it at the last;
And, for they permit and see        so many needy folks,
And love them not as our Lord bid        they lose their souls;
        *Date et dabitur vobis, etc.*
So wealth and their own wit        cumbreth full many;
Woe is him that them wieldeth        unless he well dispenses them;
        *Scientes et non facientes variis flagellis vapulabunt;*
Wisdom, saith the Book        swelleth a man's soul,
        *Sapientia inflat, etc.;*
And riches right so        unless the roots be sound;
But grace is a herb thereof        those ills to abate.
But grace groweth not        but amongst the lowly;
Patience and poverty        the place is there it groweth,
And in true-living men        and in the life-holy.

And through the gift of the Holy Ghost     as the gospel telleth,
    *Spiritus ubi vult spirat, etc.*
Clergy and Kind Wit [1]    cometh of seeing and teaching,
As the Book beareth witness     to men that can read,
    *Quod scimus, loquimur; quod vidimus, testamur.*
Of *quod scimus*, cometh Clergy     learning of heaven,
And of *quod vidimus* cometh Kind Wit     and of seeing of divers people.
But grace is a gift of God     and of great love springeth;
Knew never clerk how it cometh forth     nor Kind Wit the ways,
    *Nescit aliquis unde venit, aut quo vadit, etc.*
But yet Clergy is to be commended     and Kind Wit both,
And especially Clergy, for Christ's love     that of Clergy is root.
For Moses witnesseth that God wrote     for to teach the people,
In the old law, as the Scripture telleth     that was the law of the Jews,
That the woman who was in adultery taken     were she rich or poor,
With stones men should her strike     and stone her to death.
A woman, as we find     was guilty of that deed,
But Christ of his courtesy     through Clergy her saved;
For through the characters that Christ wrote     the Jews knew themselves
Guiltier as before God     and greater in sin
Than the woman that there was     and went away for shame.
The Clergy that there was     succoured the woman.
Holy Church knoweth this     that Christ's writing saved;
So Clergy is comfort     to creatures that repent,
And to cursed men     mischief at their end
  'For God's body might not be     of bread, without Clergy,
The which body is both     health to the righteous,
And death and damnation     to them that die evil.
As Christ's characters both comforted and     culpable showed
The woman that the Jews brought     that Jesus intended to save;
    *Nolite judicare, et non judicabimini, etc.*
Right so God's body, brethren     unless it be worthily taken,
Damneth us at the day of doom     as the characters did the Jews.
Therefore I counsel thee for Christ's sake     Clergy that thou love,
For Kind Wit is of his kin     and near cousins both
To our Lord, believe me     therefore love them, I say;
For both be as mirrors     to amend our faults,
And leaders for unlearned men     and for the lettered both.
  'Therefore attack thou never logic     law, nor his customs,

---

[1] See page 205.

Nor contradict clerks    I counsel thee for ever.
For as a man may not see    that lacketh his eyes,
No more can a clerk    unless he learnt it first through books.
Although men made books    God was the master
And Holy Spirit the teacher    and said what men should write.
And right as sight serveth a man    to see the high street,
Right so leadeth letters    unlearned men to Reason.
And as a blind man in battle    beareth weapon to fight,
And hath no luck with his axe    his enemy to hit,
No more can a man of Kind Wit    unless clerks him teach,
Come for all his Kind Wit    to Christendom and be saved;
This is the coffer of Christ's treasure    and clerks keep the keys,
To unlock it at their liking    and to the unlearned people
Give mercy for their misdeeds    if men it will ask
Humbly and gently    and pray it of grace.
    '*Archa dei* in the old law    Levites it kept;
Had never unlearned man leave    to lay hand on that chest,
Only if he were priest or priest's son    patriarch or prophet.
    'Saul, for he sacrificed    sorrow him befell,
And his sons also    for that sin came to harm,
And many more other men    that were not Levites,
That with *archa dei* travelled    in reverence and in worship,
And laid hand thereon to lift it up    and lost their life after.
Therefore I counsel all creatures    no Clergy to despise,
Nor set little by their science    whatever they do themselves.
Take we their words for worth    for their witness be true.
And meddle we not much with them    to move any wrath,
Lest strife chafe us    to chop each man the other;
        *Nolite tangere christos meos, etc.*
    'For Clergy is keeper    under Christ of heaven;
Was there never a knight    but Clergy him made.
But Kind Wit cometh    of all kinds of seeing,
Of birds and of beasts    of tastes of truth, and of deceits.
    'Men before us    used to mark
The wonders that they saw    their sons for to teach,
And held it a high science    their ways to know.
But through their science truly    was never a soul saved,
Nor brought by their books    to bliss nor to joy;
For all their knowing of nature    comes but of diverse sights.
    'Patriarchs and prophets    reproved their science,
And said, their words and their wisdom    were but folly;

As to the Clergy of Christ     they counted it but a trifle;
   *Sapientia hujus mundi, stultitia est apud Deum.*
For the high Holy Ghost     heaven shall cleave asunder,
And love shall leap out after     into this low earth,
And cleanness shall seize it     and clerks shall it find;
   *Pastores loquebantur ad invicem.*
   'He speaketh there of rich men right naught     nor of right wise,
Nor of lords that were unlearned men     but of the highest learned men,
   *Ibant magi ab oriente, etc.*
If any friar were found there     I give you five shillings;
Nor in no begger's cot     was that child born,
But in a burgess's ¹ place     of Bethlehem the best;
   *Sed non erat locus ei in diversorio ; et pauper non habet diversorium.*
   'To shepherds and to poets     appeared that angel,
And bade them go to Bethlehem     God's birth to honour,
And sung a song of solace     *Gloria in excelsis Deo!*
Rich men snored then     and at their rest were,
When it shone on the shepherds     a declarer of bliss.
   'Clerks knew it well     and came with their presents,
And did their homage honourably     to him that was almighty,
Why I have told thee all this—     I took full good heed
How thou contradicted Clergy     with crabbed words,
"How that unlearned men more readily     than lettered were saved,
Than clerks or clever men     of Christian people."
   'And thou said sooth of some     but see in what manner:—
Take two strong men     and in Thames cast them,
And both naked as a needle     neither safer than the other,
The one hath knowledge     and can swim and dive,
The other is ignorant of that labour     learned never to swim;
Which thinkest thou of those two     in Thames is in most dread?
He that never dived     nor naught knows of swimming,
Or the swimmer that is safe     if so himself pleases,
Where his fellow floats forth     as the flood pleaseth,
And is in dread to drown     that never did swim?'
   'He that swim can not,' I said     'it seemeth to my wits.'
   'Right so,' quoth the man     'reason it showeth,
That he that knoweth Clergy     can sooner arise
Out of sin and be safe     though he sin oft,
If he likes and pleases     than ignorant person.
For if the clerk be wise     he knoweth what is sin.
                    ¹ See page 205.

And how contrition without confession    comforteth the soul,
And thou seest in the psalter    in psalms one or two,
How contrition is commended    for it snatcheth away sin;

> *Beati quorum remissae sunt iniquitates, et quorum tecta sunt peccata,*
> *etc.*

And this comforteth each clerk    and saveth him from despair,
In which flood the fiend    tries a man hardest;
There the unlearned lieth still    and looketh for Lent,
And hath no contrition ere he come to shrift    and then can he little tell,
And as his master teacheth him    believeth and holdeth:
And that is according to parson or parish priest    and, perchance both
Unlearned to teach ignorant men    as Luke beareth witness,

> *Dum caecus ducit caecum, ambo in foveam cadunt.*

'Woe was for him marked    that must wade with the ignorant!
Well may the child bless    him that set him to books;
That living according to the writing    saved him life and soul!
*Dominus pars hereditatis meae*    is a merry verse,
That has taken from Tyburn    twenty strong thieves; [1]
Where untaught thieves be strung up    look how they be saved!
The thief that had grace of God    on Good Friday as thou sayest,
Was, for he yielded him a believer to Christ on the cross    and acknow-
ledged him guilty,
And grace asked of God    that to grant it is ready
To them that humbly pray it    and mean to amend themselves.
But though that thief had heaven    he had not high bliss,
As Saint John and other saints    that deserved had better.
Right as some man gives me meat more than enough    and sets me on the
floor,
I have meat more than enough    but not so much honour
As those that sit at side table    or with the lords of the hall.
But sit as a beggar table-less    by myself on the ground.
So it fareth for that felon    that on Good Friday was saved;
He sits neither with Saint John    Simon, nor Jude,
Nor with maidens nor with martyrs    confessors nor widows,
But by himself solitary    and served on the ground.
For he that is once a thief    is evermore in danger,
And at the law's pleasure    to live or to die;

> *De peccato propitiato, nolo esse sine metu.*

And for to serve a saint    and such a thief together,
It were neither reason nor right    to reward them both alike.

[1] See page 205.

'And right as Trajan the true knight    dwelt not so deep in hell,
That our Lord had him not lightly out    so believe I the thief be in heaven.
For he is in the lowest heaven    if our belief be true,
And well at ease he lolleth there    by the law of holy church,
  *Quia reddit uniquique juxta opera sua, etc.*
 'And why that one thief on the cross    yielded himself believer
Rather than that other thief    though thou wouldst question,
All the clerks under Christ    could not give the reason;
  *Quare placuit, quia voluit.*
And so I sayest for thee    that seekest after the whys,
And argued with Reason    rebuking as it were,
And of the flowers in the wood    and of their fair hues,
Whereof they catch their colours    so clear and so bright,
And wishest of birds and of beasts    and of their breeding to know,
Why some be low down and some aloft    thy liking it were,
And of the stones and of the stars    thou studiest, as I believe,
However beast or bird    hath such strong wit;
Clergy nor Kind Wit    knew never the cause,
But Kind knoweth the cause himself    and no creature else.
He is the magpie's patron    and putteth it in her ear,
That where the thorn is thickest    to build and to breed;
And Kind taught the peacock    to breed in such a way,
And taught Adam    to know his private parts,
And taught him and Eve    to cover them with leaves.
 'Unlearned men many times    masters they question,
Why Adam covered not first    his mouth that eat the apple,
Rather than his body low down    the unlearned ask thus the clerks;
Kind knoweth why he did so    but no clerk else.
But of birds and beasts    men of old time
Examples took and patterns    as telleth these poets,
And that the fairest fowl    foulest engendereth,
And feeblest fowl    that flieth or swimmeth;
And that is the peacock and the peahen    proud rich men they betoken
For the peacock, if men pursue him    can not fly high;
For the trailing of his tail    is he overtaken soon,
And his flesh is foul flesh    and his feet too,
And unlovely of voice    and hateful for to hear.
 'Right so the rich    if he his riches hoard,
And giveth it not till his death-day    the tail of all sorrow.
Right as the quills of the peacock    pain him in flight,
So is possession pain    of pence and of nobles

To all that them holdeth     till their tail be plucked.
And though the rich repent then     and bewail the time,
That ever he gathered so greatly     and gave thereof so little,
Though he cry to Christ then     with keen will, I believe
His voice be in our Lord's ear     like a magpie's chattering.
And when his body shall come     in cave to be buried,
I believe it will pollute full foully     the earth all about,
And all the others where it lieth     are envenomed through his poison.
By the peacock's feet is understood     as I have learned in Avianus,[1]
Executors, false friends     that fulfil not his will
That was written, and they were witnesses     to do right as it laid down.
Thus the poet proves that the peacock     for his feathers is reverenced,
Right so is the rich     by reason of his goods.
     'The lark, that is a lesser bird     is more lovely of voice,
And well away of wing     swifter than the peacock,
And of flesh, by many times     fatter and sweeter.
To lowly-living men     the lark is compared;
Aristotle the great clerk     such tales he telleth;
Thus he likens in his logic     the least bird there is.
And whether he be saved or not saved     that truth knows no cleric,
Not of Socrates nor of Solomon     no writing can tell.
But God is so good, I hope     that since he gave them wits
To teach us ways therewith     (that teach us to be saved,
And the better for their books)     to pray we are beholden,
That God for his grace     give their souls rest;
For lettered men were ignorant yet     but for the learning of their books.'
     'All these clerks,' quoth I then     'that on Christ believe,
Say in their sermons     that neither Saracens nor Jews,
Nor no creature of Christ's likeness     without christening is saved.'
     '*Contra*,' quoth Imaginative then     and began to frown,
And said, '*Salvabitur vix justus in die judicii.*
*Ergo salvabitur*,' quoth he     and said no more Latin.
'Trajan was a true knight     and took never christening,
And he is safe, so saith the book     and his soul in heaven.
For there is baptism of water     and baptism in blood-shedding,
And through fire is baptism     and that is firm belief;
     *Advenit ignis divinus, non comburens, sed illuminans, etc.*
'But truth that trespassed never     transgressed not against his law,
But liveth as his law teacheth     and believeth there be no better,
And if there were, he would amend     and in such will dieth,
                         [1] See page 205.

Would never true God     but recognized truth;
And whether it be or be not     the strength is great of truth,
And a hope hanging therein     to have reward for his truth.

> For, *Deus dicitur quasi dans vitam aeternam suis, hoc est, fidelibus; et alibi:*
>
> *Si ambulavero in medio umbrae mortis, etc.*

The gloss granteth upon that verse     a great reward for truth.
And wit and wisdom,' quoth that wight     'was at some time a treasure,
To keep with a commonwealth     no wealth was held better,
And much mirth and manhood'     and right with that he vanished.

# PASSUS XIII

And I awaked therewith    nearly out of my mind,
And as a fellow that free were    forth began I to walk
In manner of a mendicant    many a year after,
And of this dream many times    much thought I had.
First, how Fortune me failed    at my most need,
And how that Age menaced me    should we ever meet;
And how that friars followed    folk that were rich,
And folk that were poor    at little price they set,
And no corpse in their churchyard    nor in their church was buried,
Unless alive he bequeathed them aught    or should help pay their debts.
And how this covetousness overcame    clerks and priests,
And how that unlearned men be led    unless our Lord them help
Through ignorant curates    to incurable pains.
And how that Imaginative    in dream me told,
Of Kind and of his cleverness    and how courteous to beasts,
And how loving he is to beasts    on land and on water;
Forsakes he no living thing    less nor more;
The creatures that creep    of Kind be engendered.
And then how Imaginative said    *vix justus salvabitur*,
And when he had said so    how suddenly he passed.

    I lay down long in this thought    and at last I slept,
And, as Christ willed, there came Conscience    to comfort me that time,
And bade me come to his court    with Clergy should I dine.
And as Conscience of Clergy spoke    I came the more readily,
And there saw a master    what man he was I knew not,
That low bowed    and courteously to Scripture.
Conscience knew him well    and welcomed him fair;
They washed and wiped    and to the dinner.
But Patience in the palace stood    in pilgrim's clothes,
And prayed meat for charity    for a poor hermit.

    Conscience called him in    and courteously said,
'Welcome, wight, go and wash    thou shalt sit soon.

    This master was made sit    as for the most worthy,
And then Clergy and Conscience    and Patience came after.

Patience and I    were put to be mates,
And sat by ourselves    at a side table.

  Conscience called for meat    and then came Scripture,
And served them thus soon    of sundry meats many,
Of Augustine, of Ambrose    of all the four evangelists;
  *Edentes et bibentes quae apud eos sunt.*
But this master nor his man    no ordinary flesh eat,
But they eat food of more cost    messes and soups;
Of that which men mis-won    they made them well at ease.
But their sauce was over sour    and unsavourly ground,
In a mortar, *post mortem*    of many bitter pains,
Unless they sing for those souls    and weep salt tears:
  *Vos qui peccata hominum comeditis, nisi pro eis lacrimas et orationes*
    *effunderitis, ea quae in deliciis comeditis, in tormentis evometis.*
Conscience full courteously then    commanded Scripture
Before Patience bread to bring    and me that was his mate.
He set a sour loaf before us    and said, '*Agite poenitentiam,*'
And then drew us drink    *diu perseverans.*
'As long,' quoth I, 'as I live    and my body endures!'
'Here is proper service,' quoth Patience    'there fareth no prince better';
And then he brought us forth a mess of other meat    of *miserere-mei-*
                                                      *Deus;*
And he brought us of *beati-quorum*    of *beatus-vir*'s making,
*Et-quorum-tecta-sunt    peccata* in a dish
Of secret shrift, *dixi*    and *confitebor tibi!*
'Bring Patience some pittance'    quietly quoth Conscience;
And then had Patience a pittance    *pro-hac-orabit-ad-te-omnis-sanctus-in-*
                                      *tempore-opportuno;*
And Conscience cheered us    and told us merry tales,
  *Cor contritum et humiliatum, Deus, non despicies.*
  Patience was proud    of that proper service,
And made him mirth with his meat    but I mourned ever,
For this doctor on the high dais    drank wine so fast;
  *Vae vobis qui potentes estis ad bibendum vinum!*
He ate many sundry meats    messes and puddings,
Tripes and wild boar    and eggs fried with fat.
Then said I to myself    so that Patience it heard,
'It is not four days since that this man    before the dean of St Paul's,
Preached of penances    that Paul the apostle suffered,
*In fame et frigore*    and blows of scourges;
  *Ter caesus sum et a Judeis quinquies quadregenas, etc.*

'But one word they skip over     at each time that they preach,
That Paul in his epistle     to all the people told;

> *Periculum est in falsis fratribus.*

Holy writ bids men beware     I will not write it here
In English, in case     it should be repeated too often,
And grieve therewith good men     but grammarians shall read;

> *Unus quisque a fratre se custodiat, quia, ut dicitur, periculum est in*
> *falsis fratribus.*

'But I knew never man that as friar went     before men in English
Take it for their text     and tell it plainly.
They preach that penance     is profitable to the soul
And what mischief and pain     Christ for man suffered.
But this God's glutton,' quoth I     'with his great cheeks,
Hath no pity on us poor     he performeth evil;
That he preacheth he doeth not,'     to Patience I told,
And wished heartily     with will full eager,
That dishes and platters     before this same doctor,
Were molten lead in his maw     and Mahomet [1] inside him!
'I shall demand of this jerry     with his pot belly,
To tell me what penance is     of which he preached readily.'—
Patience perceived what I thought     and winked at me to be still,
And said, 'Thou shalt see thus soon     when he may no more,
He shall have a penance in his paunch     and puff at each word,
And then shall his guts grumble     and he shall gape after;
For now he hath drunken so deep     he will know soon,
And prove it by their Apocalypse     and by the passion of Saint Advisa,[2]
That neither bacon nor brawn     boiled meat nor messes
Is neither fish nor flesh     but food for a penitent.
And then shall he testify by the Trinity     and take his fellow to witness,
What he found in a frail     for a friar's living,
And unless the first line be lying     believe never again!
And then is the time to take up     and to ask this doctor
Of Do-well and of Do-better     and if Do-best be any penance.'—
    And I sat still, as Patience said     thus soon this doctor,
As ruddy as a rose     rubbed his cheeks,
Coughed and exclaimed     and Conscience him heard,
And told him of a Trinity     and towards us he looked.
'What is Do-well, sir doctor?' quoth I     'Is Do-well any penance?'
'Do-well?' quoth this doctor—     and took the cup and drank—
'Do no evil to thy fellow Christian     as lies in thy power.'

------

[1] See page 206.                    [2] See page 206.

'By this day, sir doctor,' quoth I   'then be ye not in Do-well;
For ye have harmed us two   in that ye eat the pudding,
Messes, and other meat   and we no morsel had!
And if ye fare so in your infirmary   it is strange methinketh,
Unless strife be where charity should be   if young children dared
                                                                complain!
I would exchange my penance with yours   for I am following Do-well!'
   Then Conscience courteously   a gesture he made,
And winked upon Patience   to pray me to be still,
And said himself, 'Sir doctor   if it be your will,
What is Do-well and Do-better?   ye thinkers know.'
   'Do-well,' quoth this doctor   'do as clerks teach,
And Do-better is he that teacheth   and travaileth to teach others,
And Do-best doth himself so   as he saith and preacheth:—
      *Qui facit et docuerit, magnus vocabitur in regno caelorum.*'
   'Now thou, Clergy,' quoth Conscience   'say what is Do-well.'
'I have seven sons,' he said   'serve in a castle,
There the lord of life dwelleth   to teach them what is Do-well;
Till I see those seven   and myself accord with them,
I am unfitted,' quoth he   'to any wight to explain it.
For one Piers the Plowman   hath impugned us all,
And set all sciences at nought   save love alone,
And no text taketh   to maintain his cause,
But *dilige Deum*   and *Domine, quis habitabit, etc.*
And he saith that Do-well and Do-better   are two absolutes,
Which absolutes, with faith   find out Do-best,
Which shall save man's soul   thus saith Piers the Plowman.'
   'I can naught hereon,' quoth Conscience   'but I know well Piers;
He will not against holy writ speak   I dare well undertake;
Then pass we over till Piers come   and prove this in deed.
Patience hath been in many places   and perchance knoweth
That no clerk can   as Christ beareth witness;
      *Patientes vincunt, etc.*'
'At your request,' quoth Patience then   'if no man displeases;
*Disce*,' quoth he, '*doce   dilige inimicos.*
*Disce*, and Do-well   *doce*, and Do-better;
*Dilige*, and Do-best   thus taught me once
A beloved that I loved   Love was her name.
"With words and with works," quoth she   "and will of thine heart,
Thy soul love faithfully   all thy life-time;
And so thou learn thee to love   for the Lord's love of heaven,

   I 57¹

Thine enemy in all ways     treat as thyself.
Cast coals on his head     and all kind speeches,
Both with works and with words     try his love to win;
And lay on him thus with love     till he laugh on thee;
Unless he bow to this beating     blind may he be!
But for to do thus with thy friend     folly it were,
For he that loveth thee truly     little of thine coveteth.
True love coveteth naught     no goods but speech,
With half a lamp-line [1] in Latin     *ex vi transitionis*."
     'I bear about herein     fast bound, Do-well,
In a sign of the Saturday     that first set the calendar,
And all the wit of the Wednesday     of the next week after;
The fullness of the moon     is the might of both.
And herewith am I welcome     where I have it with me.' [2]
     'Undo it, let this doctor judge     if Do-well be therein;
For, by him that me made     might never poverty,
Pain, nor mischief     nor man with his tongue,
Cold, nor care     nor company of thieves,
Nor either heat, nor hail     nor no hell's spirit,
Nor either fire nor flood     nor fear of thine enemy
Trouble thee any time     if thou take it with thee;
          *Caritas nihil timet.*
And indeed, have God my soul!     if thou wilt it crave,
There is not either emperor nor empress     earl, king, nor baron,
Pope, nor patriarch     that pure reason shall not make
The master of all those men     through might of this riddle;
Not through witch-craft, but through it     (if thou wish it thyself)
Shall king and queen     and all the commons after
Give thee all that they may give     as for the best guardian,
And, as thou judgest, will they do     all their days after;
          *Patientes vincunt, etc.*'
     'It is but a "Dido,"' quoth this doctor     'a popular tale.
All the wit of this world     and mighty men's strength
Can not make a peace     between the pope and his enemies,
Nor between two Christian kings     can no wight peace make,
Profitable to either people'     and pushed the table from him,
And took Clergy and Conscience     to council, as it were,
So that Patience then must pass     for pilgrims know well how to lie.
     But Conscience spoke aloud     and courteously said,
'Friends, farewell'     and fair spake to Clergy,

'For I will go with this man     if God give me grace,
And be pilgrim with Patience     till I have tried more men.'
    'What?' quoth Clergy to Conscience    'are ye covetous now
After new year's gifts or presents     or eager to read riddles?
I shall bring you a Bible     a book of the old law,
And teach you, if you like     the least point to know,
That Patience the pilgrim     perfectly knew never.'
    'Nay, by Christ,' quoth Conscience to Clergy    'God thee requite,
For all that Patience me proffers     proud am I little.
But the will of the wight     and the will of folk here
Hath moved my mind     to mourn for my sins.
The good will of a wight     was never bought to the full;
For there is no treasure comparable     to a true will.
Had not Magdalen more     for a box of salve,
Than Zacheus when he said     *dimidium bonorum meorum do pauperibus?*
And the poor widow     for a pair of mites,
Than all those that offered     into *gazophilacium*?'
    Thus courteously Conscience     first took leave of the friar,
And then softly he said     in Clergy's ear,
'I would rather, by our Lord     if I live should,
Have patience perfectly     than half thy pack of books!'
Clergy of Conscience     no leave would take,
But said full soberly     'Thou shalt see the time,
When thou art weary for walking     and glad of my counsel.'
    'That is sooth,' said Conscience    'so me God help!
If Patience be our fellow     and friend of us both,
There is no woe in this world     that we should not amend,
And conform kings to peace     and all people's lands,
Saracens and Syria     and so all the Jews
Turn into the true faith     and into one creed.'
    'That is true,' quoth Clergy    'I see what thou meanest,
I shall dwell as I do     my duty to show forth,
And train children     and other folk teach,
Till Patience have proved thee     and perfect thee made.'
    Conscience then with Patience passed forth     pilgrims as it were.
Then had Patience, as pilgrims have     in his pouch victuals,
Sobriety, and simple speech     and steadfast faith,
To comfort him and Conscience     if they come in a place
Where unkindness and covetousness are     hungry countries both.
    And as they went by the way     of Do-well they talked;
They met with a minstrel     as me then thought.

Patience approached him first    and prayed him he should tell
To Conscience, what craft he knew    and to what country he went.

'I am a minstrel,' quoth that man    'my name is *Activa Vita*:
All idleness I hate    for Active is my name.
A confectioner, would ye know    and serve many lords,
And few robes I receive    or furred gowns.
Could I lie to make men laugh    then I should get
Either mantle or money    amongst lords' minstrels.
But as I can neither play tabor nor trumpet    nor tell no tales,
Pipe, nor fiddle    at feasts, nor harp,
Joke nor juggle    nor gently play.
Nor neither dance nor leap    nor sing with the gittern,
I have no good gifts    from these great lords,
For no bread that I bring    save a benison on the Sunday,
When the priest tells the people    their *pater noster* to pray
For Piers the Plowman    and those that his profit serve.
And that am I, Active    that idleness hates,
For all true toilers    and tillers of the earth;
From Michaelmas to Michaelmas    I supply them with wafers.

'Beggars and bidders    of my bread crave,
Vagabonds and friars    and folk with tonsures.
I find bread for the pope    and provender for his palfrey,
And I have never of him    have God my truth,
Neither provender nor parsonage    yet of the pope's gift,
Save a pardon with a peace of lead    with two heads amidst! [1]
Had I a clerk that could write    I would send him a petition,
That he send me under his seal    a salve for the pestilence,
And that his blessing and his bulls    boils might destroy:

> *In nomine meo daemonia ejicient, et super aegros manus imponent, et*
> *bene habebunt.*

And then would I be ready to the people    pastry for to make,
And willing and busy    about bread and drink
For him and for all his    found I that his pardon
Might heal a man    as I believe it should.
For since he hath the power    that Peter himself had,
He hath the pot with the salve    sothly, as me thinketh:

> *Argentum et aurum non est mihi; quod autem habeo, hoc tibi do*
> *nomine Domini, surge et ambula.*

'But if might of miracle fails him    it is because men be not worthy
To have the grace of God    and no guilt of the pope.

[1] See page 206.

For may no blessing do us good    unless we will amend,
No man's mass make peace    amongst Christian people,
Till pride be completely destroyed    and that through lack of bread.
　'For ere I have bread of meal    oft much I sweat.
And ere the commons have corn enough    many a cold morning;
So, ere my wafers be made    much woe I endure.
　'All London, I believe    liketh well my wafers,
And lower when they lack them—    it is not long ago,
There were miserable commons    when no cart came to town
With baked bread from Stratford [1]    then began beggars to weep,
And workmen afraid enough    this will be remembered long.
In the date of our drought    in a dry April,
A thousand and three hundred    twice thirty and ten,
My wafers then were scarce    when Chichester was mayor.'
　I took good notice, by Christ    and Conscience too,
Of Haukyn the active man    and how he was clothed.
He had a coat of Christendom    as holy church believeth,
But it was marred in many places    with many sundry patches,
Of pride here a patch, and there a patch    of rude speech,
Of scorning and of scoffing    and of discourteous bearing,
As in apparel and in comporting    proudly amongst the people,
Otherwise than he is    with heart or sight showing;
Willing that all men think    he is what he is not.
For which he boasteth and braggeth    with many bold oathes,
And unwilling to be reproved    by any man living,
And so singular by himself    in the sight of the people,
Was none such as himself    nor none so pope-holy,[2]
Habited as a hermit    an order all to himself,
Religion without rule    and reasonable obedience;
Attacking lettered men    and unlearned men both,
Praising true living    and a liar in soul;
In thought and observation    imagination and study,
As best for his body be    and have a bad name;
And meddles he everywhere    where he hath no business,
Wishing men to think    his wit were the best,
Or his crafty skill    or of clerks he the wisest,
Or strongest on steed    sturdiest under girdle,
And loveliest to look on    and truest in deeds,
And none so holy as he    nor of life cleaner,
Or fairest of features    of form and of stature,

---

[1] See page 206.　　　　[2] See page 206.

And most skilled of song      or cunning of hand,
And generous to give      and loss thereby to suffer;
And if he giveth aught poor men      tell what he dealt them;
Poor in possessions      in purse and in coffer,
And as lion to look on      and lordly of speech.
Boldest of beggers      a boaster that naught hath,
In town and in tavern      telling tales,
And saying things that he never saw      and for truth swearing it;
Of deeds that he never did      speaking and boasting,
And of works that he well did      to witness and say—
'Lo! if ye believe me not      or think that I lie,
Ask him or him      and he you can tell,
What I suffered and saw      and sometimes had,
And what I could do and knew      and what kin I come of.'
All he wishes that men knew      of his works and words,
Which might please the people      and praise himself:

> *Si hominibus placerem, Christi servus non essem;*
> *Et alibi: nemo potest duobus dominis servire.*

'By Christ,' quoth Conscience then      'thy best coat, Haukyn,
Hath many stains and spots      it must be washed.'
'Yea, whoso took heed,' quoth Haukyn      'behind and before,
What is on back and what on front      and by the two sides,
Men would find many creases      and many foul patches.'
      And he turned about quickly      and then I took heed,
It was fouler many times      than it first seemed.
It was spotted with wrath      and wicked will,
With envy and evil speech      provoking to fight,
Lying and laughing      and chiding with tongue;
All that he knew wicked      of any wight, he tells it,
And blames men behind their back      and wishes them misfortune;
And what he knows of Will      tells it to Wat,
And the thing Wat heard      Will heard after,
And made of friends foes      through a false tongue,
'Either with might of mouth      or through man's strength
I avenge me many times      or else fret myself
Within, as a seamstress shears';—      wretched man and cursed!

> *Cujus maledictione os plenum est, et amaritudine; sub lingua ejus labor*
> *et dolor:*
> *Et alibi: filii hominum, dentes eorum arma et sagittae, et lingua eorum*
> *gladius acutus:—*

'There is no man that I love      lasts any time,

For tales that I tell    no man trusteth me,
And when I may not have the mastery    with melancholy I am seized,
So that I catch cramp    heart spasms sometimes,
Or an ague in such an anger    and sometimes a fever,
That holdeth me all a twelve month    till that I despise
Leechcraft of our Lord    and trust in a witch,
And say, that no clerk can cure me    nor Christ, as I believe,
As the cobbler of Southwark    or of Shoreditch Dame Emma! [1]
And say, that no God's word    did me never good,
But through a charm had I good luck    and my chief healing!'
    I looked more carefully    and then saw it was soiled
With liking of lechery    as by looking of his eye.
For each maid that he met    he made her a sign
Seeming to sin-ward    and sometimes began to taste
About the mouth, or beneath    beginneth to grope,
Till either's will waxeth keen    and to the work they go,
As well in fasting days and Fridays    and forbidden nights;
And as well in Lent as out of Lent    all times alike,
Such works with them    be never out of season;
Till they might no more    and then had merry tales,
And how that lechers love    laugh and jest,
And of their harlotry and whoredom    in their old age tell.
    Then Patience perceived    places of his coat
Were grimy through covetousness    and unnatural desiring;
More to goods than to God    the man his love gave,
And imagined how    he them might have
With false measures and means    and with false witness;
He gave for love of the interest    and loth to do right,
And waited to see which    way to beguile,
And mixed his merchandise    and made a good show;—
'The worst within was    clever I called it,
And if my neighbour had any hind    or any beast else,
More profitable than mine    many sleights I made,
How I might have it    all my wit I cast,
And if I had it not by other ways    at last I stole it,
Or secretly his purse shook    unpicked his locks,
Or by night or by day    about was I ever,
Through guile to gather    the goods that I have.
    'If I went to the plough    I pinched so narrowly,
That a foot of land or a furrow    steal I would,

[1] See page 206.

From my next neighbour    take of his earth;
And if I reaped, I would reach over    or gave them orders that reaped,
To seize to me with their sickles    what I sowed never.

'And whoso borrowed of me    rued the time,
With presents privately    or payed some amount.
So, willy nilly    take I would;
And both to kith and kin    I was mean with what I had.

'And whoso bargained for my goods    abuse I would,
Till he proffered to pay me    a penny or two
More than it was worth    and yet would I swear,
That it cost me much more    and swore many oaths.

'On holy days at holy church    when I heard Mass,
Had I never will, knows God    genuinely to beseech
Mercy for my misdeeds    I mourned more
For loss of goods, believe me    than for my body's guilts;
Thus, if I had deadly sin done    I dreaded not that so sore,
As when I lent and believed it lost    or it was long ere it was payed.
So if I showed any kindness    my fellow Christian to help,
Upon a cruel covetousness    my heart began to suffer.
And if I sent over sea    my servants to Bruges,
Or into Prussia my prentice    my profit to look after,
To deal with money    and make exchanges,
Might never me comfort    in the mean time,
Neither Mass nor matins    nor no manner of sights,
Nor never penance performed    nor *pater noster* said,
My mind was more    on my goods, in the balance,
Than on the grace of God    and his great helps:
        *Ubi thesaurus tuus, ibi et cor tuum.*'
And also the glutton with great oaths    his garment had soiled,
And foully muddied it    with false speech;
When no need was    he took God's name in vain,
Swore thereby very oft    and all sweated his coat.
And more meat eat and drank    than nature could digest—
'I caught sickness sometimes    for my frequent surfeits;
And then I dreaded to die    in deadly sin'—
So that into despair he fell    and thought not to be saved,
The which is sloth so strong    that no skill can help it,
Nor no mercy heal    the man that so dieth.

    Which be the ways    that bringeth a man to sloth?
It happens when a man mourneth not for his misdeeds    nor maketh no
                                                    sorrow,

But the penance that the priest enjoineth    performeth badly,
Doth no alms-deeds    dreads him of no sin,
Liveth against the faith    and no law holdeth;
Each day is holiday with him    or a high feast day;
And if aught will hear    it is a harlot's tongue.
When men speak of Christ    or of cleanness of soul,
He waxeth wroth and will naught hear    but words of mirth.
Penance and poor men    and the passion of saints
He hateth to hear thereof    and all that tell it.
These be the ways, beware    that bringeth a man to despair!
Ye lords and ladies    and legates of holy church,
That feed wise fools    flatterers and liars,
And have liking to listen to them    to make you laugh;
    *Vae vobis qui ridetis, etc.:*
And give them meat and goods    and poor men refuse,
In your death-dying    I dread me full sore,
Lest those three kinds of men    to much sorrow you bring:
    *Consentientes et agentes pari poena punientur.*
Patriarchs and prophets    and preachers of God's word
Save through their sermons    man's soul from hell;
Right so flatterers and fools    are the fiend's disciples,
To entice men through their tales    to sin and harlotry.
But clerks that know holy writ    should teach lords,
What David saith of such men    as the psalter telleth:
    *Non habitabit in medio domus meae, qui facit superbiam et qui loquitur*
        *iniqua.*
Should no jester have audience    in hall nor in chambers,
Where wise men are    God's word witnesseth;
Nor no vain man    amongst lords be allowed.
    Clerks and knights    welcome king's minstrels,
And for love of the lord    listen to them at feasts;
Much more, methinketh    rich men should
Have beggars before them    the which be God's minstrels,
As he saith himself    Saint John beareth witness:
    *Qui vos spernit, me spernit.*
Therefore I say to you rich    revels when ye make
For to solace your souls    such minstrels to have:
The poor, not a wise fool    sitting at the high table,
And a learned man, to teach thee    what our Lord suffered,
For to save thy soul    from Satan thine enemy,
And fiddle to thee, without flattering    of Good Friday the story;

And a blind man for a jester    or a bed-ridden woman,
To cry for a largesse before our Lord    your good fame to show!
These three kinds of minstrels    make a man to laugh,
And, at his death-dying    they give him great comfort,
That in his life listened to them    and loved them here.
These solace the soul    till he comes to
A well good hope, for he wrought so    amongst true saints.
But flatterers and fools    through their foul words,
Lead those that love them    to Lucifer's feast,
With *turpiloquio*, a lay of sorrow    and Lucifer's fiddle.
    Thus Haukyn the active man    had soiled his coat,
Till Conscience accused him thereof    in a courteous manner
Why he had not washed it    or cleaned it with a brush.

# PASSUS XIV

'I HAVE but one whole garment,' quoth Haukyn      'I am the less to blame
Though it be soiled and seldom clean      I sleep therein at nights;
And also I have a housewife      servants and children—
　　*Uxorem duxi, et ideo non possum venire—*
That will bespot it many a time      inspite of my checks!
It hath been washed in Lent      and out of Lent both,
With the soap of sickness      that seeketh out wondrous deep,
And with the loss of goods      loth for to offend
God or any good man      by aught that I could;
And was shriven by the priest      that gave me, for my sins,
As penance patience      and poor men to feed,
All for care of my Christianity      in cleanness to keep it.
And could I never, by Christ      keep it clean an hour,
That I soiled it not with looking      or some idle speech,
Or through deed or through word      or will of mine heart,
That I dirtied it not foul      from morning till eve.'
　'And I shall teach thee,' quoth Conscience      'of contrition to make,
That shall scrape thy coat      of all kinds of filth,
　　*Cordis contritio, etc.:—*
Do-well shall wash it and wring it      through a wise confessor,
　　*Oris confessio, etc.:—*
Do-better shall beat it and scour it      as bright as any scarlet,
And dye it with good will      and God's grace to amend thee,
And then send thee to satisfaction      for to sew it after,
　　*Satisfactio*, Do-best.
Shall never fog besmirch it      nor moth after bite it,
Nor fiend nor false man      befoul it in thy life;
Shall no herald nor harper      have a fairer garment
Than Haukyn the active man      if thou do my teaching;
Nor no minstrel be valued more      amongst poor and rich,
Than Haukyn's wife the waferer      with his *activa vita*.'
　'And I shall provide the paste,' quoth Patience      'though here is no
　　　　　　　　　　　　　　　　　　　　　　　　ploughing,
And flour to feed folk with      as best be for the soul,
Though never grain growed      nor grape upon vine.

123

For all that liveth and looketh     livelihood will I find,
And enough shall none lack     of things that they need.
We should not be too busy     about our livelihood,
    *Ne solliciti sitis, etc.: volucres coeli Deus pascit, etc.: patientes vincunt,*
      *etc.'*

    Then laughed Haukyn a little     and lightly began to swear,
'Whoso believeth you, by our Lord     I believe he be not blessed!'
'No,' quoth Patience patiently     and out of his pouch took
Food of great virtue     for all manner of beasts,
And said, 'Lo! here is livelihood enough     if our belief be true!
For lent never was life     but livelihood was given,
Whereof or wherefrom     or whereby to live.
    'First the wild worm     under wet earth,
Fish to live in the flood     and the fire the cricket,
The curlew by means of the air     most cleanest flesh of birds,
And beasts by grass and by grain     and by green roots,
Meaning that all men     might the same way
Live through true belief     and love, as God witnesseth;
    *Quodcunque petieritis a patre in nomine meo, etc.; et alibi,*
    *Non in solo pane vivit homo, sed in omni verbo, quod procedit de ore Dei.'*
    I looked what livelihood it was     that Patience so praised,
And it was a piece of the *pater noster     fiat voluntas tua.*
    'Have, Haukyn!' quoth Patience     'and eat this when thee hungereth,
Or when thou art benumbed with cold     or pinest with thirst.
Shall not gyves thee grieve     nor great lords' wrath,
Prison nor punishment     for—*patientes vincunt.*
If thou be sober     of sight and of tongue,
In eating and in handling     and in all thy five wits,
Darest thou never care for corn     nor linen cloth nor woollen,
Nor for drink, nor death dread     but die when God liketh,
Through hunger or through heat     at his will be it;
For if thou livest after his law     the shorter life the better
*Si quis amat Christum     mundum non diligit istum.*
For through his breath beasts grow     and go abroad,
    *Dixit et facta sunt, etc.:*
*Ergo* through his breath must     men and beasts live,
As holy writ witnesseth     when men say grace,
    *Aperis tu manum tuam, et imples omne animal benedictione*
    'It is found that forty winters     folk lived without tilling,
And out of the stone sprang the water     that folk and beasts drank.
And in Elijah's time     heaven was closed,

That no rain rained        thus read men in books,
That many winters men lived    and no food won by tilling.
Seven slept, as saith the book    seven hundred winters,
And lived without livelihood    and at last they woke,
And if men lived according to measure    should never more be fault
Amongst Christian creatures    if Christ's words be true.
But unkindness *caristia* maketh    amongst Christian people,
And over plenty maketh pride    amongst poor and rich;
But measure is so much worth    it cannot be too dear,
For the mischief and mischance    amongst men of Sodom
Waxed through plenty of bread    and of pure sloth;

> *Otiositas et abundantia panis peccatum turpissimum nutrivit.*

For they measured not    of that they eat and drank,
Did deadly sin    that the devil liked,
So vengeance fell upon them    for their vile sins;
They sunk into hell    those cities each one.
Therefore measure we us well    and make our faith our strong shield,
And through faith cometh contrition    conscience knows well.
Which driveth away deadly sin    and makes it venial.
And though a man may not speak    contrition may him save,
And bring his soul to bliss    if so that faith beareth witness,
That, whilst he lived, he believed    on the law of holy church;
*Ergo* contrition, faith, and conscience    is truly Do-well,
And surgeons for deadly sins    when shrift of mouth faileth.

'But shrift of mouth more worthy is    if man be inly contrite;
For shrift of mouth slayeth sin    be it never so deadly;
*Per confessionem* to a priest    *peccata occiduntur,*
Where contrition doth but drive it down    into a venial sin,
As David saith in the psalter    *et quorum tecta sunt peccata.*
But satisfaction seeketh out the root    and both slayeth and maketh
                                                    void,
And, as it never had been    to naught bringeth deadly sin,
So it never after is seen, nor hurts    but seemeth a wound healed.'

'Where dwelleth Charity?' quoth Haukyn    'I knew never in my life
Man that with him spake    widely as I have travelled!'

'Where perfect truth and poverty of heart is    and patience of tongue,
There is Charity, the chief chamberlain    for God himself!'

'Is patient poverty,' quoth Haukyn    'more pleasing to our Master
Than riches rightfully won    and reasonably spent?'

'But *quis est ille*?' quoth Patience    'quick *laudabimus eum*!
Though men talk of riches    right to the world's end,

I knew never man that rich was     that when he reckon should,
When it drew to his death-day     did not dread him sore,
And that at reckoning in arrears fell     rather than out of debt.
Where the poor dare plead     and prove by pure reason,
To have allowance of his Lord     by the law he it claimeth,
Joy that never joy had     of righteous Judge he asketh,
And saith, "Lo! birds and beasts     that no bliss knoweth,
And wild worms in woods     through winters thou them grievest,
And makest them well nigh meek     and mild for want,
And after thou sendest them summer     which is their sovereign joy,
And bliss to all that be     both wild and tame."
Then may beggars, as beasts     for good wait,
That all their life have lived     in suffering and want.
Unless God sent them some time     some manner of joy,
Either here or elsewhere     would it never be just;
For to bad fortune was he wrought     that never was for joy created.
Angels that in hell now be     had joy at some time,
And Dives on dainties lived     and in *douce vie*;
Right so reason showeth     that those men that were rich,
And their mates also lived     their life in mirth.
     'But God is of a wondrous will     as natural wit shows,
To give many man his reward     ere he it hath deserved.
Right so doeth God by some rich     a pity me it thinketh,
For they have their hire here     a heaven as it were,
And great pleasure in living     without labour of body;
And when he dieth, be disallowed     as David saith in the psalter,
          *Dormierunt, et nihil invenerunt;*
And in another place also     *velut somnium surgentium,*
          *Domine, in civitate tua, et ad nihilum rediges.*
     'Alas! that riches should deprive     and rob man's soul
From the love of our Lord     at his last end!
Labourers that have their hire in advance     are evermore needy,
And seldom dieth he out of debt     that dines ere he deserve it,
And till he have done his duty     and his day's work.
For when a workman hath wrought     then may men see the truth,
What he is worth for his work     and what he hath deserved;
And naught take before     for dread of disapproval.
So I say to you rich     it beseemeth not that ye shall
Have heaven in your life here     and heaven hereafter;
Right as a servant taketh his salary before     and then would claim more,
As he that none had     and hath his hire at the last.

It may not be, ye rich men    or Matthew on God lieth;
> *Vae! deliciis ad delicias difficile est transire.*

'But if ye rich have pity    and reward well the poor,
And live as law teacheth    deal truly with all,
Christ of his courtesy    shall comfort you at the last,
And reward all with double riches    that pitiful hearts have.
And as a hind that had his hire    ere he began,
And when he hath done his work well    men give him more reward,
Giveth him a coat above his covenant    right so Christ giveth heaven
Both to rich and to not rich    that mercifully live;
And all that do their work well    have double hire for their labours,
Here forgiveness of their sins    and heaven's bliss hereafter.

'But it is but seldom seen    as by holy saints' books,
That God rewarded double rest    to any rich wight.
For much mirth is amongst the rich    as to meat and clothing,
And much mirth in May is    amongst wild beasts,
And so long as summer lasts    the solace endureth.
But beggars about midsummer    breadless they sup,
And it is in winter for them worse    for wet-shod they go.
Athirst sore and ahungered    and foul rebuked,
And berated by rich men    so that pity it is to hear.
Now, Lord, send them summer    and some manner of joy.
Heaven after their hence-going    that here had such want!
For all mightest thou have made    none meaner than another,
And equally clever and wise    if thee well had liked.
And have pity on these rich men    that reward not thy prisoners;
Of the good that thou them givest    *ingrati* be many;
But, God, of thy goodness    give them grace to amend.
For may no famine be to them hard    drought, nor wet,
Nor neither heat nor hail    if they have their health,
Of that they wish and want    lacketh them not here.

'But poor people, thy prisoners    Lord, in the pit of misfortune,
Comfort those creatures    that much care suffer
Through famine, through drought    all their days here,
Woe in winter time    for wanting of clothes,
And in summer time seldom    sup to the full;
Comfort thy sorrowful    Christ, in thy kingdom,
For how thou comfortest all creatures    clerks bear witness,
> *Convertimini ad me, et salvi eritis:*

'Thus, *in genere* of his humanity    Jesus Christ spoke,
To robbers and to thieves    to rich and to poor.

Thou taughtest them in the Trinity     to take baptism,
And be clean through that christening     from all kinds of sins;
And if it happens through folly     to fall into sin after,
Confession, and acknowledgement     and craving thy mercy
Should amend us as many times     as man can desire.
But if the devil should plead against this     and punish us in conscience,
Christ would take the acquittal quickly     and to the evil one show it,
     *Pateat, etc., per passionem Domini,*
And repel so the devil     and prove us to be under his pledge.
But the parchment of this patent     of poverty be most,
And of pure patience     and perfect faith.
From pomp and from pride     the parchment departs,
And above all from all people     unless they be poor of heart.
Else is all idleness     all that ever we wrote,
*Pater nosters* and penance     and pilgrimages to Rome.
Unless our alms-giving and spending     spring of a true will,
All our labour is lost     lo! how men write
On the windows at the friars     vainly, if false be the foundation;
Therefore Christians should be rich in common     none covetous for
                                                         himself.

     'For the seven sins that there be     assail us ever,
The fiend accompanies them all     and gives them help,
But with riches that villain     chiefly men beguileth.
For where that riches reign     subservience followeth,
And that is pleasant to pride     in poor and in rich.
And the rich is reverenced     by reason of his riches,
Where the poor is but behind     and perchance knows more
Of wit and of wisdom     that far away is better
Than riches or royalty     and the rather heard in heaven.
For the rich hath much to reckon     and right soft walketh,
The high way heavenwards     oft riches closeth,
     *Ita impossible diviti, etc.,*
There the poor presses before the rich     with a pack at his back,
     *Opera enim illorum sequuntur illos.*
Importunes, as beggars do     and boldly he demands,
For his poverty and his patience     a perpetual bliss;
     *Beati pauperes, quoniam ipsorum est regnum caelorum.*
     'And Pride in riches reigneth     rather than in poverty,
Sooner in the master than in the man     some dwelling he hath.
But in poverty where patience is     Pride hath no might,
Nor none of the seven sins     can stay there long,

Nor have power in poverty    if patience it follows.
For the poor is always quick    to please the rich,
And ready at his bidding    for his bread's sake;
And obedience and boasting    are ever at war,
And each hateth the other    in all manner of works.

'If Wrath wrestle with the poor    he hath the worse;
For if they both plead    the poor is but feeble,
And if he chide or quarrel    it turns out worst for him;
For lowly he looketh    and lowly is his speech,
That meat or money    of other men must ask.

'And if Gluttony grieve poverty    he gains the less,
For his pay will not reach    rich meats to buy;
And if his gluttony be to good ale    he goeth to cold bed,
And his head uncovered    uneasily awry;
For when he straineth him to stretch    the straw is his sheets;
So for his gluttony and his great sloth    he hath a grievous penance,
That is woe when he waketh    and weepeth for cold,
And sometimes for his sins    so he is never merry,
Without mourning amongst it    and mishap as well.

'And if Covetousness would catch the poor    they can not come together,
And round the neck especially    neither embrace the other.
For men knoweth well that Covetousness    is of a keen will,
And hath hands and arms    of a long length,
And poverty is but a little thing    reaches not to his navel,
And good encounter was there never    between the long and the short.

'And though Avarice would anger the poor    he hath but little might,
For poverty hath but pouches    to put his goods in,
Where Avarice hath aumbries    and iron-bound coffers;
And which be easier to break open    less noise it maketh,
A beggar's bag    or an iron-bound coffer!

'Lechery loveth him not    for he giveth but little silver,
Nor doth he not dine delicately    nor drink wine oft.
A straw for the stews!    they would stand not, I trow,
Had they nothing but from poor men    their houses were un-tiled!

'And though Sloth pursue poverty    and serves not God well,
Mischance is his master    and maketh him to think,
That God is his greatest help    and no one else,
And his servant, as he saith    and of his train too.
And wherever he be    he beareth the sign of poverty,
And in that company our Saviour    saved all mankind.

K 57<sup>1</sup>

Therefore all poor that patient are     may claim and ask
After their ending here     bliss of heaven's kingdom.
Much bolder may he ask     that here could have his will
In land and in lordship     and pleasures of the body,
And for God's love leaveth all     and liveth as a beggar;
And as a maid for man's love     her mother forsaketh,
Her father and all her friends     and follows her mate,
Much is such a maid to be loved     by him that such a one taketh,
More than a maiden is     that is married through brokerage,
As by assent of sundry parties     and silver as well,
More for covetousness of goods     than human love between both:—
So it fareth by each person     that possessions forsaketh,
And puts himself to be patient     and poverty weddeth,
The which is kin to God himself     and to his saints.'
'Have God my truth,' quoth Haukyn     'ye praise poverty hard;
What is poverty with patience,' quoth he     'properly in meaning?'
'*Paupertas*,' quoth Patience     '*est odibile bonum,*
     *Remotio curarum, possessio sine calumnia, donum Dei, sanitatis mater;*
     *Absque sollicitudine semita, sapientiae temperatrix, negotium sine*
     *damno;*
     *Incerta fortuna, absque sollicitudine felicitas.*'
'I cannot construe all this,' quoth Haukyn     'ye must teach me this in
                           English.'
'In English,' quoth Patience, 'it is hard     well to expound it;
But somewhat I shall say it     so thou understand.
(1) Poverty is the first point     that Pride most hateth,
And it is good that by good skill     terrifies Pride.
Right as contrition is a comforting thing     conscience knows well,
And a sorrow for himself     and a solace to the soul,
So poverty indeed     penance, and joy,
Is to the body     pure spiritual health,
     *Ergo paupertas est odibile bonum,*
And contrition comfort     and *cura animarum.*
(2) Seldom sits poverty     the truth to declare,
Or as justice to judge men     enjoined is no poor man,
Nor to be a magistrate above men     nor minister under kings;
Seldom is any poor man put     to punish any people;
     *Remotio curarum.*
*Ergo* poverty and poor men     perform the commandment,
     *Nolite judicare quemquam.*     The third:—
(3) Seldom becomes any poor man rich     but of rightful heritage;

Winneth he naught with weights false    nor with unsealed measures,
Nor borroweth of his neighbours    except what he can pay back,
   *Possessio sine calumnia.*

(4) The fourth is a fortune    that makes the soul flourish
With sobriety from all sin    and also yet more;
It restrains the flesh    from follies full many,
And extra comfort    Christ's own gift,
   *Donum Dei.*

(5) The fifth is mother of health    a friend in all temptations,
And for the land ever a healer    a lover of all cleanness,
   *Sanitatis mater.*

(6) The sixth is a path of peace    yea, through the pass of Alton [1]
Poverty might pass    without peril of robbing,
For there that poverty passeth    peace followeth after,
And ever the less that he beareth    the braver he is of heart;
Therefore saith Seneca    *paupertas est absque sollicitudine semita.*
And a brave man of heart    amongst a gang of thieves;
   *Cantabit pauper coram latrone viator.*

(7) The seventh is a well of wisdom    and few words showeth,
For lords allow him little    nor listen to his reason,
He tempereth the tongue truth-ward    and no treasure coveteth;
   *Sapientiae temperatrix.*

(8) The eighth is a loyal labourer    and loth to take more
Than he may well deserve    in summer or in winter,
And if he trades, he feels no loss    if he charity gains;
   *Negotium sine damno.*

(9) The ninth is sweet to the soul    no sugar is sweeter;
For patience is bread    for poverty himself,
And sobriety sweet drink    and good doctor in sickness,
Thus taught me a lettered man    for our Lord's love,
Saint Augustine, a blessed life    without over concern,
For body and for soul    *absque sollicitudine felicitas.*
Now God, that all good giveth    grant his soul rest,
That thus first wrote to teach men    what poverty meant!'
  'Alas!' quoth Haukyn the active man then    'that, after my christening
I had not been dead and buried    for Do-well's sake!
So dangerous it is,' quoth Haukyn    'to live and to do sin.
Sin followeth us ever,' quoth he    and sorrowful waxed,
And wept water with his eyes    and bewailed the time,
That ever he did a deed    that dear God displeased;

       [1] See page 206.

Swooned and sobbed     and sighed full oft,
That ever he had land or lordship     less or more,
Or mastery over any man     other than himself.
'I am not worthy, knows God,' quoth Haukyn     'to wear any clothes,
Neither shirt nor shoes     save for shame one,
To cover my body,' quoth he     and cried mercy fast,
And wept and wailed     and therewith I awoke.

## PASSUS XV

BUT after my waking    it was wondrous long,
Ere I could truly    know what was Do-well.
And so my wit waxed and waned    till I a fool were,
And some blamed my life    approved it few,
And held me as a wretch    and loth to reverence
Lords or ladies    or any man else,
As persons in fur    with pendants of silver;
To serjeants nor to such    said not once,
'God save you, lords!'    nor bowed fair;
So that folk held me a fool    and in that folly I raved,
Till Reason had pity on me    and rocked me asleep,
Till I saw, as it sorcery were    a marvellous thing withal,
One without tongue and teeth    told me whither I should go,
And whereof I came and of what kind    I begged him at last.
If he were Christ's creature    for Christ's love to tell.

'I am Christ's creature,' quoth he    'and by Christians in many a place,
In Christ's court known    and of his kin a part.

'It is neither Peter the porter    nor Paul with his falchion,
That will forbid me the door    knock I never so late.
At midnight, at midday    my voice is known,
So that each creature of his court    welcometh me fair.'

'What are ye called,' quoth I, 'in that court    amongst Christian
people?'

'The whiles I quicken the body,' quoth he    'called am I *Anima*;
And when I will and would    *Animus* I am named;
And for that I think and know    called am I *Mens*;
And when I make moan to God    *Memoria* is my name;
And when I make judgements    and do as truth teacheth,
Then is *Ratio* my right name    Reason in English;
And when I feel what folk telleth    my first name is *Sensus*,
And that is wit and wisdom    the well of all crafts;
And when I challenge or challenge not    permit or refuse,
Then am I Conscience called    God's clerk and his notary;
And when I love loyally    our Lord and all others,
Then is Love my name    and in Latin *Amor*;

133

And when I fly from the flesh     and forsake the corpse,
Then am I spirit speechless     and *Spiritus* then I am called.
Austin and Isidore     each of them both
Named me thus by name     now thou may choose,
How thou desirest to call me     now thou knowest all my names.

> *Anima pro diversus actionibus diversa nomina sortitur: dum vivificat*
> *corpus, Anima est; dum vult, Animus est; dum scit, Mens est; dum*
> *recolit, Memoria est; dum judicat, Ratio est; dum sentit, Sensus*
> *est; dum amat, Amor est; dum negat vel consentit, Conscientia est;*
> *dum spirat, Spiritus est.'*

'Ye be as a bishop,' quoth I     jesting that time,
'For bishops blessed     they bear many names,
*Praesul* and *pontifex*     and *metropolitanus*,
And other names a heap     *episcopus* and *pastor*.'
'That is sooth,' said he     'now I see thy will!
Thou would'st know and understand     the cause of all their names,
And of mine, if thou mightest     methinketh by thy speech!'
'Yea, sir,' I said     'if so no man were grieved,
All the sciences under sun     all the subtle crafts
I would I knew and understood     by nature in my heart!'
'Then art thou imperfect,' quoth he     'and one of Pride's knights;
For such a lust and liking     Lucifer fell from heaven:

> *Ponam pedem meum in aquilone, et similis ero altissimo*.

It is against nature,' quoth he     'and all kind of reason,
That any creature should know all     except Christ alone.
Against such Solomon speaketh     and despiseth their wits,

> And saith, *sicut qui mel comedit multum, non est ei bonum: sic qui*
> *scrutator est majestatis, opprimitur a gloria.*

To English men this means     that may speak and hear,
The man that much honey eateth     his maw it cloyeth;
And the more that a man     of good matter heareth,
Unless he do thereafter     it doth him double harm:
*Beatus est,* saith Saint Bernard     *qui scripturas legit,*
*Et verba vertit in opera*     fully to his power.
Covetousness to understand     and to know science
Pulled out of paradise     Adam and Eve;

> *Scientiae appetitus hominem inmortalitatis gloria spoliavit.*

And right as honey is evil to digest     and cloyeth the maw,
Right so those that through reason     would the root know
Of God and of his great mights     his graces it hindereth.

[1] See page 206.

For in the liking lieth a pride     and a covetousness of the body,
Against Christ's counsel     and all clerks' teaching,
    'That is, *non plus sapere quam opertet sapere.*
Friars and many other masters     that to ignorant men preach,
Ye touch on matters immeasurable     to tell of the Trinity,
So that oft times the unlearned people     of their faith doubt.
Better if abandoned many     doctors such teaching,
And told men of the ten commandments     and touched on the seven sins,
And of the branches that burgeoneth from them     and bring men to hell,
And how that folk in follies     mispend their five wits,
As well friars as other folk     foolishly spend
In housing, in clothing     and high learning to show,
More for pomp than for pure charity     the people know the truth
That I lie not, lo!     for lords ye please,
And reverence the rich     the rather for their silver;
    *Confundantur omnes qui adorant sculptilia; et alibi:*
      *Ut quid diligitis vanitatem, et quaeritis mendacium?*
Go to the gloss of the verse     ye great clerks;
If I lie on you in my ignorant wit     lead me to burning!
For as it seemeth, ye forsake     no man's alms,
Of usurers, of whores     of avaricious chapmen,
And bow to these lords     that may lend you nobles,
Against your rule and religion     I take record by Jesus,
That said to his disciples     *ne sitis personarum acceptores.*
    'Of this matter I might     make a long book,
But of curates of Christian people     as clerks bear witness,
I shall tell it for truth's sake     take heed whoso liketh!
As holiness and honesty     out from holy church spread
Through loyal living men     that God's law teach,
Right so out from holy church     all evils spread,
Where imperfect priesthood is     preachers and teachers.
And see it by example     in summer time on trees,
Where some boughs be leaved     and some beareth none;
There is a mischief in the root     of such manner boughs.
Right so parsons and priests     and preachers of holy church,
That are root of the right faith     to rule the people;
But where the root is rotten     reason knows the truth,
Shall never flower nor fruit     nor fair leaf be green.
Therefore, would ye lettered leave     the lechery of clothing,
And be kind, as befits clerks     and courteous with Christ's goods,
True of your tongue     and of your tally both,

And hate to hear harlotry     and not to receive
Tithes of untrue thing     tilled or chaffered,
Then loth were unlearned men     unless they your lore followed,
And amend them that misdo     more for your examples,
Than for to preach and practise not     hypocrisy that seemeth.
For hypocrisy in Latin     is likened to a dunghill,
That was covered with snow     and snakes within;
Or to a wall that was white-limed     and was foul within.
Right so many priests     preachers and prelates,
Ye are blanched with *belles paroles*     and with clothes also,
But your works and your words thereunder     are full unlovely.
  '*Johannes Chrysostomus* [1]     of clerks speaketh and priests,
    *Sicut de templo omne bonum progreditur, sic de templo omne malum
      procedit.*
    *Si sacerdotium integrum fuerit, tota floret ecclesia; si autem corruptum
      fuerit, omnis fides marcida est.*
    *Si sacerdotium fuerit in peccatis, totus populus convertitur ad peccandum.*
    *Sicut cum videris arborem pallidam et marcidam, intelligis quod vitium
      habet in radice,*
    *Ita cum videris populum indisciplinatum et irreligiosum, sine dubio
      sacerdotium ejus non est sanum.*
  'If unlearned men wist     what this Latin meaneth,
And who was my authority     much wonder methinketh,
Unless many a priest bore     instead of their daggers and their brooches,
A set of beads [2] in their hand     and a book under their arm.
Sir John and Sir Geoffrey [3]     have a girdle of silver,
A dagger, or a knife     with studs guilded.
But a breviary that should be his plow     *placebo* to say,
Had he never a service to save silver by     saith it with evil will!
Alas! ye ignorant men     much lose ye by priests,
But a thing that wickedly is won     and with false sleights,
Was never wisdom of wise God     save wicked men it had;
The which are priests imperfect     and preachers after silver,
Executors and subdeans     summoners and their lovers.
This which with guile was got     ungraciously is spended;
So harlots and whores     are helped with such goods,
And God's folk for lack thereof     ruined and destroyed.
  'Curates of holy church     as clerks that be avaricious,
Lightly what they leave     rascals it have,
Or die intestate     and then the bishop entereth,

      [1] See page 206.          [2] See page 206.          See page 206.

And maketh merry therewith    and his men both,
And say, "he was a niggard    that no goods might spare
To friend nor to stranger    the fiend have his soul!
For a wretched house he held    all his life time;
And what he spared and locked up    spend we with mirth."
For learned, for unlearned    that loth is to spend,
Thus go their goods    when the spirit is fled.
But for good men, God wot    great dole men make,
And bemoan good meat-givers    and in mind have,
In prayers and in penances    and in perfect charity.'
    'What is Charity?' quoth I then    'a childlike thing,' he said;
        '*Nisi efficiamini sicut parvuli, non intrabitis in regnum caelorum;*
Without childishness or folly    a free liberal will.'
    'Where should men find such a friend    with so free a heart?
I have lived in the land,' quoth I    'my name is Long Will,[1]
And found I never full charity    before nor behind!
Men be merciful    to mendicants and to poor,
And will lend where they believe    honestly to be payed.
    'But charity that Paul praiseth best    and most pleasant to our Saviour,
        As, *non inflatur, non est ambitiosa, non quaerit quae sua sunt,*
I saw never such a man    so me God help,
That would not ask after his own    and other whiles covet
Things that he needed not    and take if he might!
Clerks teach me that Christ    is in all places;
But I saw him never truly    but as myself in a mirror,
        *Ita in aenigmate, tunc facie ad faciem.*
And so I trow truly    by what men telleth of charity,
It is not champions' contest    nor trade, as I think.'
    'Charity,' quoth he, 'chaffereth not    nor challengeth, nor craveth.
As proud of a penny    as of a pound of gold,
And is as glad of a gown    of a gray wool
As of a tunic of Tharsian silk    or of choice scarlet.
He is glad with all the glad    and good to all wicked,
And believeth and loveth all    that our Lord made.
Curseth he no creature    nor can he bear wrath,
Nor no liking hath to lie    nor laugh men to scorn.
All that men saith, he holds it true    and in peace taketh,
And all manner of mischiefs    in mildness he suffereth;
Coveteth he no earthly good    but bliss of heaven's kingdom.'
    'Hath he any rents or riches    or any rich friends?'

        [1] See page 206.

'Of rents nor of riches     recketh he never.
For a friend findeth him     that faileth him never at need;
*Fiat-voluntas-tua*     finds him evermore.
And if he suppeth, he eats but a sop     of *spera-in-Deo*.
He can portray well the *pater noster*     and paint it with *aves*,
And otherwhiles is his wont     to wend in pilgrimage,
Where poor men and prisoners lie     their pardon to have.
Though he bear them no bread     he beareth them sweeter livelihood,
Loveth them as our Lord biddeth     and looketh how they fare.
     'And when he is weary of that work     then will he sometimes
Labour in a laundry     well the length of a mile,
And go to youth     and eagerly address
Pride with all its appurtenances     and pack them together,
And soak them in his breast     and beat them clean,
And labour on them long     with *laboravi-in-gemitu-meo*,
And with warm water at his eyes     wash them after.
And then he singeth when he doth so     and sometimes saith weeping,
     *Cor contritum et humiliatum, Deus, non despicies.*'
     'By Christ, I would that I knew him,' quoth I     'no creature rather!'
'Without help of Piers Plowman,' quoth he     'his person seest thou never.'
'Do clerks know him,' quoth I     'that keep holy church?'
     'Clerks have no knowing,' quoth he     'but by works and by words.
But Piers the Plowman     perceiveth more deeper
What is the will and wherefore     that many wights suffer,
     *Et vidit Deus cogitationes eorum.*
For there are full proud-hearted men     patient of tongue,
And polite as of bearing     to burgesses and to lords,
And to poor people     have pepper in the nose,
And as a lion he looketh     where men blame their works.
     'For there are beggars and bidders     beadsmen as it were,
Looketh as lambs     and seem life-holy,
But it is more to have their meat     with such an easy manner,
Than for penance and perfectness     the poverty that such have.
Therefore by sight nor by clergy     know shalt thou him never,
Neither through words nor works     but through will alone.
And that knoweth no clerk     nor creature on earth,
But Piers the Plowman     *Petrus, id est, Christus.*
For he is not among rascals     nor vagabond hermits,
Nor among anchorites, where a box hangeth [1]     all such they deceive.
Fie on deceivers     and *in fautores suos*!

          [1] See page 206.

For charity is God's champion     and as a good child mild,
And the merriest of mouth     at meat where he sitteth.
The love that lieth in his heart     maketh him light of speech,
And is companionable and cheerful     as Christ himself bids,
> *Nolite fieri sicut hypocritae, tristes, etc.*

For I have seen him in silk     and sometimes in russet,
Both in grey and in fur     and in gilt armour,
And as gladly he gave     to people that needed.
Edmund and Edward     both were kings,[1]
And saints considered     when charity them followed.
I have seen charity also     sing and read,
Ride and run     in ragged weeds,
But bidding as beggars     beheld I him never.
But in rich robes     soonest he walketh,
Capped and annointed     and his crown shaved,
And cleanly clothed     in lawn and in silk of Tartary.
And in a friar's frock     he was found once,
But it is far agone     in Saint Francis' time;
In that sect since     too seldom hath he been known.
Rich men he recommendeth     and of their robes taketh,
That without guile     lead their lives,
> *Beatus est dives, qui, etc.*

In king's court he cometh oft     where the counsel is true,
But if covetousness be of the counsel     he will not come therein.
In court among jesters     he cometh but seldom,
For brawling and back-biting     and bearing of false witness.
In the consistory before the commissary     he cometh not full oft,
For their law lasteth over-long     unless they take silver;
And matrimony for money     make and unmake,
And what Conscience and Christ     have knit fast,
They undo it unworthily     those doctors of law.
Amongst archbishops and other bishops     and prelates of holy church,
To dwell among them     his wont was some time,
And Christ's patrimony to the poor     deal out in portions.
But Avarice hath the keys now     and keepeth for his kinsmen,
And for his executors and his servants     and some for their children.
    'But I blame no man     but Lord, amend us all,
And give us grace, good God     charity to follow!
For whoso might meet with him     such manners him pleaseth,
Neither he blameth nor curseth     boasteth, nor praiseth,

---

[1] See page 206.

Taketh, nor loseth      nor looketh stern;
Craveth, nor coveteth      nor crieth after more,
 *In pace in idipsum dormiam, etc.*
The most livelihood that he liveth by      is love of God's passion,
Neither he asketh, nor beggeth      nor borroweth to repay;
Misdoth he no man      nor with his mouth grieveth.

 'Amongst Christian men      this mildness should last;
In all manner of trials      have this at heart—
That though they suffered all this      God suffered for us more,
In example we should do so      and take no vengeance
On our foes that do us falseness      that is our Father's will.
For well may every man know      if God had willed himself,
Should never Judas nor Jew      have Jesu put on rood,
Nor have martyred Peter nor Paul      nor in prison held.
But he suffered in example      that we should suffer also,
And said to such that suffer would      that *patientes vincunt.*

 '*Verbi gratia,*' quoth he      'and true examples many,
In *Legenda Sanctorum*      the life of holy saints,
What penance and poverty      and passion they suffered,
In hunger, in heat      in all manner of trials.
Anthony and Giles [1]      and other holy fathers
Wonned in wilderness      amongst wild beasts;
Monks and mendicants      men by themselves,
In caves and in caverns      seldom speak together.
But neither Anthony nor Giles      nor hermit that time
Of lions nor of leopards      livelihood took,
But of fowls that fly      thus find men in books.
Except that Giles      after a hind cried,
And through the milk of that mild beast      the man was sustained;
And day by day had he her not      his hunger for to slake,
But seldom and sundry times      as saith the book and teacheth.

 'Anthony some days      about noon-time,
Had a bird that brought him bread      that he lived by;
And though the man had a guest      God found for them both.

 'Paul *primus heremita* [2]      had enclosed himself,
So that no man might him see      for moss and for leaves;
Fowls him fed      many winters withal,
Till he founded friars      of Austin's order.
Paul, after his preaching      baskets he made,
And won with his hands      what his belly needed.

   [1] See page 207.   [2] See page 207.

Peter fished for his food     and his fellow Andrew;
Some they sold and some they cooked     and so they lived both.
And also Mary Magdalen     by roots lived and dews,
But most through devotion     and thought of God almighty.
I could not these seven days     say them all,
That lived thus for our Lord's love     many long years.
But there was not lion nor leopard     that on land went,
Neither bear, nor boar     nor other beast wild,
That fell not at their feet     and fawned with their tails.
And if they could have talked     by Christ, as I trow,
They would have fed that folk     before wild fowls.
For all the courtesy that beasts know     they showed that folk oft
In pleasing and in reverencing     where they on land went.
But God sent them food by fowls     and by no fierce beasts,
In meaning that meek things     mild things should feed;
As who saith, religious     righteous men should support,
And lawful men to life-holy men     livelihood bring.
And then would lords and ladies     be loth to offend,
And to take of their tenants     more than truth wills,
If they found that friars     would forsake their alms,
And tell them to bear it     whence it was borrowed.
For we be God's fowls     and abide always,
Till birds bring us     what we should live by.
For had ye soup and bread enough     and penny ale to drink,
And a dish there-midst     of some manner of sort,
Ye had right enough, ye religious     and so your rule me told:

> *Nunquam, dicit Job, rugit onager cum herbam habuerit? aut mugiet bos*
> *cum ante plenum praesepe steterit?*
>
> *Brutorum animalium natura te condemnat, qui cum eis pabulum com-*
> *mune sufficiat; ex adipe prodiit iniquitas tua.*

'If unlearned men knew this Latin     they would look to whom they give,
And considered before     five days or six,
Ere they amortized to monks     or canons their rents.
Alas! lords and ladies     ignorant counsel have ye
To give from your heirs     what your forefathers you left,[1]
And give to pray for you     to such as be rich,
And be founded and endowed even     to pray for others.
Who performeth this prophecy     of the people that now live,

> *Dispersit, dedit pauperibus, etc.?*

If any people perform that text     it is these poor friars!

[1] See page 207.

For what they beg around     in building they spend,
And on themselves some     and such as be their labourers,
And from them that have they take     and give them that have not.
     'But clerks and knights     and commoners that be rich,
Many of you fareth     as if I a forest had,
That were full of fair trees     and I considered and thought
How I might more therein     amongst them set.
Right so, ye rich     ye robbeth those that be rich,
To help them that help you     and give where no need is.
As whoso filled a cask     from a fresh river,
And went forth with that water     to wet with the Thames.
Right so, ye rich     ye robbeth and feedeth
Them that have as ye have     them ye make at ease.
     'But religious that rich be     should rather feast beggars
Than burgesses that rich be     as the book teacheth;
     *Quia sacrilegium est res pauperum non pauperibus dare.*
     *Item: peccatoribus dare, est daemonibus immolare.*
     *Item: monache, si indiges et accipis, potius das quam accipis;*
          *si autem non eges, et accipis, rapis.*
     *Porro non indiget monachus, si habeat quod naturae sufficit.*
Therefore I counsel all Christians     to conform them to charity;
For charity without demanding     unchargeth the soul,
And many a prisoner from purgatory     through his prayers he delivereth.
But there is a fault in the folk     that the faith keep;
Wherefore folk are the feebler     and not firm of belief.
As in counterfeit is an evil alloy     and yet looketh it like sterling,
The mark of that money is good     but the metal is feeble;
So it fareth by some folk now     they have fair speech,
Crown and christening     the king's mark of heaven,
But the metal, that is man's soul     with sin is foul alloyed;
Both lettered and unlearned     be now alloyed with sin,
That no man loveth the other     nor our Lord, as it seemeth.
For through war and wicked works     and weathers unreasonable,
Weather-wise shipmen     and wise clerks also
Have no belief in the sky     nor the lore of philosophers.
     'Astronomers all days     in their art fail,
That whilom warned before     what should befall after.
Shipmen and shepherds     that with ship and sheep went,
Wist by the welkin     what should betide;
As of weathers and winds     they warned men oft.
Tillers that tilled the earth     told their masters,

By the seed that they sowed     what they sell might,
And what to lend and what to live by     the land was so true.
Now faileth the folk of the flood     and of the land both,
Shepherds and shipmen     and so do these tillers;
Neither they see nor know     one course before another.
Astronomers also     are at their wits' end;
Of that was calculated by the elements     the contrary they find.
Grammar, the ground of all     beguileth now children;
There is none of these new clerks     whoso taketh heed,
That can versify fair     nor formally write;
Nor not one among a hundred     that an author can construe,
Nor read a letter in any language     but in Latin or in English.
Go now to any degree     and unless Guile be master,
And Flatterer his fellow     under him to work,
Much wonder methinketh     amongst us all.
Doctors of decrees     and of divinity masters,
That should learn and know     all kinds of knowledge,
And answers to arguments     and also to a *quodlibet* [1]
(I dare not say it for shame)     if such were opposed,
They would fail in their philosophy     and in physic both.
Wherefore I am afeared     of folk of holy church,
Lest they skip over as others do     in offices and in hours; [2]
But if they skip over, as I hope not     our belief sufficeth;
As clerks at Corpus Christi feast     sing and read,
That *sola fides sufficit*     to save with unlearned people.
   'And so may Saracens be saved     scribes and Jews;
Alas then! that our law-givers     might live as they teach us,
And, for their living, that unlearned men     be more loth God to offend.
For Saracens have somewhat     similar to our belief,
For they love and believe     on one person Almighty;
And we, learned and ignorant     on one God believe.
But one Mahomet, a man     into mis-belief
Brought Saracens of Syria     and see in what manner.
This Mahomet was a Christian man     and because he might not be a
                                    pope, [3]
Into Syria he sought     and through his subtle wits
Tamed a dove     and day and night her fed;
The corn that she cropped     he cast it in his ear.
And if he among the people preached     or in places came,
Then would the dove come     to the clerk's ear,

        [1] See page 207.          [2] See page 207.          [3] See page 207.

In meaning after meat          thus Mahomet her enchanted,
And made folk then fall on knees          for he swore in his preaching
That the dove that came so          came from God of heaven
As messenger to Mahomet          men for to teach
And thus through wiles of his wit          and a white dove,
Mahomet in mis-belief          men and women brought,
So that learned there and unlearned too          live in his laws,
And so our Saviour suffered          the Saracens thus beguiled,
Through a Christian clerk          accursed in his soul;
But for dread of the death          I dare not tell truth,
How English clerks a dove feed          that Covetousness is called,
And follow Mahomet's custom          so that no man useth truth.

   'Anchorites and hermits          and monks and friars
Resemble apostles          through their perfect living.
Would never the faithful father          that his ministers should
Of tyrants that plague true men          take any alms,
But do as Anthony did          Dominic and Francis,
Benet and Bernard          the which them first taught
To live by little and in low houses          by true men's alms,
Grace should grow and be green          through their good living,
And folk should find          that be in divers sickness,
The better for their praying          in body and in soul.
Their prayers and their penances          to peace should bring
All that be at strife          if beadsmen were true;
    *Petite et accipietis, etc.*
Salt saveth cattle          say the wives;
    *Vos estis sal terrae, etc.*
The heads of holy church          if they holy were,
Christ calleth them salt          for Christian souls;
    *Et si sal evanuerit, in quo salietur.*
But fresh flesh or fish          when it salt lacketh,
It is unsavoury, indeed          seethed or baked.
So is man's soul sothly          that seeth no good example
From them of holy church          that the high way should teach,
And be guide, and go before          as a good standard-bearer,
And encourage them that behind be          and give them good proof.

   'Eleven holy men          all the world turned
Into true belief          the more methinketh,
Should all manner of men          we have so many masters,
Priests and preachers          and a pope above,
Who God's salt should be          to save man's soul.

'All was heathenness some time    England and Wales,
Till Gregory sent clerks    to come here and preach.
Austin at Canterbury    christened the king,
And through miracles, as men may read    all that march he turned
To Christ and to Christendom    and cross to honour,
And baptized folk fast    and the faith taught
More through miracles    than through much preaching,
As well through his works    as with holy words,
And told them what baptism    and faith was in meaning.

'Cloth that cometh from the weaving    is not comely to wear,
Till it is fulled under foot    or on fulling-stocks,
Washed well with water    and with teasles scratched,
Tucked, and tented    and put under tailor's hand.
And so it fareth by a child    that born is of womb,
Till it be christened in Christ's name    confirmed by the bishop,
It is heathen as to heavenward    and helpless in the soul.

'Heathen means after heath    and untilled earth;
As in wild wilderness    waxeth wild beasts,
Rude and irrational    running without cruppers.

'Ye mind well how Matthew saith    how a man made a feast;
He fed them with no venison    nor pheasants baked,
But fouls that went not from him    but followed his whistling;

  *Ecce altilia mea et omnia parata sunt, etc.;*

And with calves' flesh he fed    the fold that he loved.
The calf betokeneth cleanness    in them that keep laws.
For as the cow with her milk    the calf nourisheth to an ox,
So love and loyalty    true men sustaineth,
And maidens and mild men    mercy desire;
Right as the cow-calf    coveteth sweet milk,
So do righteous men    mercy and truth.
And by the hand-fed fowls    this folk understand,
That loth be to love    without teaching of examples.
Right as poultry in a courtyard    come to men's whistling,
In search of meat    follow men that whistle,
Right so uncouth men    that little reason know,
Love and believe    by lettered men's doings,
And by their words and their works    think and trow.
And, as those fowls to find    food after whistling,
So hope they to have    heaven through their whistling.
And by the man that made the feast    the majesty is signified;
That is, God of his grace    giveth all men bliss;

L 57¹

With weathers and with wonders    he warneth us with a whistler,
Where that his will is    to worship us all,
And feed us and feast us    for evermore together.
     'But who be that excuseth    they are parsons and priests,
That heads of holy church be    that have their will here,
Without toil, the tithe wield    that true men work for,
They will be wroth that I write thus    but to witness I take
Both Matthew and Mark    and *memento Domini David;*
     *Ecce audivimus eam in Ephrata, etc.*
What pope or prelate now    performeth what Christ said,
     *Ite in universum mundum et praedicate, etc.?*
     'Alas! that men so long    on Mohamet should believe,
So many prelates to preach    as the pope maketh,
Of Nazareth, of Nineveh    of Nepthali, and Damascus,[1]
That they go not as Christ teacheth    since they wish for their titles,
To be pastors and preach    the passion of Jesus,
And as himself said    so to live and die;
     *Bonus pastor animam suam ponit, etc.;*
And said for salvation    of Saracens and others.
For Christians and unchristened    Christ said to preachers
     *Ite vos in vineam meam.*
And since that these Saracens    scribes, and Jews
Have a bit of our belief    the more, methinketh,
They would turn, whoso travail would    to teach them of the Trinity,
     *Quaerite et invenietis, etc.*
     'It is ruth to read    how righteous men lived,
How they defouled their flesh    forsook their own will,
Far from kith and from kin    evil-clothed went,
Badly bedded    no book but conscience,
Nor no riches but the rood    to rejoice them in;
     *Absit nobis gloriari, nisi in cruce Domini nostri, etc.*
     'And then was plenty and peace    amongst poor and rich;
And now is ruth to read    how the red noble
Is reverenced over rood    received for the worthier
Than Christ's cross, that overcame    death and deadly sin!
And now is war and woe    and whoso "why" asketh,
It is covetousness after that cross    the crown shows in gold.
Both rich and religious    that rood they honour,
That on groats is engraven    and on gold nobles.
For covetousness of that cross    men of holy church

[1] See page 207.

Shall turn as Templars [1] did    the time approacheth fast.
Know ye not, wise men    how those men honoured
More treasure than truth?    I dare not tell the soth;
Reason and rightful judgement    those religious judge.
Right so, ye clerks    for your covetousness, ere long,
Shall they judge *dos ecclesiae*    and your pride depose;
      *Deposuit potentes de sede, etc.*
If knighthood and kind wit    and common conscience
Together love loyally    believe it well, ye bishops,
The lordship of lands    for ever shall ye lose,
And live as *Levitici*    as our Lord you teacheth,
      *Per primitias et decimas.*
      'When Constantine of courtesy    holy church endowed
With lands and subjects    lordships and rents,
An angel me heard    on high at Rome cry,
"*Dos ecclesiae* this day    hath drunk venom,
And those that have Peter's power    are poisoned all."
A medicine must be thereto    that may amend prelates,
That should pray for the peace    possession them hindereth,
Take their lands, ye lords    and let them live by tithes.
If possession be poison    and imperfect men make,
Good it were to discharge them    for holy church's sake,
And purge them of poison    ere more peril fall.
      'If priesthood were perfect    the people would amend,
That cross Christ's law    and Christendom despise.
For all paynims pray    and perfectly believe
On the holy great God    and his grace they ask,
And make their moan to Mahomet    their message to offer.
And thus in a faith liveth that folk    and by a false mediator,
And that is pity for righteous men    that in the realm live,
And a peril to the pope    and prelates that he maketh,
That bear bishop's names    of Bethlehem and Babylon;
When the high king of heaven    sent his son to earth,
Many miracles he wrought    man to convert;
In example that men should see    that by grave reason
Men might not be saved    but through mercy and grace,
And through penance and passion    and perfect belief;
And became man of a maid    and *metropolitanus*,[2]
And baptized and bishoped    with the blood of his heart
All that willed, and would    with their mind believe it,

            [1] See page 207.                    [2] See page 207.

Many a saint since     hath suffered to die,
All for to confirm the faith     in many countries died,
In India and in Alexandria     in Armenia and Spain,
In doleful death died     for their faith's sake;
In salvation of the faith     Saint Thomas [1] was martyred,
Amongst unnatural Christians     for Christ's love he died,
And for the right of all this realm     and all realms Christian.
Holy church is honoured     highly through his dying,
He is a pattern to all bishops     and a bright mirror,
And sovereignly to such     that of Syria bear the name,
That hop about in England     to hallow men's alters,
And creep amongst curates     and confess against the law,
    *Nolite mittere falcem in messem alienam, etc.*
Many man for Christ's love     was martyred in Rome
Ere any Christianity was known there     or any cross honoured.
    'Every bishop that beareth cross     by that he is held,
Through his province to pass     and to his people to show him,
Tell them and teach them     on the Trinity to believe,
And feed them with spiritual food     and needy folk to help.
But Isaiah of you speaketh     and Hosea both,
That no man should be bishop     unless he has both,
Bodily food and spiritual food     and give where there is need;
    *In domo mea non est panis neque vestimentum, et ideo nolite constituere*
        *me regem.*
Hosea saith for such     that sick be and feeble,
    *Inferte omnes decimas in horreum meum, ut sit cibus in domo mea.*
But we Christian creatures     that on the cross believe,
Are firm as in the faith     God forbid else!
And have clerks to keep us therein     and them that shall come after us.
    'And Jews live in true law     our Lord wrote it himself,
In stone, for it steadfast was     and stand should ever—
*Dilige Deum et proximum*     is perfect Jewish law—
And gave it to Moses to teach men     till Messiah come;
And on that law they live yet     and hold it the best.
    'And yet knew they Christ     that Christianity taught,
For a perfect prophet     that many people saved
From strange ills     they say it oft,
Both of miracles and marvels     and how he men feasted
With two fishes and five loaves     five thousand people;
And by that eating men might well see     that Messiah he was.
                    [1] See page 207.

And when he raised up Lazarus    that laid was in grave,
And under stone dead and stank    with loud voice him called,
    *Lazare, veni foras,*
Dead he rose and moved    right before the Jews.
But they said and swore    with sorcery he wrought,
And studied to destroy him    and destroyed themselves;
And through his patience their power    to pure naught he brought;
    *Patientes vincunt.*
Daniel of their undoing    divined and said,
    *Cum sanctus sanctorum veniat, cessabit unxio vestra.*
  'And yet believe those wretches    that he was *pseudo-propheta,*
And that his lore be lyings    and blame it all,
And hope that he be to come    that shall them relieve,
Moses again, or Messiah    their masters still prophecy.
  'But Pharisees and Saracens    Scribes and Greeks
Are folk of one faith    the Father God they honour;
And since the Saracens    and also the Jews
Know the first clause of our belief    *Credo in Deum patrem omnipotentem,*
Prelates of Christian provinces    should prove, if they might,
Teach them by little and little    *et in Jesum Chrĭstum, filium,*
Till they can speak and spell    *et in Spiritum Sanctum,*
And render it and record it    with *remissionem peccatorum,*
    *Carnis resurrectionem, et vitam aeternam. Amen.*'

'Now fair befall you!' quoth I then   'for your fair showing,
For Haukyn's love the active man   ever I shall you love;
But yet I am in doubt   what charity means.'
'It is a full excellent tree,' quoth he   'truly to tell.
Mercy is the root thereof   the middle trunk is pity.
The leaves be true words   the law of holy church,
The blossom be courteous speech   and benign looking;
Patience is called the pure tree   and poor simple of heart,
And so, through God and through good men   groweth the fruit charity.'
'I would travel,' quoth I, 'this tree to see   twenty hundred miles,
And for to have my fill of that fruit   forsake all other food.
Lord,' quoth I, 'does any wight know   whereabouts it groweth?'
   'It groweth in a garden,' quoth he   'that God made himself,
Amidst man's body   the root is of that trunk;
Heart is called the garden   that it groweth in,
And *Liberum Arbitrium*   hath the land to farm,
Under Piers the Plowman   to hoe it and to weed it.'
'Piers the Plowman!' quoth I then   and all for pure joy
That I heard named his name   soon I swooned after,
And lay long in a lone dream   and at last me thought,
That Piers the Plowman   all the place me showed,
And bade me gaze on the tree   on top and on root.
With three piles was it under-propped   I perceived it soon.
'Piers,' quoth I, 'I pray thee   why stand these piles here?'
   'Against winds, if thou would'st know,' quoth he   'to keep it from
         falling;
    *Cum ceciderit justus, non collidetur; quia Dominus supponit manum
     suam;*
And, in blossom time, nip the flowers   unless the piles help.
The World is a wicked wind   to them that seek truth,
Covetousness cometh of that wind   and creepeth among the leaves,
And nearly destroys the fruit   through many fair sights.
Then with the first pile I strike him down   that is, *potentia-Dei-Patris*.
The Flesh is a fell wind   and in flowering time
Through liking and lusts   so loud he begins to blow,

That it nourisheth foolish sights     and sometimes words,
And wicked works thereof     worms of sin,
And biteth the blossoms     right to the bare leaves.
Then take I to the second pile     *sapientia-Dei-Patris,*
That is, the passion and the power     of our prince Jesus,
Through prayers and through penances     and God's passion in mind,
I save it till I see it ripen     and somewhat fruited.
And then tries the Fiend     my fruit to destroy,
With all the wiles that he can     and shaketh the root,
And casteth among the crop     unfriendly neighbours,
Backbiters mischief-making     brawlers and quarrellers,
And layeth a ladder thereto     of lies are its rungs,
And fetcheth away my flowers sometimes     before both my eyes.
But *Liberum Arbitrium*     hinders him sometimes,
Who is lieutenant to look to it well     by leave of myself;
     *Videatis qui peccat in Spiritum Sanctum, nunquam remittetur, etc.;*
     *Hoc est idem, qui peccat per liberum arbitrium non repugnat.*
But when the Fiend and the Flesh     forth with the World
Threaten behind me     my fruit for to steal,
Then *Liberum Arbitrium*     seizes the third pile,
And striketh down the demon     purely through grace
And help of the Holy Ghost     and thus have I the mastery.'
     'Now fair fall you, Piers,' quoth I     'so fair you describe
The power of these posts     and their own might.
But I have thoughts in a multitude     of these three piles,
In what wood they were     and where that they grew;
For are they all alike long     none less than another,
And to my mind, as methinketh     from one source they grew,
And of one greatness     and green of grain they seem.'
     'That is true,' said Piers     'so it may befall;
I shall tell thee at once     what this tree is.
The ground where it groweth     Goodness is called,
And I have told thee what the tree is named     the Trinity it meaneth'—
And sternly he looked on me     and therefore I spared
To ask him any more thereof     and asked him full fair
To describe the fruit     that so fair hangeth.
'Here now hangeth,' quoth he     'if I needs must,
Matrimony I mention     a moist fruit withal.
Then continence is near the top     like a sweet grafted pear,
Then beareth the crop good fruit     and cleanest of all,
Maidenhood, angels' pears     and soonest will be ripe,

And sweet without swelling    sour is it never.'
I prayed Piers to pull down    an apple, if he would,
And suffer me to try    what savour it had.
And Piers threw up among the crop    and then it began to cry,
And he shook widowhood    and it wept after.
And matrimony was moved    it made a foul noise,
I was sorry when Piers rocked it    it lamented so ruefully.
For ever as they dropped down    the devil was ready,
And gathered them all together    both great and small,
Adam and Abraham    and Isaiah the prophet,
Sampson and Samuel    and Saint John the Baptist;
Bore them forth boldly    nobody stopped him,
And made of holy men his hoard    in *limbo inferni*,
Where is darkness and dread    and the devil master.
And Piers for pure anger    one pile he seized,
And hit after him    happen how it might,
*Filius* by the Father's will    and grace of *Spiritus Sanctus*,
To go rob that ruffian    and take the fruit from him.

    And then spoke *Spiritus Sanctus*    in Gabriel's mouth,
To a maid called Mary    a meek one withal,
'That one Jesus, a justice's son    must rest in her chamber,
Till *plenitudo temporis*    fully come were,
That Piers' fruit flowered    and came to be ripe.
And then should Jesus joust for that    by judgement of arms,
Which should take the fruit    the Fiend or himself.'
The maid mildly then    to the messenger consented,
And said courteously to him    'Lo me, his handmaiden
For to do his will    without any sin';
        *Ecce ancilla Domini; fiat mihi secundum verbum tuum, etc.*
And in the womb of that girl    was he forty weeks,
Till he grew a child through her flesh    and of fighting knew
To have fought with the Fiend    ere full time came.
And Piers the Plowman    perceived the fullness of time,
And taught him medicine    his life for to save,
So that though he were wounded by his enemy    to heal himself;
And he did try his surgery    on them that sick were,
Till he was a perfect practitioner    if any harm fell,
And he sought out the sick    and sinful both,
And healed sick and sinful    both blind and lame,
And common women converted    and to good turned;
        *Non est sanis opus medicus, sed infirmis, etc.*

Both lepers and the dumb    and those with bloody flux,
Oft he healed such    he held it no great skill,
Save when he healed Lazarus    that had lain in the grave,
*Quatriduanus* dead    alive did he walk.
But as he made that mastery    *moestus coepit esse*,
And wept water with his eyes    there saw it many.
Some that the sight saw    said at the time,
That he was giver of life    and lord of high heaven.
The Jews argued against it    and judged by laws,
And said he wrought through witchcraft    and with the devil's might,
     *Daemonium habes, etc.*
'Then are ye churls,' quoth Jesus    'and your children both,
And Satan your saviour    yourselves now ye witness.
For I have saved yourselves,' saith Christ    'and your sons after,
Your bodies, your beasts    and blind men helped,
And fed you with fishes    and with five loaves,
And left over baskets full of broken meat    bear away whoso would';—
And he attacked the Jews manfully    and threatened to beat them,
And struck them with a cord    and cast down their stalls,
That in church bartered    or changed any money,
And said it in sight of them all    so that all heard,
'I shall overturn this temple    and throw it down,
And in three days after    build it anew,
And make it as much or more    in all ways,
As ever it was, and as large    wherefore I command you,
Of prayers and of perfectness    call this place;
     *Domus mea domus orationis vocabitur.*'
Envy and evil will    was in the Jews;
They cast about and contrived    to kill him when they might,
Each day after another    their time they awaited.
Till it befell on a Friday    a little before Passover,
The Thursday before    when he made his maundy,
Sitting at supper    he said these words—
'I am sold through one of you    he shall the time rue
That ever he his saviour sold    for silver or aught else.'
     Judas quarrelled with that    but Jesus him told,
It was himself truely    and said '*tu dicis.*'
Then went he forth, that wicked man    and with the Jews met,
And told them a token    how to know Jesus,
And which token to this day    too much is used,
That is, kissing and fair countenance    and unkind will;

And so it was by Judas then     that Jesus was betrayed.
'*Ave, rabi*,' quoth that wretch     and right to him he went,
And kissed him, to be caught thereby     and killed of the Jews.
Then Jesus to Judas     and to the Jews said,
'Falseness I find     in thy fair speech,
And guile in thy glad cheer     and gall is in thy laughing.
Thou shalt be mirror to many     men to deceive,
But the worst and thy wickedness     shall fall upon thyselves;
    *Necesse est ut veniant scandala; vae homini illi per quem scandalum*
      *venit!*
Though I by treason be taken     at your own will,
Suffer my apostles in peace     and in peace to go.'
On a Thursday in darkness     thus was he taken
Through Judas and the Jews     Jesus was his name;
That on the Friday following     for mankind's sake
Jousted in Jerusalem     a joy to us all.
On cross upon Calvary     Christ gave battle,
Against death and the devil     destroyed both their mights,
Died, and death undid     and day of night made.

    And I awoke therewith     and wiped my eyes,
And after Piers the Plowman     pried and stared.
Eastwards and westwards     I searched hard,
And went forth as an idiot     in country to espy
After Piers the Plowman     many a place I sought.
And then met I with a man     on a mid-Lenten Sunday,
As hoar as a hawthorne     and Abraham he was called.
I asked him first     from whence he came,
And of what part he was     and whither he was going.
    'I am Faith,' quoth that man     'it befits not to lie,
And of Abraham's house     a herald at arms.
I seek after a person     that I saw once,
A full bold bachelor     I knew him by his blazon.'
'What beareth that man?' quoth I then     'so bliss thee betide!'
'Three persons in one     none longer than another,
Of one size and might     in measure and in length;
What one doth, all do     and each doth by his one.
The first hath might and majesty     maker of all things;
*Pater* is his own name     a person by himself.
The second of that sire is     truth, *Filius*,
Warden of those who wisdom have     was ever without beginning.
The third is called Holy Ghost     a person by himself,

The light of all that life hath     on land and in water,
Comforter of creatures     of him cometh all bliss.
So three belongeth to a lord     that lordship claimeth,
Might, and a mediator     to know his own might,
Of him and of his servant     and what they suffer both.
So God that beginning had never     when him good thought,
Sent forth his son     as for servant at that time,
To work here     till issue were sprung,
That is, children of charity     and holy church the mother.
Patriarchs and prophets     and apostles were the children,
And Christ and Christendom     and Christian holy church.
Meaning that man must     on one God believe,
And where he liked and loved     in three persons himself showed.
  ‘And that it may be so and soth     manhood it showeth,
Wedlock and widowhood     with virginity named,
In token of the Trinity     was taken out of one man.
Adam father of us all     Eve was of himself,
And the issue that they had     it was of them both,
And either is the other’s joy     in three different persons,
And in heaven and here     one single name;
And thus is mankind or manhood     of matrimony sprung,
And it betokeneth the Trinity     and true belief.
Mighty is matrimony     that multiplieth the earth,
And betokeneth truely     tell if I dare,
Him that first formed all     the Father of heaven.
The Son, if I it dare say     resembleth well the widow,
        *Deus meus, Deus meus, ut quid dereliquisti me?*
That is, creator became creature     to know what was both;
As widow without wedlock     was never yet seen,
No more might God be man     unless he mother had;
So widow without wedlock     may not well stand,
Nor matrimony without wife     is not much to praise;
        *Maledictus homo qui non reliquit semen in Israel, etc.*
Thus in three persons     is perfectly manhood,
That is, man and his mate     and the mother’s children,
And is naught but offspring of one generation     before Jesus Christ in
                                                                                        heaven,
So is the Father forth with the Son     and free will of both;
        *Spiritus procedens a Patre et Filio;*
Which is the Holy Ghost of all     and all is but one God.
Thus in a summer I him saw     as I sat in my porch;

I rose up and reverenced him     and right fair him greeted;
Three men to my sight     I made well at ease,
Washed their feet and wiped them     and afterwards they eat
Calves' flesh and a cake of bread     and knew what I thought;
Full true tokens between us are     to tell when me liketh.
First he tried me     if I loved better
Him, or Isaac mine heir     the which he told me to kill.
He knew my will by him     he will me it allow,
I am full certain in soul thereof     and my son both.
I circumcised my son     then for his sake;
Myself and my household     and all that male were
Bled blood for that lord's love     and hope to bless the time.
My trust and my faith     is firm in this belief;
For himself promised me     and my issue both
Land and lordship     and life without end;
To me and to mine issue     more yet he me granted,
Mercy for our misdeeds     as many times as we ask;

  *Quam olim Abrahae promisisti, et semini ejus.*

And then he sent to me to say     I should do sacrifice,
And do him worship with bread     and with wine both,
And called me the foundation of his faith     his folk for to save,
And defend them from the fiend     folk that on me believed.
Thus have I been his herald     here and in hell,
And comforted many a sorrowful     that for his coming wait.
And thus I seek him,' he said     'for I heard said lately
Of a man that baptised him     John the Baptist was his name,
That to patriarchs and prophets     and to other people in darkness
Said that he saw him     that should save us all;

  *Ecce agnus Dei, etc.*'

 I had wonder at his words     and of his wide clothes;
For in his bosom he bore a thing     that he blessed ever.
And I looked on his lap     a leper lay therein
Amongst patriarchs and prophets     playing together.
'What awaitest thou?' quoth he     'and what would'st thou have?'
'I would know,' quoth I then     'what is in your lap?'
'Lo!' quoth he, and let me see     'Lord, mercy!' I said,
'This is a present of much price     what prince shall it have?'
'It is a precious present,' quoth he     'but the fiend it hath claimed,
And me therewith,' quoth that man     'may no pledge redeem us,
Nor no man be our bail     nor bring us from this danger;
Out of the fiend's pound     no surety may us fetch,

Till he come that I speak of    Christ is his name,
That shall deliver us some day    out of the devil's power,
And better pledge for us lay    than we be all worthy,
That is, life for life    or lie thus ever
Lolling in my lap    till such a lord us fetch.'
  'Alas!' I said, 'that sin    so long shall stay
The might of God's mercy    that might us all amend!'
I wept for his words    with that I saw another
Rapidly run forth    the same way he went.
I asked him first    from whence he came,
And what he was called and whither he was going    and willingly he told.

# PASSUS XVII

'I AM Spes,' quoth he, 'a scout    and I spy after a knight.
That gave me a commandment . upon the mount of Sinai,
To rule all realms with    I bear the writ here.'
'Is it sealed?' I said    'may men see thy letters?'
'Nay,' he said, 'I seek him    that hath the seal to keep;
And that is, cross and Christendom    and Christ thereon to hang.
And when it is sealed so    I know well the truth,
That Lucifer's lordship    last shall no longer.'
'Let see thy letters,' quoth I    'that we might the law know.'
Then plucked he forth a patent    a piece of hard rock,
Whereon were written two words    on this wise glossed,
     *Dilige Deum et proximum tuum, etc.*
This was the text truly    I took full good notice;
The gloss was gloriously written    with a gilt pen,
     *In his duobus mandatis tota lex pendet et prophetia.*
'Be here all thy lord's laws?' quoth I    'Yea, believe me well,' he said,
'And whoso doth according to this writ    I will undertake,
Shall never devil him hurt    nor death in soul grieve.
For though I say it myself    I have saved with this charm
Of men and of women    many score thousands.'
'He saith soth,' said the herald    'I have found it oft;
Lo here in my lap    that believed on that charm,
Joshua and Judith    and Judas Maccabeus,
Yea, and sixty thousand more besides    that be not seen here.'
    'Your words are wonderful,' quoth I then    'which of you is truest,
And firmest to believe on    for life and for soul?
Abraham saith that he saw    holy the Trinity,
Three persons individually    separate from each other,
And all three but one God    thus Abraham me taught,
And hath saved that believed so    and were sorry for their sins,
He cannot say how many    and some are in his lap.
What needed it then    a new law to begin,
Since the first sufficeth    to salvation and to bliss?
And now cometh *Spes*, and speaketh    who hath espied the law,
And telleth naught of the Trinity    that gave him his letters,

158

"To believe and love    on one Lord almighty,
And then right as myself    love all other people."
The man that walketh with one staff    he seemeth in greater health
Than he that walketh with two staves    in sight of us all.
And right so, by the rood!    reason me showeth,
It is lighter for unlearned men    one lesson to know,
Than for to teach them two    and hard enough to learn the least!
It is full hard for any man    on Abraham to believe,
And well away worse yet    for to love a rascal!
It is lighter to believe    in three lovely persons
Than for to love and to believe    as well wretches as the true.
Go thy ways,' quoth I to *Spes*    'so me God help!
Those that learn thy law    will a little while follow it!'

    And as we went thus on the way    conversing together
Then saw we a Samaritan    sitting on a mule,
Riding full speedily    the same way we were going,
Coming from a country    that men called Jericho;
To a joust in Jerusalem    he hurried away fast.
Both the herald and Hope    and he met at once
Where a man was wounded    and by thieves attacked.
He could neither walk nor stand    nor stir foot nor hands,
Nor help himself truly    for half alive he seemed,
And as naked as a needle    and none to help near him.

    Faith had first sight of him    but he hurried on the other side,
And would not come near him    by nine lands' length.

    Hope came trotting after    that had so boasted,
How he with Moses' commandment    had many men helped;
But when he had sight of that man    aside he began to draw,
Fearfully, by this day! as duck    doth from a falcon.

    But so soon as the Samaritan    had sight of this man,
He alighted from his horse    and led him by his hand,
And to the wight he went    his wounds to behold,
And perceived by his pulse    he was in peril to die,
And unless he had succour quickly    rise should he never;
And hurried to his bottles    and both he broached;
With wine and with oil    his wounds he washed,
Anointed him and bound his head    and in his lap him laid,
And led him then on his horse    to *Lex Christi*, a grange,
Well six miles or seven    from the new market;
Harboured him at a hostelry    and to the host called,
And said, 'Here, keep this man    till I come the jousts,

And lo here is silver,' he said      'for salve for his wounds.'
And he gave him two pence      for upkeep as it were,
And said, 'What he spendeth more      I make thee good hereafter;
For I may not stay,' quoth that man      and horse he bestrides,
And hastened him Jerusalem-ward      the straight way to ride.
     Faith followeth after fast      and sought to meet him,
And *Spes* quickly him sped      to succeed if he could,
To overtake him and talk to him      ere they to town came.
And when I saw this, I stayed not      but started to run,
And followed that Samaritan      that was so full of pity,
And asked him to be his page      'Gramercy,' he said,
'Thy friend and thy fellow,' quoth he      'thou findest me at need.
And I thanked him then      and after I him told,
How that Faith flew away      and *Spes* his fellow both,
For sight of the sorrowful man      that robbed was by thieves.
'Hold them excused,' quoth he      'their help may little avail;
May no medicine on earth      the man to health bring,
Neither Faith nor fine Hope      so festered be his wounds,
Without the blood of a child      born of a maid.
And be he bathed in that blood      baptised, as it were,
And then plastered with penance      and passion of that baby,
He should stand and walk      but stalwart will he be never,
Till he have eaten all the child      and his blood drunk.
For went never wight in this world      through that wilderness,
But he was robbed or rifled      rode he there or walked,
Save Faith, and his fellow      *Spes*, and myself,
And thyself now, and such      as follow our works.
For outlaws in the wood      and under banks lurk,
And can each man see      and good note take,
Who is behind and who in front      and who be on horse,
For they hold him hardier on horse      than he that is on foot.
For they saw me, that am Samaritan      follow Faith and his fellow
On my steed that is called *Caro*      (of mankind I took it),
He was fearful, that villain      and hid him *in inferno*.
But ere this day three days      I dare undertake,
That he is fettered, that felon      fast with chains,
And never after grieve a man      that goeth this same way;
     *O mors, ero mors tua, etc.*,
And then shall Faith be forester here      and in this wood walk,
And direct common men      that know not the country,
Which is the way that I went      and forth to Jerusalem.

And Hope the hostelry's man shall be     where the man lieth healing;
And all that feeble and faint be     that Faith cannot teach,
Hope shall lead them forth with love     as his letter telleth,
And welcome them and heal     through holy church's faith,
Till I have salve for all sick     and then I shall return,
And come again through this country     and comfort all sick
That crave it or covet it     and cry thereafter.
For the child was born in Bethlehem     that with his blood shall save
All that live in faith, and follow     his fellow's teaching.'

   'Ah! sweet sir!' I said then     'am I to believe,
As Faith and his fellow     informed me both?
In three persons separable     that endless were ever,
And all three but one God     thus Abraham me taught;—
And Hope afterwards     he bade me to love
One God with all my strength     and all men after,
Love them like myself     but our Lord above all.'
'According to Abraham,' quoth he     'that herald at arms,
Set fast thy faith     and firm believe.
And, as Hope told thee     I command thee love
Thy fellow Christians evermore     equally with thyself.
And if conscience speak against it     or kind wit either,
Or heretics with arguments     thine hand thou them show;
For God is like a hand     hear now and know it.

   'The Father was first, as a fist     with one finger folding,
Till he loved and pleased     to unloosen his finger,
And proffer it forth as with a palm     to what place it would.
The palm is purely the hand     and proffereth forth the fingers
To minister and to make     what the might of the hand willeth,
And betokeneth truly     tell whoso liketh,
The Holy Ghost of heaven     he is as the palm.
The fingers that free be     to fold and to serve,
Betokeneth sothly the Son     that sent was to earth,
That touched and tasted     at teaching of the palm
Saint Mary a maid     and mankind took upon him;
        *Qui conceptus est de Spiritu Sancto, natus, etc.*
The Father is then as a fist     with finger to touch,
        *Quia omnia traham ad meipsum, etc.,*
All that the palm perceiveth     profitable to feel.
Thus are they all but one     as it a hand were,
And three different sights     in one showing.
The palm, for he putteth forth fingers     and the fist both,

   M 57¹

Right so readily     reason it showeth,
How he that is Holy Ghost     Sire and Son witnesseth.
And as the hand holds hard     and all things fast
Through four fingers and a thumb     forth from the palm,
Right so the Father and the Son     and Saint Spirit the third
Hold all the wide world     within them three,
Both sky and the wind     water and earth,
Heaven and hell     and all that there is in.
Thus it is, needeth no man     to think otherwise,
That three things belong     in our Lord of heaven,
And are separately by themselves     but apart were never,
No more than my hand may     move without fingers.
And as my fist is a full hand     folded together,
So is the Father fully God     former and shaper,
     *Tu fabricator omnium, etc.*,
And all the might with him is     in making of things.
     'The fingers form a full hand     to portray or paint
Carving and compassing     as craft of the fingers;
Right so is the Son     the science of the Father,
And fully God, as is the Father     no feebler nor no stronger.
     'The palm is truly the hand     hath power by himself,
Otherwise from the closed fist     or workmanship of fingers;
For the palm hath power     to move out all the joints,
And to unfold the folded fist     and the fingers' purpose.
So is the Holy Ghost God     neither greater nor less
Than is the Sire and the Son     and of the same might,
And all are they but one God     as is mine hand and my fingers,
Unfolded or folded     my fist and my palm,
All is but a hand     however I look at it.
     'But who is hurt in the hand     even in the midst,
He may hold right naught     reason it showeth;
For the fingers, that fold should     and the fist make,
For pain of the palm     power them faileth
To clutch or to grasp     to clip or to hold.
Were the middle of my hand     maimed or pierced,
I should hold right naught     of that I might reach to.
But though my thumb and my fingers     both were flayed,
And the middle of my hand     without ill ease,
In many kinds of ways     I might myself help,
Both move and mend     though all my fingers ached.
By this, methinketh     I see an evidence,

That whoso sinneth against the Holy Spirit     absolved will he be never,
Neither here nor elsewhere     as I heard tell,
> Qui peccat in Spiritum Sanctum, nunquam, etc.,

For he pricketh God as in the palm     that *peccat in Spiritum Sanctum*.
For God the Father is as a fist     the Son is as a finger,
The Holy Ghost of heaven     is, as it were, the palm.
So whoso sinneth against the Holy Spirit     it seemeth that he grieveth
God, where he grasps with     and would his grace quench.

'And to a torch or a taper     the Trinity is likened;
As wax and a wick     are entwined together,
And then a fire flames     forth out of both;
And as wax and wick     and hot fire together
Foster forth a flame     and a fair light,
So doth the Sire and the Son     and also *Spiritus Sanctus*
Foster forth amongst folk     love and faith,
That all kinds of Christians     cleanseth of sins.
And as thou seest sometimes     suddenly a torch,
The blaze thereof blown out     yet burneth the wick,
Without flame or light     the match burns,
So is the Holy Ghost God     and grace without mercy
To all unkind creatures     that covet to destroy
Loyal love or life     that our Lord made.
And as glowing embers     glad not those workmen,
That work and watch     on winter nights,
So much as a torch or a candle     that caught hath fire and blazeth,
No more doth Sire nor Son     nor Saint Spirit together,
Grant grace     nor forgiveness of sins,
Till the Holy Ghost begin     to glow and to blaze.
So the Holy Ghost     gloweth but as an ember,
Till that faithful love     light on him and blow,
And then flameth he as fire     on Father and on *Filius*,
And melteth their might into mercy     as men may see in winter
Icicles in eaves     through heat of the sun,
Melt in a minute while     into mist and to water;
So grace of the Holy Ghost     the great might of the Trinity
Melteth into mercy     to the merciful, and to none other.
And as wax without more     on a warm coal
Will burn and blaze     be they together,
And solace them that would see     that sit in darkness,
So will the Father forgive     folk of mild hearts
That ruefully repent     and restitution make,

In as much as they may      amend and repay.
And if it suffice not for assets      that in such a will dieth,
Mercy for his meakness      will make good the remnant.
And as the wick and fire      will make a warm flame
For to mirth men with      that in murk sit,
So will Christ of his courtesy      if men cry him mercy,
Both forgive and forget      and pray for us
To the Father of heaven      forgiveness to have.

'But strike fire from a flint      four hundred winters,
Unless thou have tow to take it with      tinder or twigs,
All thy labour is lost      and all thy long travail;
For may no fire flame make      fail it fuel.
So is the Holy Ghost God      and grace without mercy
To all unkind creatures      Christ himself witnesseth,

> *Amen dico vobis, nescio vos, etc.*

'Be unkind to thy fellow Christians      and all that thou canst pray,
Give and do penance      day and night ever,
And purchase all the pardons      of Pampeluna and Rome,
And indulgences enough      and be *ingratus* to thy kind,
The Holy Ghost heareth thee not      nor help thee by reason;
For unkindness quencheth him      so he can not shine,
Nor burn nor blaze clear      for blowing of unkindness.
Paul the apostle      proveth whether I lie,

> *Si linguis hominum loquar, etc.*

Therefore beware, ye wise men      that with the world dealeth,
That rich be and reason know      rule well your soul.
Be not unkind, I counsel you      to your fellow Christians.
For many of you rich men      by my soul, men telleth,
Ye burn, but ye blaze not      that is a hidden beacon;

> *Non omnis qui dicit Domine, Domine, intrabit, etc.*

'*Dives* died damned      for his unkindness
Of his meat and his money      to men that it needed.
Each rich man I warn      notice of him take,
And give your goods to that God      that Grace ariseth from.
For they that be unkind to their own      hope I none other,
But they dwell where Dives is      days without end.
Thus is unkindness the contrary      that quencheth, as it were,
The grace of the Holy Ghost      God's own kind.
For what kind doth, unkind undoes      as these cursed thieves,
Unkind Christian men      for covetousness and envy,
Slayeth a man for his property      with mouth or with hands.

For what the Holy Ghost hath to keep      those villains destroy,
The which is life and love     the light of man's body.
For every manner of good man     may be likened to a torch,
Or else to a taper     to reverence the Trinity;
And who murdereth a good man     methinketh, by my conscience,
He undoes the dearest light     that our Lord loveth.

   'But yet in many more manners     men offend the Holy Ghost;
But this is the worst way     that any wight might
Sin against the Saint Spirit     by assenting to destroy,
For covetousness of any kind of thing     what Christ dearly bought.
How might he ask mercy     or any mercy him help,
That wickedly and wilfully     would mercy destroy?
Innocence is next to God     and night and day it crieth,
"Vengeance, vengeance     forgiven be it never,
That killed us and shed our blood     un-made us, as it were;
     *Vindica sanguinem justorum!*"
Thus "vengeance, vengeance"     very charity asketh;
And since holy church and charity     charge this so strongly,
Believe I never that our Lord will love     what charity blames,
Nor have pity for any prayer     there that he maketh.'

   'I pose I had sinned so     and should now die,
And now am sorry, that so     the Saint Spirit I have offended,
Confess me, and cry his grace     God, that all made,
And mildly his mercy ask     might I not be saved?'
'Yes,' said the Samaritan     'so well thou might repent,
That righteousness through repentance     to pity might turn.
But it is but seldom seen     where truth beareth witness,
Any creature that is guilty     before a king's justice,
Be ransomed for his repentance     where all reason him damneth.
For where the injured prosecutes     the appeal is so huge,
That the king may do no mercy     till both men agree,
And both have justice     as holy writ telleth;
     *Numquam dimittitur peccatum, donec restituatur ablatum.*
Thus it fareth by such folk     that falsely all their lives
Evil live and cease not     till life them forsake;
Dread of despair     driveth away then grace,
So that mercy on their mind     may not then fall;
Good hope, that help should     to despair turneth—
Not of the powerlessness of God     that he is not able
To amend all that amiss is     and his mercy greater
Than all our wicked works     as holy writ telleth,
     *Misericordia ejus super omnia opera ejus.*

But, ere his righteousness to pity turn     some restitution behoveth;
His sorrow is satisfaction     for him that cannot pay.

   'Three things there be     that make a man by their strength
For to flee his own house     as holy writ showeth.
The one is a wicked wife     that will not be chastened;
Her partner flee-eth from her     for fear of her tongue.
And if his house be unroofed     and rain on his bed,
He seeketh and seeketh     till he sleep dry.
And when smoke and smother     smite in his eyes,
It doth him worse than his wife     or wet to sleep.
For smoke and smother     smite in his eyes,
Till he be blear-eyed or blind     and hoarse in the throat,
He coughs, and curses     that Christ give them sorrow
Who should bring in better wood     or blow till it burn.

   'These three that I tell of     be thus to understand;
The wife is our wicked flesh     that will not be chastened,
For nature cleaveth to him ever     to oppose the soul.
And though it fall, it finds reasons     that frailty made it;
And that is lightly forgiven     and forgotten both,
To man that mercy asketh     and amendment thinketh.
The rain that raineth     where we rest would,
Be sicknesses and sorrows     that we suffer oft,
As Paul the apostle     to the people taught,

     *Virtus in infirmitate perficitur, etc.*

And though that men make     much noise in their affliction,
And be impatient in their penance     pure reason knoweth,
That they have cause to complain     by nature of their sickness;
And lightly our Lord     at their lives' end,
Hath mercy on such men     that such evil suffer.
But the smoke and the smother     that smite our eyes,
That is covetousness and unkindness     that quencheth God's mercy.
For unkindness is the contrary     of all forms of reason;
For there is none sick nor sorry     nor so great wretch,
That he may not love, if him like     and give from his heart
Good will and good word     both wish and will
All manner of men     mercy and forgiveness,
And love them like himself     and his life amend.
I may no longer stay,' quoth he     and his horse he spurred,
And went away as the wind     and therewith I awoke.

LINEN-LESS [1] and wet-shod    went I forth after,
As a reckless fellow    that of no woe recks,
And went like a vagrant    all my life,
Till I waxed weary of the world    and wished to sleep again,
And leaned me about till Lent    and long time I slept;
And of Christ's passion and penance    that the people saved,
I rested and dreamed there, and snored fast    till *ramis palmarum*; [2]
Of children and of *gloria laus*    greatly me dreamed,
And how *hosanna* to the organ    old folk sang.
One like to the Samaritan    and somewhat to Piers Plowman,
Bare-foot on an ass's back    boot-less came riding,
Without spurs or spear    lively he looked,
As is the way with a knight    that cometh to be dubbed,
To get him gilt spurs    or shoes slashed.
Then was Faith in a window    and cried '*a! fili David!*'
As doth a herald at arms    when the adventurous come to joust.
Old Jews of Jerusalem    for joy they sang,
> *Benedictus qui venit in nomine Domini.*
Then I asked of Faith    what all that affair meant,
And who should joust in Jerusalem    'Jesus,' he said,
'And fetch what the Fiend claimeth    Piers' fruit the Plowman.'
'Is Piers in this place?' quoth I    and he looked on me,
'This Jesus of his nobility    will joust in Piers' arms,
In his helm and in his hauberk    *humana natura*;
That Christ be not known here    for *consummatus Deus*,
In Piers' garment the Plowman    this pricker shall ride;
For no dint shall him hurt    as *in deitate Patris*.'
'Who shall joust with Jesus?' quoth I    'Jews or scribes?'
'Nay,' quoth He, 'the foul Fiend    and falsehood and death.
Death saith he will undo    and down bring
All that liveth or looketh    in land or in water.
Life saith that he lies    and laith his life to pledge,
That for all that death can do    within three days,
He will go and fetch from the Fiend    Piers' fruit the Plowman,

And lay it where him liketh     and Lucifer bind,
And beat and down bring     sorrow and death for ever:
    *O mors, ero mors tua!'*
    Then came *Pilatus* with much people     *sedens pro tribunali,*
To see how daughtily death should do     and judge the rights of both.
The Jews and the justices     against Jesus they were,
And all their court on him cried     *crucifige* sharp.
Then put forth a robber     before Pilate, and said,
'This Jesus at our Jews' temple     japed and despised,
To undo it on one day     and in three days after
Edify it anew     (here he stands that said it)
And yet make it as much     in all manner of points,
Both as long and as large     by height and by length.'
'*Crucifige,*' quoth a catchpole     'I warrant him a witch!'
'*Tolle, tolle!'* quoth another     and took of keen thorns,
And began of keen thorn     a garland to make,
And set it hard on his head     and said in malice,
'*Ave, rabi!'* quoth that rascal     and threw reeds at him,
Nailed him with three nails     naked on the rood,
And poison on a pole     they put up to his lips,
And bade him drink his death drink     his days were done.
'And if that thou powerful be     help now thyself,
If thou be Christ, and king's son     come down off the rood;
Then shall we believe that Life thee loveth     and will not let thee die!'
'*Consummatum est,*' quoth Christ     and began for to swoon
Piteously and pale     as a prisoner that dieth;
The lord of life and of light     then layed his eyes together.
The day for dread withdrew     and dark became the sun,
The veil shook and was cleft     and all the world quaked.
Dead men for that din     came out of deep graves,
And told why that tempest     so long time lasted.
'For a bitter battle'     the dead body said;
'Life and Death in this darkness     one undoes the other;
Shall no wight know truly     who shall have the mastery,
Ere Sunday about sun-rising'     and sank with that to earth.
Some said that he was God's son     that so fair died,
    *Vere filius Dei erat iste, etc.*
And some said he was a witch     'it is good that one try,
Whether he be dead or not dead     down ere he be taken.'
    Two thieves also     suffered death that time,
Upon a cross beside Christ     so was the common law.

A catchpole came forth    and cracked both their legs,
And their arms after    of each of those thieves.
But was no boy so bold    God's body to touch;
For he was knight and king's son    nature granted that time,
That no rascal was so hardy    to lay hand upon him.
But there came forth a knight    with a keen spear ground,
Called *Longinus*, as the story telleth    and long had lost his sight.
Before Pilate and the other people    in the place he stood;
Spite his many teeth    he was made that time
To take the spear in his hand    and joust with Jesus;
For all they were afraid    that waited on horse or stood,
To touch him or to handle him    or take him down off rood.
But this blind bachelor then    struck him through the heart;
The blood sprung down by the spear    and unbarred the knight's eyes.
Then fell the knight upon knees    and cried him mercy—
'Against my will it was, lord    to wound you so sore!'
He sighed and said    'sore it methinketh;
For the deed that I have done    I deliver me to your grace;
Have on me pity, righteous Jesus!'    and right with that he wept.
    Then began Faith fiercely    the false Jews to despise,
Called them caitives    accursed for ever,
For this foul villainy    'vengeance to you all!
To make the blind beat him bound    it was a knave's counsel.
Cursed caitiff    knighthood was it never
To ill treat a dead body    by day or by night.
The prize yet hath he gained    for all his great wound.
For your champion of chivalry    chief knight of you all,
Yields him defeated in the running    right to Jesus' will.
For be this darkness done    his death will be avenged,
And ye, lordlings, have lost    for Life shall have the mastery.
And your franchise, that free was    fallen in thraldom,
And ye, churls, and your children    succeed shall ye never,
Nor have lordship in land    nor no land till,
But all barren be    and usery use,
Which is a life that our Lord    in all laws curseth.
Now your good days are done    as Daniel prophesied,
When Christ came, of their kingdom    the crown should fall;
    *Cum veniat sanctus sanctorum, cessabit unctio vestra.*'
    What with fear of this marvel    and of the false Jews,
I withdrew me in that darkness    to *descendit ad inferna.*
And there I saw sothly    *secundum scripturas,*

Out of the west        a wench, as me thought,
Came walking in the way        to Hell-ward she looked.
Mercy was called that maid        a meek thing withal,
A full benign lady        and gentle of speech.
Her sister, as it seemed        came softly walking,
Even out of the east        and westward she looked.
A full comely creature        Truth she was called,
For the virtue that her followed        afraid was she never.
When these maidens met        Mercy and Truth,
Each asked the other        of this great wonder,
Of the din and of the darkness        and how the day began to dawn,
And what a light and a brightness        lay before Hell.
'I wonder at these happenings        in faith,' said Truth,
'And am seeking to discover        what this marvel meaneth.'
'Have no wonder,' quoth Mercy        'joy it betokeneth.
A maiden called Mary        and mother without knowledge
Of any human creature        conceived through speech
And grace of the Holy Ghost        waxed great with child;
Without stain        into this world she brought him;
And that my tale be true        I take God to witness.
Since this child was born        be thirty winters passed;
Who died and death suffered        this day about midday.
And that is cause of this eclipse        that closeth now the sun,
In meaning that man shall        from darkness be drawn,
The while this light and this brightness        shall Lucifer blind.
For patriarchs and prophets        have preached hereof often,
That man shall man save        through a maiden's help,
And what was lost through tree        tree shall it win,
And what death down brought        death shall relieve.'
'What thou tellest,' quoth Truth        'is but a tale of waltrot!
For Adam and Eve        and Abraham with others,
Patriarchs and prophets·        that in pain lie,
Believe thou never that yon light        them aloft will bring,
Nor have them out of Hell        hold thy tongue, Mercy!
It is but a trifle that thou tellest        I, Truth, know the soth.
For that is once in Hell        out cometh he never;
Job the prophet, patriarch        reproveth thy sayings,
    *Quia in inferno nulla est redemptio.*'
Then Mercy full mildly        mouthed these words,
'Through experience,' quoth she        'I hope they shall be saved.
For venom undoes venom        and that I prove by reason.

For of all venoms     foulest is the scorpion,
May no medicine help     the place where he stingeth,
Till he be dead and placed thereon     the evil he destroyeth,
The first venom     through venom of himself.
So shall this death undo     I dare my life lay,
All that Death undid first     through the devil's enticing;
And right as through guile     man was beguiled,
So shall grace that began     make a good sleight;

> *Ars ut artem falleret.*'

'Now stay we,' said Truth     'I see, as methinketh,
Out of the cold of the north     not full far hence,
Righteousness come running     rest we the while;
For she knows more than we     she was ere we both.'
'That is soth,' said Mercy     'and I see here by south,
Where Peace cometh playing     in patience clothed;
Love hath coveted her long     believe I none other
But he sent her some letter     what this light meaneth,
That is over Hell thus     she us shall tell.'

When Peace, in patience clothed     approached near them twain,
Righteousness her reverenced     for her rich clothing,
And prayed Peace to tell her     to what place she went,
And in her gay garments     whom greet she thought?
'My will is to wend,' quoth she     'and welcome them all,
That many day I might not see     for murkyness of sin.
Adam and Eve     and others more in Hell,
Moses and many more     mercy shall have;
And I shall dance thereto     do thou so, sister!
For Jesus jousted well     joy beginneth to dawn;

> *Ad vesperum demorabitur fletus, et ad matutinum laetitia.*

Love, that is my lover     such letters me sent,
That Mercy, my sister, and I     mankind should save;
And that God hath forgiven     and granted me, Peace, and Mercy,
To be man's surety     for evermore after.
Lo! here the patent!' quoth Peace     '*in pace in idipsum—*
And that this deed shall endure     *dormiam et requiescam.*'

'What, ravest thou?' quoth Righteousness     'or thou art right drunk!
Believest thou that yonder light     unlock might Hell,
And save man's soul?     sister, ween it never!
At the beginning, God     gave the judgement himself,
That Adam and Eve     and all that them followed
Should die down right     and dwell in pain after,

If that they touched a tree     and the fruit ate.
Adam afterwards     against his warning,
Ate of that fruit     and forsook, as it were,
The love of our Lord     and his lore both,
And followed what the fiend taught     and his fellow's will,
Against reason, I, Righteousness     record thus with truth,
That their punishment be perpetual     and no prayer them help.
Therefore let them chew as they chose     and chide we not, sisters,
For it is helpless harm     the bite that they took.'
     'And I shall prove,' quoth Peace     'their pain must have an end,
And woe into well     must wend at last;
For had they wist of no woe     well had they not known.
For no wight knows what well is     that never woe suffered,
Nor what is called hunger     that had never lack.
If no night were     no man, as I believe,
Would know clearly     what day means;
Would never right rich man     that liveth in rest and ease
Know what woe is     except for natural death.
So God that began all     of his good will
Became man of a maid     mankind to save,
And suffered himself to be sold     to see the sorrow of dying,
The which un-knitteth all care     and commencing is of rest.
For till *modicum* meet with us     I may it well avow,
Knows no wight, as I ween     what enough means.
     'Therefore God of his goodness     the first man Adam,
Set him in solace     and in sovereign mirth;
And then he suffered him sin     sorrow to feel,
To see what well was     truly to know it.
And after, God ventured himself     and took Adam's nature,
To know what he hath suffered     in three sundry places,
Both in Heaven, and in earth     and now to Hell he thinketh,
To know what all woe is     that knew of all joy.
So it shall fare with these folk     their folly and their sin,
Shall teach them what anguish is     and bliss without end.
Knows no wight what war is     where that peace reigneth,
Nor what is indeed well     till "well-away" him teach.'
     Then was there a wight     with two broad eyes,
Book was called the *beau-père* [1]     a bold man of speech.
'By God's body,' quoth this Book     'I will bear witness,
That when this child was born     there blazed a star,

[1] See page 207.

That all the wise of this world     in one thought accorded,
That such a child was born     in Bethlehem city,
That man's soul should save     and sin destroy.
And all the elements,' quoth the Book     'hereof bear witness,
That he was God that all wrought     the welkin first showed;
Those that were in heaven     took *stella cometa*,
And kindled her as a torch     to reverence his birth;
And light followed the Lord     into the low earth.
The water witnessed that he was God     for he went on it;
Peter the apostle     perceived his going,
And as he went on the water     well him knew, and said,
     *Jube me venire ad te super aquas.*
And lo! how the sun began to lock     her light in herself,
When she saw him suffer     who sun and sea made!
The earth for heaviness     that he would suffer,
Quaked as a live thing     and all crushed the rock!
Lo! Hell might not hold     but opened when God suffered,
And let out Simeon's sons     to see him hang on rood.
And now shall Lucifer believe it     though him loth think;
For *Gigas* the giant     with a weapon made
To break and to beat down     those that be against Jesus.
And I, Book, will be burnt     but Jesus rise to live,
In all the might of man     and his mother gladden,
And comfort all his kin     and out of care bring,
And all the Jews' joy     dissolve and disjoin;
And unless they reverence his rood     and his resurrection,
And believe on a new law     be lost life and soul.'
     'Abide we,' said Truth     'I hear and see both,
How a spirit speaketh to Hell     and bids unbar the gates;
     *Attollite portas, etc.*'
A voice loud in that light     to Lucifer crieth,
'Princes of this place     unbolt and unlock!
For here cometh with crown     that king is of glory.
Then sighed Satan     and said to them all,
'Such a light, against our leave     Lazarus it fetched away;
Care and confusion     is come to us all.
If this king come in     mankind will he fetch,
And lead it where he liketh     and easily me bind.
Patriarchs and prophets     have talked hereof long,
That such a lord and a light     should lead them all hence.'
     'Listen,' quoth Lucifer     'for I this lord know,

Both this lord and this light     it is long ago I knew him.
May no death him harm     nor no devil's cunning,
And where he will, is his way     but ware him of the perils;
If he reave me of my right     he robbeth me by mastery.
For by right and by reason     those people that be here
Body and soul be mine     both good and ill.
For himself said     that sire is of heaven,
If Adam eat the apple     all should die,
And dwell with us devils     this threat he made;
And he that truth is     said these words;
And since I have been in possession     seven hundred winters,
I believe that law will not     let him in the least.'
'That is soth,' said Satan     'but I me sore dread,
For thou gained them with guile     and his garden broke,
And in semblance of a serpent     sat on the apple-tree,
And egged them on to eat     Eve by herself,
And told her a tale     of treason were the words;
And so thou haddest them out     and hither at last.
It is not easily held     where guile is the root.'
'For God will not be beguiled'     quoth Goblin, 'nor tricked;
We have no true title to them     for through treason were they damned.
'Certes, I dread me,' quoth the Devil     'lest truth will them fetch.
This thirty winter, as I ween     hath he gone and preached;
I have assailed him with sin     and at some time asked
Whether he were God or God's son?     he gave me short answer.
And thus he walked forth     this two and thirty winter,
And when I saw it was so     sleeping, I went
To warn Pilate's wife     what sort of man was Jesus;
For Jews hated him     and have done him to death.
I would have lengthened his life     for I believed, if he died,
That his soul would suffer     no sin in his sight.
For the body, while it on bones went     about was ever
To save men from sin     if they themselves would.
And now I see where a soul     cometh hitherward sailing
With glory and with great light     God it is, I know well.
I advise we flee,' quoth he     'fast all hence;
For us were better not be     than abide his sight.
For thy lies, Lucifer     lost is all our prey.
First through thee we fell     from heaven so high;
Because we believed thy lies     we leapt out all with thee,
And now for thy last lie     lost we have Adam,

And all our lordship, I believe     on land and on water;
    *Nunc princeps hujus mundi ejicietur foras.'*
    Again the light bade unlock     and Lucifer answered,
'What lord art thou?' quoth Lucifer     '*quis est iste?*'
'*Rex gloriae*'     the light soon said,
'And lord of might and of main     and all manner of virtues; *dominus*
    *virtutum;*
Dukes of this dim place     anon undo these gates,
That Christ may come in     the king's son of heaven.'
And with that breath Hell broke     and Belial's bars;
Inspite of wight or ward     wide open the gates.
Patriarchs and prophets     *populus in tenebris,*
Sang Saint John's song     '*ecce agnus Dei.*'
Lucifer might not look     so light him blinded;
And those that our Lord loved     into his light he took,
And said to Satan, 'lo! here     my soul to amend
For all sinful souls     to save those that be worthy.
Mine they be and of me     I may the better them claim.
Although reason record     and right of myself,
That if they eat the apple     all should die,
I promised them not here     Hell for ever.
For the deed that they did     thy deceit it made;
With guile thou them got     against all reason.
For in my palace, paradise     in person of an adder,
Falsely thou fetchest thence     thing that I loved.
Thus like a lizard     with a lady's visage,
Like a thief thou me robbest     the old law granteth,
That beguilers be beguiled     and that is good reason;
    *Dentem pro dente, et oculum pro oculo.*
*Ergo*, soul shall soul quit     and sin drive out sin,
And all that man hath misdone     I, man, will amend.
Member for member     by the old law made amends,
And life for life also     and by that law I claim it,
Adam and all his issue     at my will hereafter.
And what death in them undid     my death shall relieve,
And both quicken and purchase     what was destroyed through sin;
And that grace guile destroy     good faith it asketh.
So believe it not, Lucifer     that against the law I fetch them,
But by right and by reason     ransom here my lieges:
    *Non veni solvere legem, sed adimplere.*
Thou fetchest mine from my place     against all reason,

Falsely and feloniously     good faith me it taught,
To recover them through ransom     and by no reason else,
So what with guile thou got     through grace it is won.
Thou, Lucifer, in likeness     of a wicked adder,
Got by guile     those that God loved;
And I, in likeness of a man     that lord am of Heaven,
Graciously thy guile have requited     go guile against guile!
And as Adam and all     through a tree died,
Adam and all through a tree     shall turn again to life;
And guile is beguiled     and in his guile fallen:

*Et cecidit in foveam quam fecit.*

Now beginneth thy guile     against thee to turn,
And my grace to grow     ever greater and wider.
The bitterness that thou hast brewed     enjoy it thyself,
That art doctor of death     drink what thou madest!
    'For I, that am lord of life     love is my drink,
And for that drink today     I died upon earth.
I fought so, I thirst yet     for man's soul's sake;
May no drink me moist     nor my thirst slake,
Till the vintage fall     in the vale of Jehoshaphat,
And I drink right ripe must     *resurrectio mortuorum,*
And then shall I come as a king     crowned with angels,
And have out of Hell     all men's souls.
    'Fiends and fiendkins     before me shall stand,
And be at my bidding     wheresoe'er me liketh.
And to be merciful to man     then my nature asketh;
For we be bretheren of blood     but not in baptism all.
But all that be my whole bretheren     in blood and in baptism,
Shall not be damned to the death     that is without end;

    *Tibi soli peccavi, etc.*

It is not the custom on earth     to hang a felon
More than once     though he were a traitor.[1]
And if the king of that kingdom     come in that time,
Where the felon suffer should     death or otherwise,
Law wills, he give him life     if he looked on him.
And I, that am king of kings     shall come in such a time,
Where judgement to the death     damneth all wicked;
And if law wills I look on them     it lieth in my grace,
Whether they die or die not     for what they did ill.
Be it anything ransomed     the boldness of their sins,

                    [1] See page 207.

I may do mercy through righteousness     and all my words true.
And though holy writ wills that I be avenged     on them that did ill,
　　*Nullum malum impunitum, etc.*
They shall be cleansed clearly     and washed of their sins
In my prison Purgatory     till *parce* is called,
And my mercy shall be showed     to many of my bretheren.
For blood may suffer blood     both hungry and a'cold,
But blood may not see blood     bleed, without pity.
　　*Audivi arcana verba, quae non licet homini loqui.*
But my righteousness and right     shall rule all Hell,
And mercy all mankind     before me in Heaven.
For I were an unkind king     unless I my kindred helped,
And above all at such need     when help needs must come;
　　*Non intres in judicium cum servo tuo, Domine.*
Thus by law,' quoth our Lord     'lead I will from hence
Those that me loved     and believed in my coming.
And for thy lying, Lucifer     that thou told to Eve,
Thou shalt abide it bitterly'     and bound him with chains.
Ashtoreth and all the rout     hid them in corners,
They dared not look on our Lord     the boldest of them all,
But let him lead forth what he liked     and allowed him what he pleased.
　　Many hundreds of angels     harped and sung,
　　*Culpat caro, purgat caro; regnat Deus Dei caro.*
Then piped Peace     of poesy a note,
'*Clarior est solito post maxima nebula Phoebus,*
*Post inimicitias clarior est et amor.*
After sharp showers,' quoth Peace     'most glorious is the sun;
Is no weather warmer     than after watery clouds.
Nor no love dearer     nor dearer friends,
Than after war and woe     when Love and Peace be masters.
Was never war in this world     nor wickedness so keen,
That Love, if he pleased     could not bring to laughter,
And Peace through patience     all perils stopped.'
'Truce,' quoth Truth     'thou tellest us soth, by Jesus!
Clip we in covenant     and each of us kiss the other!'
'And let no people,' quoth Peace     'perceive that we chid!
For impossible is no thing     to him that is almighty.'
'Thou sayest soth,' said Righteousness     and reverently her kissed,
Peace, and Peace her     *per saecula saeculorum.*
　　*Misericordia et veritas obviaverunt sibi; justitia et pax osculatae sunt.*
Truth trumpeted then, and sang     '*Te Deum laudamus*';

And then played Love the lute    in a loud note,
  *Ecce quam bonum et jocundum, etc.*
  Till the day dawned    these damsels danced,
That men rang in the resurrection    and right with that I waked,
And called Kit my wife    and Calot my daughter—
'Arise and reverence    God's resurrection,
And creep to the cross on knees    and kiss it for a jewel! [1]
For God's blessed body    it bore for our saving,
And it frighteneth the fiend    for such is the might,
May no grisly ghost    glide near its shadow!'

[1] See page 208.

# PASSUS XIX

Thus I awoke and wrote    what I had dreamed,
And dressed me neatly    and went me to church,
To hear holy the Mass    and to be houseled after.
In midst of the Mass    when men went to the offering,
I fell again asleep    and suddenly I dreamed,
That Piers the Plowman    was painted all bloody,
And come in with a cross    before the common people,
And right like in all limbs    to our Lord Jesu;
And then called I Conscience    to teach me the truth.
'Is this Jesus the Jouster?' quoth I    'that Jews did to death?
Or it is Piers the Plowman    who painted him so red?'
Quoth Conscience, and kneeled then    'these are Piers' arms,
His colours and his coat armour    but he that cometh so bloody
Is Christ with his cross    conqueror of Christians.'
   'Why call ye him Christ?' quoth I    'since Jews call him Jesus?
Patriarchs and prophets    prophesied before,
That all kind of creatures    should kneel and bow,
Anon as men named    the name of God Jesus.
*Ergo* there is no name    like to the name of Jesus.
Nor none so needful to name    by night or by day.
For all dark devils    are adread to hear it,
And the sinful are solaced    and saved by that name,
And ye call him Christ    for what cause, tell me?
Is Christ more of might    and more worthy name
Than Jesu or Jesus    that all our joy came of?'
   'Thou knowest well,' quoth Conscience    'if thou canst reason,
That knight, king, conqueror    may be one person.
To be called a knight is fair    for men shall kneel to him;
To be called a king is fairer    for he may knights make;
But to be conqueror called    that cometh of special grace,
And of hardiness of heart    and of courtesy both,
To make lords of lads    in land that he winneth,
And free men foul thralls    that follow not his laws.
The Jews, that were gentlemen    Jesu they despised,

179

Both his lore and his law     now are they low churls.
As wide as the world is     liveth there none
But under tribute and tax     as tykes and churls.
And those that become Christians     by counsel of the Baptist,
Are franklins, free men     through baptism that they took,
And gentlemen with Jesu     for Jesus was baptised,
And upon Calvary on cross     crowned King of Jews.

'It becometh to a king     to keep and to defend,
And conqueror of conquest     his laws and his bounty.
And so did Jesus the Jews     he justified and taught them
The law of life     that last shall ever;
And defended from foul evils     fevers and fluxes,
And from fiends that in them were     and false belief.
Then was he Jesus of Jews     called gentle prophet,
And king of their kingdom     and crown bore of thorns.
And then conquered he on cross     as conqueror noble;
Might no death him undo     nor down bring,
So that he arose and reigned     and ravished hell.
And then was he conqueror called     of quick and of dead;
For he gave Adam and Eve     and others more bliss,
That long had lain before     as Lucifer's churls.

'And then he gave largely     all his loyal lieges
Places in paradise     at their going hence,
He may well be called conqueror     and that is the meaning of
Christ.[1]
But the cause that he cometh thus     with cross of his passion,
Is to teach us therewith     that when we be tempted,
Therewith to fight and defend us     from falling into sin,
And see by his sorrow     that whoso loveth joy,
To penance and to poverty     he must put himself,
And much woe in this world     accept and suffer.

'But to speak more of Christ     and how he came to that name,
Truly for to speak     his first name was Jesus.
When he was born in Bethlehem     as the Book telleth,
And came to take manhood     kings and angels
Reverenced him fair     with riches of earth.
Angels out of heaven     came kneeling and sang,
     *Gloria in excelsis Deo, etc.*
Kings came after     kneeled, and offered
Myrrh and much gold     without thanks asking,
                    [1] See page 208.

Or any kind of gift    but acknowledging him sovereign
Both of sand, sun, and sea    and after they went
To their kings' country    by counsel of angels.
And then was that word fulfilled    the which thou speakest of;
    *Omnia caelestia, terrestria, flectantur in hoc nomine Jesu.*
For all the angels of heaven    at his birth kneeled,
And all the wisdom of the world    was in those three kings;
Reason and righteousness    and pity they offered;
Wherefore and why    wise men that time,
Masters and lettered men    *Magi* them called.
The one king came with reason    signified by incense.
The second king then    truly offered
Righteousness under red gold    reason's fellow.
Gold is likened to loyalty    that last shall ever,
And reason to rich gold    to right and to truth.
The third king then came    kneeling to Jesu,
And presented him with pity    appearing as myrrh;
For myrrh is mercy in meaning    and mild speech of tongue.
Three like honest things    were offered thus at once,
Through three kin kings    kneeling to Jesu.
But for all these precious presents    our Lord Prince Jesus
Was neither king nor conqueror    till he began to grow
In the manner of a man    and that by much skill;
As it becometh a conqueror    to know many skills,
And many wiles and wit    that will be a leader;
And so did Jesu in his days    whoso had time to tell it.
Some time he suffered    and some time he hid him;
And some time he fought fast    and fled other whiles.
And sometimes he gave good    and granted health both,
Life and limb    as he pleased, he wrought.
As right is in a conqueror    so began Jesu,
Till he had all them    that he bled for.
  'In his youth this Jesus    at Jews' feast
Water into wine turned    as holy writ telleth,
And there began God    of his grace to Do-well.
For wine is likened to law    and life of holiness;
And law lacked then    for men loved not their enemies.
And Christ counselleth thus    and commandeth both,
Both to learned and unlearned    to love our enemies.
So at feast first    as I before told,
Began God, of his grace    and goodness, to Do-well:

And then was he named and called     not holy Christ, but Jesu,
A child fine, full of wit     *filius Mariae.*
For before his mother Mary     made he that wonder,
That she first and foremost     firm should believe,
That he through grace was begot     and of no person else.
He wrought that by no wit     but through word one,
According to the kind he came of     there began he Do-well.
And when he was waxed more     in his mother's absence,
He made lame to leap     and gave light to blind,
And fed with two fishes     and with five loaves
Sore hungered folk     more than five thousand.
Thus he comforted the sorrowful     and won a greater name,
The which was Do-better     wherever that he went.
For deaf through his deeds to hear     and dumb to speak he made,
And all he healed and helped     that him of grace asked.
And then was he called in country     of the common people,
For the deeds that he did     *fili David, Jesus!*
For David was doughtiest     of deeds in his time,
The maidens then sang     *Saul interfecit mille, et David decem millia;*
Therefore the country where Jesu came     called him *fili David,*
And named him of Nazareth     and no man so worthy
To be caesar or king     of the kingdom of Juda,
Over Jews a justice     as Jesus was, they thought.
Whereof Caiphas had envy     and other of the Jews,
And for to do him to death     day and night they cast about;
Killed him on cross     at Calvary on Friday,
And then buried his body     and bid that men should
Keep it from night comers     with knights armed,
For no friends should him fetch     for prophets them told,
That that blessed body     from sepulchre should rise,
And go into Galilee     and gladden his apostles,
And his mother Mary     thus men before deemed.
The knights that kept it     confessed it themselves,
That angels and archangels     ere the day dawned,
Came kneeling to the corpse     and sang, "*Christus resurgens*"
Very man before them all     and forth with them he went.
The Jews prayed them peace     and besought the knights
To tell the commons that there came     a company of his apostles,
And bewitched them as they woke     and away stole it.
But Mary Magdalen     met him by the way,
Going towards Galilee     in godhead and manhood,

And alive and looking    and she aloud cried,
In each company where she came    *"Christus resurgens!"*
Thus came it out that Christ overcame    recovered and lived;
    *Sic oportet Christum pati, et intrare, etc.;*
For what women know    may not well be judged!
Peter perceived all this    and pursued after,
Both James and John    Jesu for to seek,
Thaddeus and ten more    with Thomas of India.[1]
And as all these wise wights    were together,
In a house all shut    and their door barred,
Christ came in, and all closed    both door and gates,
To Peter and to his apostles    and said *"pax vobis!"*
And took Thomas by the hand    and taught him to grope,
And feel with his fingers    his fleshly heart.
Thomas touched it    and with his tongue said,
    *"Deus meus et dominus meus.*
Thou art my lord, I believe    God, lord Jesu!
Thou died and death suffered    and judge shall us all,
And now art living and looking    and last shall ever!"
Christ spoke then    and courteously said,
"Thomas, because thou trowest this    and truly believest it,
Blessed thou be    and be shalt for ever.
And blessed they all be    in body and in soul,
That never shall see me in sight    as thou dost now,
And loyally believe all this    I love them and bless them;
    *Beati qui non viderunt, et crediderunt, etc."*
  'And when this deed was done    Do-best he taught,
And gave Piers power    and pardon he granted
To all manner of men    mercy and forgiveness,
And might to absolve    of all manner of sins,
Under covenant that they come    and recognition pay,
To Piers' pardon the Plowman    *redde quod debes.*
Thus hath Piers power    be his pardon payed,
To bind and to unbind    both here and elsewhere,
And absolve men from all sins    save of debt alone.
Anon after on high    up into heaven
He went, and dwells there    and will come at last,
And reward him right well    that *reddit quod debet—*
Payeth perfectly    as pure truth wills.
And what person payeth it not    to punish he thinketh,
             [1] See page 208.

And judge them at doomsday    both quick and dead;
The good to the Godhead    and to great joy,
And wicked to dwell    in woe without end.'
Thus Conscience of Christ    and of the cross spoke,
And counselled me to kneel thereto    and then came, methought,
One *Spiritus Paraclitus*    to Piers and to his fellows;
In likeness of a lightning    he alighted on them all,
And made them understand and know    all kinds of language.
I wondered what that was    and shook Conscience,
And was afeared of the light    for in fire's likeness
*Spiritus Paraclitus*    over-spread them all.

   Quoth Conscience, and kneeled    'this is Christ's messenger,
And cometh from the great God    and Grace is his name.
Know now,' quoth Conscience    'and if thou canst sing,
Welcome him and worship him    with "*Veni, Creator Spiritus*."'
Then sung I that song    and so did many hundred,
And cried with Conscience    'help us, God of grace!'
And then began Grace    to go with Piers Plowman,
And counselled him and Conscience    the commons to summon—
'For I will deal today    and divide grace,
To all kind of creatures    that have their five wits,
Treasure to live by    to their lives' end,
And a weapon to fight with    that will never fail.
For Antichrist and his own    all the world shall grieve,
And encumber thee, Conscience    unless Christ thee help.
And false prophets many    flatterers and liars
Shall come, and be masters    over kings and earls,
And Pride shall be pope    prince of holy church,
Covetousness and Unkindness    cardinals him to lead.
Therefore,' quoth Grace, 'ere I go    I will give you treasure,
And a weapon to fight with    when Antichrist you assaileth.'
And gave each man a grace    to guide himself with,
That idleness encumber him not    envy, nor pride,
    *Divisiones gratiarum sunt, etc.*
   Some he gave wit    with words to show,
Wit to win their livelihood with    as the world asketh,
As preachers and priests    and prentices of law,
They honestly to live    by labour of tongue,
And by wit to show others    as Grace them would teach.
And some he taught craft    and cunning of sight,
With selling and buying    their livelihood to win,

And some he taught to labour    a loyal life and a true,
And some he taught to till    to ditch and to thatch,
To win with it their livelihood    by lore of his teaching.
And some to divine and divide    numbers to know;
And some to compass craftily    and colours to make;
And some to see and to say    what should befall,
Both of well and of woe    tell it ere it fell,
As astronomers through astronomy    and philosophers wise.
And some to ride and recover    what unrightfully was won;
He taught them to win it again    through quickness of hands,
And fetch it from false men    with Folville's laws.[1]
And some he taught to live    in longing to be hence,
In poverty and in penitence    to pray for all Christians.
And all he taught to be loyal    and each craft love the other,
And forbade them all strife    that none is among them.
'Though some be cleaner than some    ye see well,' quoth Grace,
'That he that useth the fairest craft    to the foulest I could have put
him,
Think all,' quoth Grace    'that grace cometh as my gift;
Look that none blame other    but love all as bretheren.
And who that most masteries has    be mildest of bearing,
And crown Conscience king    and make Craft your steward,
And after Craft's counsel    clothe you and feed.
For I make Piers the Plowman    my proctor and my reeve,
And registrar to receive    *redde quod debes.*
My purveyor and my plowman    Piers shall be on earth,
And for to till truth    a team shall he have.'
    Grace gave Piers a team    four great oxen;
The one was Luke, a large beast    and a mild faced,
And Mark, and Matthew the third    mighty beasts both,
And joined to them one John    most gentle of all,
The prize ox of Piers' plow    passing all other.
    And Grace gave Piers    of his goodness, four horses,
All that his oxen plowed    they were to harrow after.
One was called Austin    and Ambrose another,
Gregory the great clerk    and Jerome the good;
These four, the faith to teach    follow Piers' team,
And harrowed in a hand's space    all holy scripture,
With two harrows that they had    an old and a new,
    *Id est, vetus testamentum et novum.*

[1] See page 208.

And Grace gave grain    the cardinal virtues,
And sowed them in man's soul    and then he told their names.
*Spiritus prudentiae*    the first seed was called,
And whoso ate that    imagine he should,
Ere he did any deed    devise well the end;
And taught men a ladle to buy    with a long handle,
That mean for to keep a crock    to save the fat on top.

The second seed was called    *spiritus temperantiae.*
He that ate of that seed    had such a nature,
Should never meat nor much drink    make him to swell,
Nor should no scorner nor scold    our of reason him bring,
Nor winning, nor wealth    of worldly riches,
Waste words of idleness    nor wicked speech move;
Should no curious cloth    come on his back,
Nor no meat in his mouth    that Master John spiced.

The third seed that Piers sowed    was *spiritus fortitudinis.*
And whoso ate of that seed    hardy was ever
To suffer all that God sent    sickness and miseries;
Might no falsehood nor liar    nor loss of worldly goods
Make for him any mourning    that he was not merry in soul,
And bold and abiding    revilings to suffer,
And playeth all with patience    *et parce mihi, Domine,*
And covered him under the counsel    of Cato the wise;
*Esto forti animo, cum sis damnatus inique.*

The fourth seed that Piers sowed    was *spiritus justitiae,*
And he that ate of that seed    should be ever true
With God, and not afraid    save of guile alone.
For guile goeth so privily    that good faith at times
May not be espied    by *spiritus justitiae.*
*Spiritus justitiae*    spareth not to over-spill
Them that be guilty    and for to correct
The king, if he fall    into guilt or in trespass.
For counteth he no king's wrath    when he in court sitteth
To judge as a judge    adread was he never,
Neither of duke nor of death    that he administered not the law,
For present or for prayer    or any prince's letters;
He gives equity to all    according to his power.

These four seeds Piers sowed    and then he did them harrow
With old law and new law    that love might grow
Among the four virtues    and vices destroy.
For commonly in countries    rest harrow and weeds

Foul the fruit in the field    where they grow together;
And so do vices    virtues worthy.
Quoth Piers, 'harrow all that have common wit    by counsel of these
doctors,
And till according to their teaching    the cardinal virtues.'
'When thy grains,' quoth Grace    'begin for to ripen,
Build thee a house, Piers    to harbour in thy corn.'
'By God! Grace,' quoth Piers    'you must give timber,
And build that house    ere you hence wend.'
And Grace gave him the cross    with the crown of thorns,
That Christ upon Calvary    for mankind suffered on,
And of his baptism and blood    that he bled on rood
He made a kind of mortar    and Mercy it was called.
And therewith Grace began    to make a good foundation,
And wattled it and walled it    with his pains and his passion,
And of all holy writ    he made a roof after,
And called that house Unity    Holy Church in English.
And when this deed was done    Grace devised
A cart, called Christendom    to carry Piers' sheaves;
And gave him horses to his cart    Contrition and Confession,
And made Priesthood overseer    the while himself went
As wide as the world is    with Piers to till truth.
    Now is Piers to the plow    and Pride it espied,
And gathered him a great host    to grieve he thinketh
Conscience and all Christians    and cardinal virtues,
Blow them down and break them    and bite asunder the roots;
And sent forth Arrogance    his serjeant at arms,
And his spy Spill-love    one Speak-evil-secretly.
These two came to Conscience    and to Christian people,
And told them tidings    'that lay waste they should the seeds,
That Piers there had sown    the cardinal virtues;
And Piers' barn will be broken    and they that be in Unity
Shall come out, and Conscience    and your two horses,
Confession and Contrition    and your cart the Faith
Shall be coloured so quaintly    and covered under our sophistry,
That Conscience shall not    know by Contrition,
Nor by Confession    who is Christian or heathen,
Nor no manner of merchant    that with money dealeth,
Whether he win by honesty    or by wrong or by usury.
With such colours and cunning    cometh Pride armed,
With the lord that liveth after    the lust of the body,

To waste, on fine living    and on wicked keeping,
All the world in a while    through our wit,' quoth Pride.

    Quoth Conscience to all Christians then    'my counsel is to wend
Hastily into Unity    and hold we us there,
And pray we that a peace were    in Piers' barn the Plowman.
For truly I wot well    we be not of strength
To go against Pride    unless Grace be with us.'
And then came Kind Wit    Conscience to teach,
And cried and commanded    all Christian people,
For to delve a ditch    deep about Unity,
So that Holy Church stood on Unity    as it a pile were.
Conscience commanded then    all Christians to delve,
And make a great moat    that might be a strength,
To help Holy Church    and them that it keepeth.
Then all kinds of Christians    save common women,
Repented and refused sin    save they alone;
And false men, flatterers    usurers and thieves,
Liars and inquest mongers    that were forsworn oft,
Wittingly and wilfully    with the false held,
And for silver were forsworn    truly they knew it.
There was no Christian creature    that kind wit had,
Save shrews alone    such as I spake of,
That did not help a quantity    holiness to increase.
Some through bead bidding    and some through pilgrimage,
And others private penance    and some through alms giving.
And then welled water    for wicked works,
Bitterly running    out of men's eyes.
Cleanness of the commons    and clerks' clean living
Made Unity Holy Church    in holiness to stand.
'I care not,' quoth Conscience    'though Pride come now,
The lord of lust shall be stopped    all this Lent, I hope.
Come,' quoth Conscience    'ye Christians, and dine,
That have laboured loyally    all this Lent time.
Here is bread blessed    and God's body thereunder.
Grace through God's word    gave Piers power,
And might to make it    and men to eat it after,
In help of their health    once in a month,
Or as oft as they had need    those that had payed
To Piers' pardon the Plowman    *redde quod debes.*'
'How?' quoth all the commons    'thou counselled us to yield
All that we owe any wight    are we going to housel?'

'That is my counsel,' quoth Conscience    'and cardinal virtues,
That each man forgive other    and that wills the *pater noster*,
    *Et dimitte nobis debita nostra, etc.*,
And so to be absolved    and then be houseled.'
  'Yea, bah!' quoth a brewer    'I will not be ruled,
By Jesu! for all your jangling    with *spiritus justitiae*,
Nor according to Conscience, by Christ    while I can sell
Both dregs and draff    and draw it at a hole,
Thick ale and thin ale    for that is my nature,
And not hack after holiness    hold thy tongue, Conscience.
Of *spiritus justitiae*    thou speakest much idly!'
'Caitiff,' quoth Conscience    'cursed wretch!
Unblessed art thou, brewer    unless thee God help;
Unless thou live by lore    of *spiritus justitiae*,
The chief seed that Piers sowed    saved wilt thou be never.
Unless Conscience the commons feed    and cardinal virtues,
Believe it well they be lost    both life and soul.'
'Then is many man lost,'    quoth an ignorant vicar,
'I am a pastor of Holy Church    and came never in my time
Man to me, that me could tell    of cardinal virtues,
Or that accounted Conscience    at a cock's feather or a hen's!
I knew never cardinal    that came not from the pope,
And we clerks, when they come    for their provisions pay,
For their fur and their palfreys' meat    and pillagers that them follow.
The commons *clamat cotidie*    each man to other,
"The country is the curseder    that cardinals come in;
And where they lie and linger most    lechery there reigneth:"—
Therefore,' quoth this vicar    'by very God, I would
That no cardinal come    among the common people,
But in their holiness    hold them still
At Avignon, among the Jews    *cum sancto sanctus eris, etc.*,
Or in Rome, as their rule will    the relics to keep;
And thou, Conscience, in king's court    and should never come thence,
And Grace, that thou praisest so    guide of all clerks,
And Piers with his new plow    and also with his old,
Emperor of all the world    and that all men were Christian!
Imperfect is that pope    that all people should help,
And sends them that slay such    as he should save;
And well for Piers the Plowman    that pursueth God in doing,
*Qui pluit super justos    et injustos* at once,
And sends the sun to save    a cursed man's tilth,

As bright as to the best man      and to the best woman.
Right so Piers the Plowman      works to till
As well for a waster      and wenches of the stews,
As for himself and his servants      save that he is first served;
And travaileth and tilleth      for a traitor as hard
As for a true honest man      all times alike.

And worshipped be he that wrought all      both good and wicked,
And suffereth the sinful      till some time that they repent.
And God amend the pope      that pillages Holy Church,
And claimeth before the king      to be keeper over Christians,
Yet counteth not though Christians      be killed and robbed,
And finds folk to fight      and Christian blood to spill,
Against the old law and new      as Luke thereof witnesseth,
    *Non occides: mihi vindictam, etc.*
It seemeth, if so      he had his will,
That he recketh right naught      of all the remnant.
And Christ of his courtesy      the cardinals save,
And turn their minds to wisdom      and to weal of soul!
For the commons,' quoth this curate      'count full little
The counsel of Conscience      or cardinal virtues,
Unless they see by sight      something to win;
Of guile nor of lying      care they never a jot.
For *spiritus prudentiae*      among the people, is guile,
And all those fair virtues      as vices they seem;
Each man devises a sleight      sin for to hide,
And disguises it as a clever      and a clean living.'

    Then laughed there a lord      and 'by this light,' said,
'I hold it right and reason      of my reeve to take
All that mine auditor      or else my steward
Counselleth me by their account      and my clerk's writing.
With *spiritus intellectus*      they seek the reeve's rolls,
And with *spiritus fortitudinis*      fetch it I will.'

    And then came there a king      and of his crown said,
'I am king with crown      the commons to rule,
And Holy Church and clergy      from cursed men to defend.
And if me lacketh to live by      the law wills I take it,
Where I may soonest it have      for I am head of law;
For ye be but members      and I above all.
And since I am head of you all      I am health of you all,
And Holy Church's chief help      and chieftain of the commons.
And what I take of you two      I take it at teaching

Of *spiritus justitiae*    for I judge you all;
So I may boldly be houseled    for I borrow never,
Nor crave of my commons    but as my status asks.'
   'On condition,' quoth Conscience    'that thou canst defend
And rule thy realm in reason    right well, and in truth,
Take thou may in reason    as thy law asketh;
    *Omnia tua sunt ad defendum, sed non ad depraedandum.'*
The vicar had far to go home    and fair took his leave,
And I awakened therewith    and wrote as I had dreamed.

# PASSUS XX

THEN as I went by the way    when I was thus awaked,
Heavy-cheered I journeyed    and sad in heart;
I knew not where to eat    nor at what place.
And it came nigh the noon    and with Need I met,
That affronted me foully    and deceiver me called.
'Could'st thou not excuse thee    as did the king and others,
That thou took for thy livelihood    for clothes and for sustenance,
As by teaching and by telling    of *spiritus temperantiae*,
And thou seized no more    than Need thee taught,
And need hath no law    nor never shall fall in debt?
For three things he taketh    his life for to save,
That is, meat, when men him denieth    as he no money wieldeth,
Nor none will be his surety    nor pledge hath none to lay.
And he takes in that case    and comes thereto by sleight,
He sinneth not truly    that so winneth his food.
And though he come so to clothes    and can have no better bargain,
Need right at once    takes him under surety.
And if he wishes to lap    the law of kind wills
That he drink at each ditch    ere he for thirst died.
So Need, at great need    may take him as for his own,
Without counsel of Conscience    or cardinal virtues,
As long as he follow and guard    *spiritus temperantiae*.
For is no virtue by far    like *spiritus temperantiae*,
Neither *spiritus justitiae*    nor *spiritus fortitudinis*.
For *spiritus fortitudinis*    fails full oft,
He shall do more than measure    many time and oft,
And beat men over bitterly    and some of them too little,
And grieves men greater    than good faith wishes.
And *spiritus justitiae*    shall judge, willy nilly,
After the king's counsel    and the commons' will.
And *spiritus prudentiae*    in many a point shall fail
In what he thinks will happen    if it were not for his wit.
Weening is no wisdom    nor wise imagination,
*Homo proponit et Deus disponit*    and governeth all good virtues.
But Need is next to him    for anon he makes men meek,

And as low as a lamb    for the lack of what they need.
Wise men forsook wealth    for they would be needy,
And dwelt in wilderness    and would not be rich.
And God all his great joy    in heaven he left,
And came and took manhood    and became needy.
So needy he was, as saith the Book    in many sundry places,
That he said in his sorrow    on the rood itself,[1]
"Both fox and fowl    may fly to hole and creep,
And the fish hath fin    to swim with to rest,
But need hath seized me    so that I must need abide,
And suffer sorrow's full sorrow    that shall to joy turn."
Therefore be not abashed    to beg and to be needy;
Since he that made all the world    was by will needy,
Nor never none so needy    nor poorer died.'
    When Need had corrected me thus    anon I fell asleep,
And dreamed full marvellously    that, in man's form,
Antichrist came then    and all the crop of truth
Turned it upside-down    and overturned the root,
And made falsehood spring and spread    and increased men's needs;
In each country where he came    he cut away truth,
And made guile grow there    as he a god were.
Friars followed that fiend    for he gave them copes,
And religious reverenced him    and rang their bells,
And all the convent forth came    to welcome that tyrant,
And all his as well as him    save only fools;
Which fools were well liefer    to die than to live
Longer, since loyalty    was so rebuked.
And a false fiend Antichrist    over all folk reigned;
And those who were mild men and holy    and no mischief feared,
Defied all falseness    and folk that it used;
And whatever king them supported    knowing them any while,
They cursed, and their counsellors    whether clerk or unlearned.
    Antichrist had thus soon    hundreds at his banner,
And Pride it bore    boldly about,
With a lord that liveth    after liking of body,
That came against Conscience    that keeper was and guide
Over Christian people    and cardinal virtues.
'I counsel,' quoth Conscience then    'come with me, ye fools,
Into Unity Holy Church    and hold we us there,
And cry we to Nature    that he come and defend us,

[1] See page 208.

O 571

Fools, from this fiend's limbs     for Piers' love the Plowman.
And cry we to all the commons     that they come to Unity,
And there abide and bicker     against Belial's children.'
     Nature Conscience then heard     and came out of the planets,
And sent forth his messengers     fevers and fluxes,
Coughs and spasms     cramps and toothaches,
Rheums and running sores     and dirty scabs,
Boils and swellings     and burning agues;
Frenzies and foul evils     foragers of Nature,
Had pricked and preyed upon     the polls of people,
That fully a legion     lost their lives soon.
There was—'harrow and help!     here cometh Nature,
With Death that is dreadful     to undo us all!'
The lord that lived after lust     then aloud cried
After Comfort, a knight     to come and bear his banner.
'Alarm! alarm!' quoth that lord     'each man for himself!'
And then encountered these men     ere minstrels might pipe,
And ere heralds at arms     had named the champions.
     Age the hoary     he was in the vanguard,
And bore the banner before Death     by right he it claimed.
Nature came after     with many keen sores,
As pox and pestilences     and many people destroyed;
So Nature through corruptions     killed full many.
Death came driving after     and all to dust pashed
Kings and knights     caesars and popes;
Learned nor ignorant     he let no man stand,
Those he hit evenly     never stirred after.
Many a lovely lady     and lovers of knights
Swooned and died     for sorrow of Death's blows.
     Conscience of his courtesy     to Nature besought
To cease and hold     and see whether they would
Leave Pride privily     and be perfect Christians.
And Nature ceased then     to see the people amend.
Fortune began to flatter then     those few that were alive,
And promised them long life     and Lechery he sent
Amongst all manner of men     wedded and unwedded,
And gathered a great host     all against Conscience.
This Lechery laid on     with a laughing cheer,
And with privy speech     and painted words,
And armed him with idleness     and with high bearing.
He bore a bow in his hand     and many bloody arrows,

Were feathered with fair promise    and many a false truth.
And with his low tales    he troubled full oft
Conscience and his company    of Holy Church the teachers.
   Then came Covetousness    and cast about how he might
Overcome Conscience    and cardinal virtues,
And armed him in avarice    and greedily lived.
His weapon was all wiles    to win and to hide;
With lyings and with deceits    he beguiled the people.
Simony sent him    to assail Conscience,
And he preached to the people    and prelates they made,
To hold with Antichrist    their temporal power to save;
And he came to the king's counsel    as a bold baron,
And kneeled to Conscience    in court before them all,
And made Good Faith flee    and False to abide,
And boldly bore down    with many a bright noble
Much of the wit and wisdom    of Westminster hall.
He jogged to a justice    and jousted in his ear,
And overturned all his truth    with 'take-this-recompense.'
And to the court of the arches hastily    he went anon after,
And turned civil law into simony    and then won over the official;
For a mantle of miniver    he made true matrimony
Depart ere death came    and divorces made.
   'Alas!' quoth Conscience, and cried then    'would Christ, of his
grace,
That Covetousness were Christian    that is so keen a fighter,
And bold and abiding    while his purse lasteth!'
And then laughed Life    and had his clothes decorated,
And armed him in haste    in worthless words,
And held Holiness a joke    and Kindness a waster,
And looked on Loyalty as a churl    and Liar a free man;
Conscience and counsel    he counted it folly.
Thus rallied Life    at a little fortune,
And pricked forth with Pride    praiseth he no virtue,
He careth not how Nature slew    and shall come at last,
And kill all earthly creatures    save Conscience alone.
Life leapt aside    and took him a lover,
'Health and I,' quoth he    'and highness of heart
Shall make thee dread not    either Death or Age,
And to forget sorrow    and care naught of sin.'
This Life liked    and his lover Fortune,
And they begot in their glory    a vagabond at last,

One that much woe wrought     Sloth was his name.
Sloth waxed wondrous fast     and soon was of age,
And wedded one Wanhope     a wench of the stews;
Her sire was a jury-man     that never swore truth,
One Thomas Two-tongue     attainted at each inquest.
This Sloth was wary in war     and a sling made,
And threw dread of despair     a dozen miles around.
For care Conscience then     cried upon Age,
And bade him try to fight     and frighten Wanhope.
        And Age took good hope     and hastily shifted himself,
And waved away Wanhope     and with Life he fighteth.
And Life fled for fear     to Physic for help,
And besought him for succour     and of salve had,
And gave him gold, good measure     that gladdened his heart
And they gave him in return     a glass hood.
Life believed that leech-craft     would stay Age,
And drive away Death     with medicines and drugs.
        And Age adventured against Life     and at last he hit
A physician with a furred hood     so that he fell into a palsy
And there died that doctor     ere three days after.
'Now I see,' said Life     'that surgery nor physic
May not a mite avail     to meddle against Age.'
And in hope of his health     good heart he took,
And rode so to Revel     a rich place and a merry;
The company of comfort     men called it sometimes.
And Age came anon after me     and over my head went,
And made me bald in front     and bare on the crown,
So hard he went over my head     it will be seen ever.
'Sir evil-taught Age,' quoth I     'ill ways go with thee!
Since when was the way     over men's heads?
Had'st thou been polite,' quoth I     'thou would'st have asked leave!'
'Yea! dear lazy-bones!' quoth he     and laid on me with age,
And hit me under the ear     hardly can I hear;
He buffeted me about the mouth     and beat out my teeth,
And fettered me in gout     I may not go at large.
And of the woe that I was in     my wife had pity,
And wished full well     that I were in heaven.
For the limb that she loved me for     and glad was to feel,
On nights indeed     when we naked were,
I might not in no manner     make it serve her will,
So Age and she truly     had it enfeebled.

And as I sat in this sorrow     I saw how Nature passed,
And Death drew nigh me     for dread I began to quake,
And cried to Nature     out of care me to bring.
'Lo! Age the hoary     hath me beset,
Avenge me, if your will be     for I would be hence.'
'If thou wilt be avenged     wend into Unity,
And hold thee there ever     till I send for thee,
And look thou learn some craft     ere thou come thence.'
'Counsel me, Nature,' quoth I     'what craft is best to learn?'
'Learn to love,' quoth Nature     'and leave all others.'
'How shall I come to goods so     to clothe me and to feed?'
'If thou love truly,' quoth he     'lack shall thee never
Meat nor worldly weeds     while thy life lasteth.'
And there, by counsel of Nature     I began to roam
Through Contrition and Confession     till I came to Unity;
And there was Conscience constable     Christians to save,
And it was besieged sothly     with seven great giants,
That with Antichrist held     hard against Conscience.
    Sloth with his sling     a hard assault he made,
Proud priests came with him     more than a thousand,
In cloaks and peaked shoes     and pissers' long knives,
Came against Conscience     with Covetousness they held.
'By Mary,' quoth a cursed priest     of the march of Ireland,
'I count no more Conscience     if so I catch silver,
Than I do to drink     a draught of good ale!'
And so said sixty     of the same country;
And shot against him with shot     many a sheaf of oaths;
And broad hooked arrows     God's hurt, and his nails,
And had almost Unity     and holiness down.
    Conscience cried, 'help     Clergy, or else I fall
Through imperfect priests     and prelates of holy church.'
Friars heard him cry     and came him to help,
But as they knew not well their craft     Conscience forsook them.
Need came then near     and Conscience he told
That they come for covetousness     to have cure of souls—
'And if they are poor, by chance     for patrimony them lacketh,
They will flatter, to fare well     folk that be rich;
And since they chose chill     and low poverty,
Let them chew as they chose     and charge them with no cure!
For oftener he lieth     that livelihood must beg,
Than he that laboureth for livelihood     and giveth to beggars.

And since friars forsook     earthly felicity,
Let them be as beggars     or live by angels' food!'
    Conscience at this counsel then     began to laugh,
And courteously comforted them     and called in all friars,
And said, 'sirs, sothly     welcome be ye all
To Unity and Holy Church     but one thing I you pray,
Hold you in Unity     and have no envy
Of learned or of unlearned     but live after your rule.
And I will be your bail     ye shall have bread and clothes,
And other necessities enough     you shall no thing lack,
If that ye leave logic     and learn for to love.
For love left they lordship     both land and school,
Friar Francis and Dominic     for love to be holy,
And if ye coveteth a cure     Kind will you teach,
That in measure God made     all manner of things,
And set them at a certain     and at a fixed number,
And named names new     and numbered the stars;
        *Qui numerat multitudinem stellarum, et omnibus eis nomina, etc.*
Kings and knights     that keep and defend,
Have officers under them     and each of them numbered;
And if they wage men to war     they write them in number,
Or will no money them pay     travail they never so sore.
All others in battle     be held robbers,
Thieves and plunderers     in each place cursed.
Monks and nuns     and all men of religion
Their order and their rule wills     to have a fixed number.
Of unlearned and of learned     the law wills and asketh
A fixed number for a certain order     save only among friars!
Therefore,' quoth Conscience, 'by Christ     kind wit me telleth,
It is wicked to pay you     ye grow out of number!
Heaven hath an even number     and hell is without number;
Therefore I would indeed     that ye were in the register,
And your number under notary's seal     and neither more nor less!'
    Envy heard this     and bade friars go to college,
And learn logic and law     and also the contemplative life,
And preach to men of Plato     and prove it by Seneca,
That all things under heaven     ought to be in common.
    And yet he lieth, as I believe     that to the ignorant so preacheth,
For God made to men a law     and Moses it taught,
        *Non concupisces rem proximi tui.*
And evil is this held     in parishes of England,

For parsons and parish priests    that should the people shrive,
Be pastors called    to know and to heal,
All that be their parishioners    penance to enjoin,
And they should be ashamed at their confession    but shame makes
                                            them go,

And flee to the friars    as false folk do to Westminster,
That borrow and bear it thither    and then ask friends
Earnestly for forgiveness    or a further year's loan.
But while he is in Westminster    he will be ahead,
And make him merry    with other men's goods.
And so it fareth with many folk    that to the friars confesseth,
As jurymen and executors    they will give the friars
A portion to pray for them    and make themselves merry
With the residue and the remnant    for which other men laboured,
And leave the dead man in debt    to the day of doom.

   Envy therefore    hated Conscience,
And friars for philosophy    he founded them colleges
The while Covetousness and Unkindness    Conscience assailed.
In Unity Holy Church    Conscience held him,
And made Peace porter    to bar the gates
Against all tale tellers    and idle tattlers.
Hypocrisy and he    a hard battle they had.
Hypocrisy at the gate    hard began to fight,
And wounded very wickedly    many a wise teacher,
That with Conscience accorded    and with cardinal virtues.
Conscience called a leech    that could well shrive,
'Go salve those that sick be    and through sin wounded.'
Shift shaped a sharp salve    and made men do penance
For their misdeeds    that they wrought had,
So that Piers was payed    *redde quod debes.*

   Some liked not this leech    and letters they sent,
If any surgeon were in the town    that softer could plaster.
Sir Lief-to-live-in-lechery    lay there and groaned;
For fasting of a Friday    he behaved as he would die.
'There is a surgeon in this town    that soft can handle,
And more of physic knows by far    and fairer he plastereth;
One friar Flatterer    is physician and surgeon.'
Quoth Contrition to Conscience    'let him come to Unity,
For here is many a man    hurt through Hypocrisy.'
'We have no need,' quoth Conscience    'I know no better leech
Than parson or parish priest    confessor or bishop,

Save Piers the Plowman that hath power over them all,
And indulgences may give unless debt prevent it.
I will allow,' quoth Conscience 'since ye desire,
That friar Flatterer be fetched and physic you sick.'

 The friar heard hereof and hied fast
To a lord for a letter leave to have to cure,
As if a curate he were and came with his letters
Boldly to the bishop and his brief had,
In countries where he came into confessions to hear;
And came where Conscience was and knocked at the gate.
Peace unbarred it was porter of Unity,
And in haste asked 'what his will were?'
'In faith,' quoth this friar 'for profit and for health
Speak I would with Contrition and therefore come I hither.
'He is sick,' said Peace 'and so are many others,
Hypocrisy hath hurt him full hardly will they recover.'
'I am a surgeon,' said the man 'and salves can make;
Conscience knoweth me well and what I can do too.'
'I pray thee,' quoth Peace then 'ere thou pass further,
What art thou called? I pray thee hide not thy name.'
'Certes,' said this fellow 'sir *Penetrans-domos*.'
'Yea, go thy ways,' quoth Peace 'by God, for all thy physic,
Unless thou know some craft thou comest not herein!
I knew such a one once not eight winters past,
Came in thus coped at a court where I dwelt,
And was my lord's leech and my lady's both.
And at last this begging friar when my lord was out,
He salved so our women till some were with child!'
Mild-speech told Peace open the gates—
'Let in the friar and his fellow and make them fair cheer.
He may see and hear so it may befall,
That Life through his lore shall leave Covetousness,
And be afeared of Death and withdraw him from Pride,
And accord with Conscience and kiss each the other.'
 Thus through Mild-speech entered the friar,
And came in to Conscience and courteously him greeted.
'Thou art welcome,' quoth Conscience 'canst thou heal the sick?
Here is Contrition,' quoth Conscience 'my cousin, wounded;
Comfort him,' quoth Conscience 'and take care of his sores.
The plasters of the parson and powders bite sore,
He lets them lie over long and loth is to change them;

From Lent to Lent     he lets his plasters bite.'
'That is over long,' quoth this friar     'I believe I shall amend it';—
And goeth and graspeth Contrition     and gave him a plaster
Of 'a privy payment     and I shall pray for you,
For all that ye be held for     all my life time,
And make you my lady     in mass and in matins,
As friars of our fraternity     for a little silver.'
Thus he goeth and gathereth     and lieth where he shriveth,
Till Contrition had clean forgotten     to cry and to weep,
And lie awake for his wicked works     as he was wont to do.
For comfort of his confessor     Contrition he left,
That is sovereignest salve     for all kind of sins.
    Sloth saw that     and so did Pride,
And came with a keen will     Conscience to assail.
Conscience cried then     and bade Clergy help him,
And also Contrition     for to keep the gate.
'He lieth and dreameth,' said Peace     'and so do many others;
The friar with his physic     this folk hath enchanted,
And plastered them so pleasantly     they dread no sin.'
'By Christ,' quoth Conscience then     'I will become a pilgrim,
And walk as wide     as all the world lasteth,
To seek Piers the Plowman     that Pride will destroy,
And that friars may have provision     that for need flatter,
And oppose me, Conscience     now Kind me avenge,
And send me good fortune and health     till I have Piers the Plowman!'
And so he cried after grace     till I began to wake.

*Explicit hic dialogus Petri Plowman.*

# NOTES

[Page 2.] *Friars*.  The friars preachers: Dominicans (Black friars), Franciscans (Grey friars or friars Minor), Carmelites (White friars), and the Augustinians (Austin friars).  They were mendicant, peripatetic, pastoral, and preaching clergy with certain monastic obligations, and so to be distinguished from the monks, who are not essentially priests and whose activities do not normally extend beyond the monastery walls.  Langland is by no means the only medieval writer to castigate the particular abuses which their way of life and uncontrolled numbers gave rise to.

[Page 2.] *Pardoner*.  A pardoner was licensed by ecclesiastical authority to preach and collect money for a specified object (e.g. to build a church or a bridge), for contributing to which a pardon (see note to page 18) was attached. This name and office was abolished entirely by the Council of Trent in 1563.

[Page 3.] *Bachelors*.  Bachelors, masters, and doctors signify priests with various degrees—such as B.A., M.A., Ph.D., as we still know them—obtained from a university.  The normal education of a priest was gained at a university, and the division between learning and the priesthood was hardly, in theory, conceivable; so we find Langland using 'Clergy' to signify both simultaneously. The whole idea of secular knowledge as against an especial form of priestly education has grown to its modern proportions steadily since the Renaissance, the Reformation, the scientific movement, and the reactions they produced in the Christian church.

[Page 4.] The general moral of this ancient fable of 'belling the cat' is clear. In its special application here the rats are the burgesses and weighty commons, the mice the lesser folk, the cat King Edward III, the kitten his grandson, the future Richard II.

[Page 10.] *Natural knowing*.  Langland has 'kind knowing,' and a treatise could be written on the use and meaning of the word 'kind' both in medieval literature and later.  It always has a connection with that which is natural and proper to the person in question as such, to a person as a man, for instance, or to God as God.  'Kind' as a noun can mean nature just, or the God who is the life of nature.  Here 'kind knowing' means an instinctive knowledge, proper to a man, of the first general principles of moral action; not conscience, but the principles conscience judges by.

[Page 13.] *Meed*.  Meed is reward; not necessarily a bad thing, but often misused and hence becoming something like bribery or, in a more general sense, graft.

[Page 14.] *Summoners*.  Officers who called persons before the ecclesiastical courts.  Such a court was the *Arches*, which is still in existence.  This court dealt with such things as deciding the validity of marriages, on which only the church could pronounce, and it appears to have been particularly open to blatant bribery and corruption.

[Page 17.] *Paulines*.  Referred to in medieval writing both as friars and hermits.

[Page 18.] *Pardons*.  Pardons, or indulgences, originated in the early days of Christianity as remissions of the sometimes very rigorous and public penances imposed on individuals for heinous offences.  In the Middle Ages, and still, they are remissions of the temporal punishment due to those sins of which the guilt has been forgiven (normally by confession and absolution), granted by the Church and ratified by God. Because of the origin, the amount of remission is expressed in terms of time, i.e. a hundred days (originally a hundred days off your long public penance). The common medieval custom of granting indulgences in return for, say, alms-giving to some good cause, was obviously easily abused, and all such indulgences or pardons where revoked by Pope Pius V, in 1567.

[Page 25.] *Regum.* The Book of Kings.

[Page 26.] *Placebo.* A colloquial term for the Office of the Dead. 'David' in the next line means the psalms, which were commonly all ascribed to David. The psalms form a major part of the office, the daily prayer of the Church; and of course the passage is telling priests to say or sing the office as they should instead of spending their time in sport.

[Page 27.] This sort of prophecy, with its semi-magical incantation, was popular. They may or may not have been intended to be clear at the time; they certainly are not to us. This one refers to the conversion of the Jews, infidels and Mohammedans at some future date; 'the full of the moon' is the full moon of Easter, the time of our redemption.

[Page 31.] *Recordare.* A name, from the first word of the introit—the 'entering' psalm at the beginning of the Mass, which varies according to the day—from the Mass for avoidance of death and plague.

[Page 33.] *Pestilences.* A reference to the recurrent epidemics of the plague, the 'Black Death,' which decimated the population of England during the fourteenth century, causing, among other things, widespread social changes. The 'south-west wind' in the following line is usually identified with a great storm on 15th January 1362, and thus becomes a significant clue in attempts to date the poem.

[Page 33.] *Women's punishment.* This is probably the ducking-stool, the popular and uncomfortable punishment for a scold.

[Page 36.] *Diapenidion.* An emollient medicine.

[Page 36.] *Limiters and lectors.* A limiter was a friar with a limited district in which to beg. A lector is probably the holder of an academic degree, that is, a Lector in Sacred Theology.

[Page 37.] Here is no question of ordaining women. Many abbesses and prioresses of the Middle Ages exercised complete temporal jurisdiction and tried to stretch their spiritual authority to match it, especially by claiming to 'hear confessions.' These had to be restrained by church authorities.

[Page 39.] *Rood of Bromholm.* One of the many English shrines of popular pilgrimage. Walsingham is also mentioned, which is becoming a centre of pilgrimage again in the twentieth century with its increasing revival of medieval Catholic practices.

[Page 41.] *'New fair' game.* Explanations of this game seem hardly clearer than Langland's own description. It was obviously a game of barter, and was known to be highly popular.

[Page 43.] *Benedicite.* The first word of grace before meat.

[Page 44.] *Love-days.* In fact, law-days; days set apart for manorial courts, hence days of reconciliation and concord. The term 'love-days' is used commonly for any days chosen for settling disputes by arbitration.

[Page 45.] *Dismas.* The name popularly and traditionally given to the good thief on Calvary.

[Page 46.] *Suit.* That is, Christ's bodily flesh, the same suit and the same armorial device as worn by human beings.

[Page 47.] A list of the various 'trophies' brought home by pilgrims to show what shrines they had visited. Ampullas were small flasks containing holy water—they were stamped with a sign showing the shrine they came from; such signs were the shells of Galicia and the keys of Rome. The vernicle was also commonly worn by pilgrims; it is the image of the face of our Lord from the veil of St Veronica who, traditionally, wiped the face of our Lord when he was on his way to Calvary, an impression of his countenance being left, miraculously, on the veil she used.

[Page 49.] *Waferer.* A maker of small wafers of bread and cakes.

[Page 50.] *Bull.* A papal rescript or edict.

[Page 53.] *Memento.* A prayer for the named dead in the Mass, *memento* being the first word of that prayer.

[Page 54.] *Religion.* A term used for a religious order, now obsolete; 'a religious' is still used to denote a member of a religious order.

[Page 58.] *Collops.* Apparently slices of salt meat, though it is not clear how the eggs come in.

[Page 59.] Another prophecy, with the distinction of the unconscious truth of one of its fanciful touches. About fifty years later the Maid of Orleans— Joan of Arc—did have the mastery.

[Page 60.] A pardon *a poena et a culpa* is a plenary indulgence, i.e. a remission not of part but all the temporary punishment due to forgiven sin. (See note to page 18.)

[Page 64.] *Biennials and triennials.* The saying of Masses for the dead over a period of two or three years.

[Page 66.] *Wit.* This term seldom, if ever, bears the modern meaning. It signifies intelligence, cleverness, intellectuality, brain, according to the context.

[Page 67.] *New year's gift.* The meaning here is a free gift; there seems, however, to have been a regular system of gifts at the new year, given, for instance, to the king's officers, which were 'free' but not overlooked by the prudent man.

[Page 70.] *Kind.* The God of nature. (See note to page 10.)

[Page 70.] *Anima.* The soul.

[Page 73.] This refers to the legend of the time that Cain was conceived during the period of penitence and fasting imposed on Adam and Eve after their expulsion from Eden. It should be remembered, to understand Langland's thought, that it was common medieval practice and considered of great merit, for husbands and wives to refrain from intercourse during times of penitence and general fasting such as Lent, and especially if there was any particular reason for doing penance.

[Page 74.] The Dunmow flitch was apparently as well known in Langland's day as it is in ours, and perhaps regarded more seriously.

[Page 76.] *Margery pearls.* That is, simply pearls. 'Margery,' an anglicized version of the Greek for 'pearl,' is a bit of poetic tautology.

[Page 77.] *Bernard.* St Bernard of Clairvaux, 1091–1153, saint, philosopher, and theologian, famous in his own time, and throughout the Middle Ages.

[Page 78.] The custom of preaching in the open air at St Paul's Cross was carried on after the Reformation; Latimer, for instance, preached there. A preacher was sure there of a good public hearing and a certain fame, if not necessarily great influence.

[Page 78.] *Worm.* Snake or serpent; the word had a more general sense at the time than we give it.

[Page 80.] *The seven arts.* A reference to the system of education at the universities. 'Arts' has not our connotation, but is in distinction to the higher studies of philosophy and theology. The seven arts consisted of the trivium: grammar, logic, and rhetoric; and the quadrivium: music, arithmetic, geometry, and astronomy.

[Page 82.] *Austin.* St Augustine of Hippo, 354–430, one of the four great 'fathers' of the early Western church, the others being St Ambrose, St Gregory the Great, and St Jerome. The works of all of them would be looked to as weighty, if not final, authorities, but St Augustine has always had the greatest popular influence.

[Page 83.] *Archa dei.* The Ark of the Covenant.

[Page 84.] *Constantine.* The fourth-century Roman emperor, Constantine the Great, whose conversion to Christianity by bringing to the Church the power and the wealth of the Western empire had such a profound and not in all ways happy effect on its development.

[Page 91.] A reference to the privacy of the confessional.

[Page 92.] *Trajan.* The great Roman emperor, A.D. 98–117. The reference is to a popular story, which may be found in that delightful work Caxton's translation of the Golden Legend, that Pope Gregory the Great held the memory of Trajan in such esteem and love that he plied God with prayers until Trajan's soul was delivered from hell. The whole passage shows Langland considering the question that troubled the mind of the Middle Ages very much, that of the salvation of the righteous heathen, for whom no explicit place had been made in the Church's economy of redemption. Langland's conclusion is that it is possible, but that, typically, it is through their own good works rather than the prayers even of the most holy of the faithful.

[Page 102.] *Roquemadour.* A much-loved shrine of our Lady in the Dordogne, with a long history. Charlemagne, in the eighth century, is supposed to have visited it, and Roland, his knight, left his sword there as an offering on the altar of the chapel of St Michael.

[Page 102.] *Felicia.* Probably a reference to the romance of Guy of Warwick, in which she is Sir Guy's wife and behaves with such disdain and contempt towards her husband that he leaves her, to her disgrace, after forty days. Rosamund, in the next line, was the mistress of King Henry II. Her story is well known; Tennyson, for instance, treats of it in his play 'Becket.'

[Page 103.] *Kind Wit.* Two of the most difficult words in *Piers Plowman* together (see notes to page 10 and page 66). Here the interpretation is something like 'instinctive understanding' of the sort that comes from experience and study.

[Page 105.] This seems an odd gloss on the stable at Bethlehem of St Luke's gospel. It is possibly derived from the word *domum* used in St Matthew's account of the coming of the wise men from the east. If this was thought of as a house and that house identified as the inn, i.e. the best house of a small town, and our Lord was born in the stable of that inn, then the idea is possible; but it can hardly be said to be more than a strained explanation.

[Page 106.] A reference to the 'neck verse' which saved many a rogue from hanging. So close was the connection between learning and the clergy that the power of reading a verse from the Bible could be used as evidence of being in holy orders—not necessarily as a priest, but minor orders, deacon or subdeacon. The clergy were exempt from capital punishment, so it was a useful thing to be able to prove. This was most probably often merely a recognized convention, used to mitigate the extreme rigour of penalties for lesser crimes such as theft.

[Page 108.] *Avianus.* This term signifies simply a collection of fables. Avianus lived in the fourth century and wrote fables in Latin verse, but his name was used loosely to cover any writings of this nature.

[Page 112.] *Mahomet.* As a popularly considered infidel Mahomet's name was sometimes used as here to signify a devil; Langland elsewhere shows a somewhat more exact knowledge of Mohammedan beliefs.

[Page 112.] The apocalypse meant here is the Apocalypse of the Gluttons by Walter Mapes, a kind of parody of St John's Apocalypse. Saint Advisa was fed with fine white bread from heaven, the implication presumably being that such heavenly food is the only delicacy penitents should seek.

[Page 114.] *Lamp-line.* There seems to be no satisfactory explanation of this simple phrase. It *could* refer to a Latin inscription of some benevolent nature on the little lamps often kept burning before a shrine or statue (W. W. Skeat's suggestion), but there is nothing to say that it does.

[Page 114.] This riddle resembles the fanciful prophecies. It signifies generally baptism (the 'sign of the Saturday,' i.e. Holy Saturday before Easter Sunday on which day, traditionally, people were baptized into the Christian Church); repentance ('the wit of the Wednesday of the next week after,' i.e. the teaching of the epistle of the Wednesday after Easter); with Easter signified, as before, by 'The fullness of the moon.'

[Page 116.] The two heads are those of St Peter and St Paul on the seal (which in fact is the 'bull' itself) of a papal edict.

[Page 117.] *Stratford.* That is, the Stratford by London (Chaucer's Strat-ford-atte-Bowe) where lived many of the bakers who supplied London with bread.

[Page 117.] *Pope-holy.* 'Pious' as we tend to use that word to-day: super-ficially and perhaps hypocritically devout.

[Page 119.] Dame Emma of Shoreditch was presumably a well-known dabbler in the magic arts.

[Page 131.] *The pass of Alton.* At the time that part of Hampshire was heavily afforested, and this was a favourite spot for highway robbers and associated with them rather as Hampstead Heath was with highwaymen in the eighteenth century. The pass—passage or roadway—would be much used by travellers to and from Winchester, which was then an important city.

[Page 134.] This passage gives an account of the qualities or attributes of the soul (*Anima*) according to Catholic theology.

[Page 136.] *Johannes Chrysostomus.* John the 'Golden-mouthed.' The great saint and renowned preacher of the Eastern Church. He lived from about 344 to 407.

[Page 136.] *A set of beads.* Beads was common usage for what we now call the rosary; a 'set of beads' is a more extended way of saying it. 'Bidding one's beads' is saying the rosary.

[Page 136.] *Sir John and Sir Geoffrey.* The title 'sir' was used as one of respect, and often given, as here, to priests.

[Page 137.] *Long Will.* One of the small pieces of biographical information that can be gleaned from the text of the poem.

[Page 138.] That is, a box in which the charitable could put alms for the benefit of these anchorites, who were hermits in the sense of living alone in some sort of cell, but who had not retired to any 'wilderness' but on the contrary had their dwellings often in very public places.

[Page 139.] *Edmund and Edward.* St Edmund, King of East Anglia before the unification of the Anglo-Saxon states in England; martyred in 870. St Edward is the great king, Edward the Confessor, 1004–1066; he was patron of England before he was superseded by the chivalric but not entirely historical figure of St George.

[Page 140.] *Anthony, Giles.* St Anthony was one of the first hermits who lived in Egypt from, remarkably, 251 until 356. St Giles we would more accurately call a monk; he lived in Provence in the seventh and early eighth centuries, and was an extremely popular saint in the Middle Ages.

[Page 140.] *Paul, primus heremita.* Like St Anthony a hermit of Egypt, and celebrated as the first of them. Also like St Anthony the traditional dates of his life (230–342) suggests that the eremitical life was a peculiarly healthy one. The Paul mentioned almost immediately afterwards is of course the apostle.

[Page 141.] Langland refers here, as elsewhere, to the practice of leaving money for prayers to be said and Masses offered for the soul of the dead person. This, in view of the Catholic doctrine that the souls of the dead who have not gone straight to heaven can be helped in their state of expiation by the prayers of those still on earth, is reasonable. But in the Middle Ages the financial aspect of it, at least, had reached unreasonable proportions.

[Page 143.] *Quodlibet.* The method of thought, reasoning, and argument used by medieval philosophers and theologians, known as 'scholastic' and associated above all with St Thomas Aquinas, derived to a great extent from Aristotle. It was based on close reasoning, and question and answer. *Quodlibet* refers to a general question from anyone, which a master or doctor of divinity should be prepared to answer.

[Page 143.] *Offices and hours.* That is, the official daily prayer of the church, made up of psalms, prayers, lessons, and hymns; called 'hours' because appointed to be said or sung at set hours of the day.

[Page 143.] This account of Mahomet is Langland's version of a popular contemporary, and of course unfounded, story.

[Page 146.] This does not mean that these bishops actually had sees in these districts, although Langland is suggesting that if they were true Christians they should at least be preaching to the heathen there. These were a form of courtesy title given to certain prelates.

[Page 147.] *Templars.* A famous ecclesiastico-military order of a peculiarly medieval type which arose during the crusades. It became wealthy, although it cannot be said that its finances were mismanaged, and aroused the enmity especially of the powerful. After a great deal of intrigue and confusion it was suppressed by Pope Clement V in 1312.

[Page 147.] *Metropolitanus.* We would say 'archbishop,' here as it were archbishop of the whole world.

[Page 148.] *Saint Thomas.* St Thomas of Canterbury martyred in 1170 as an outcome of his struggle with King Henry II. His shrine in Canterbury Cathedral was one of the most popular in the Middle Ages. Already to Langland, as to many since, he is the symbol of the rights and well-being of the Church in face of the encroachment of the State.

[Page 167.] *Linen-less.* Langland has 'wolleward,' i.e. with wool next to the skin; he means without underlinen, so that his upper garment touched his skin.

[Page 167.] *Ramis palmarum.* Palm Sunday. *Ramis palmarum* and *gloria laus* are references to the entry of Christ into Jerusalem as described in St John's gospel, and also to the antiphons and hymn sung at the procession of palms before Mass on Palm Sunday.

[Page 172.] *Beau-père.* This name was sometimes given to a friar who was an authorized confessor. Here it probably signifies authority and benevolence.

[Page 176.] It may be wondered how such a thing was possible. The lines could be ironical; but more probably it is a reference to the custom of reprieving a criminal upon whom the penalty had been improperly carried out, especially if the king were near by and could be appealed to.

[Page 178.] A reference not simply to any performance of humble thanksgiving, but more specifically to the ceremony of creeping to the cross performed normally on Good Friday, in which worshippers process to a cross often genuflecting as they go, and kiss the foot of the cross.

[Page 180.] That of course is *not* the meaning of Christ—the meaning is 'anointed.' But Langland was not the only one, nor the first, to give it the signification of conqueror or king.

[Page 183.] *St Thomas of India.* There was a venerable tradition that the apostle Thomas preached the gospel in India.

[Page 185.] *Folville's laws.* This probably means something like 'lynch laws,' i.e. a form of popular justice which is not necessarily evil, and indeed serves a useful purpose in a community where the king's writ does not always run.

[Page 193.] Langland's words are a rather beautiful paraphrase and elaboration of something our Lord did say, but not of course on the cross.